Praise for *The Boy Is Gone*

"The saga of the General's passage from boy to man is a tale of two civilizations caught in the creative and destructive form of contact we call colonialism. . . . Anyone wishing to broaden their understanding of what lies beneath the veil of stereotypes and Hollywood distortions of Africa, or who would enjoy meeting a character of uncommon intellect and grace, should read this book."

> —Theodore Rosengarten, author of *All God's Dangers: The Life of Nate Shaw* (National Book Award winner)

"The General's story . . . will meet scholarly tests but will enchant a much wider audience . . . and will inform and broaden the views of Western readers about Kenya's important anticolonial Mau Mau movement at a time when all Americans, through President Obama, have a need to know more about that country's history."

> —Peter H. Wood, author of *Black Majority: Negroes in Colonial South Carolina*

"The oral history is just stunning. . . . [Huttenbach] has had the incredible good fortune to find a natural storyteller who is in the same league as Ned Cobb and Nisa. And in rendering the voice and the story comprehensible to ordinary readers, [she] has created a work of art."

> —Susan Millar Williams, coauthor of *Upheaval in Charleston: Earthquake and Murder on the Eve of Jim Crow*

"Laura Lee did what every one of us in the African history field has always wanted to do. She actually lived with the family of her subject. They ate together, worked together (picking tea), stayed together. There is simply no better way for a White outsider to penetrate the core of Meru history."

> —Jeffrey A. Fadiman, author of *When We Began, There Were Witchmen: An Oral History from Mount Kenya*

"Those of us who teach African history are always looking for accessible and engaging books to assign our students. Africa is a vast unknown to most American college students. Most of us have developed strategies of easing them into the subject gently. Huttenbach's book will fit the bill."

—John Edwin Mason, professor of African history at the University of Virginia and author of *One Love, Ghoema Beat: Inside the Cape Town Carnival*

THE BOY IS GONE

Africa in World History

SERIES EDITORS: DAVID ROBINSON AND JOSEPH C. MILLER

James C. McCann
Stirring the Pot: A History of African Cuisine

Peter Alegi
African Soccerscapes: How a Continent Changed the World's Game

Todd Cleveland
Stones of Contention: A History of Africa's Diamonds

Laura Lee P. Huttenbach
The Boy Is Gone: Conversations with a Mau Mau General

John M. Mugane
The Story of Swahili

Forthcoming

Charles Ambler
Mass Media and Popular Culture in Modern Africa

THE BOY IS GONE

Conversations with a Mau Mau General

Laura Lee P. Huttenbach

OHIO UNIVERSITY PRESS   ATHENS

Ohio University Press, Athens, Ohio 45701
ohioswallow.com
© 2015 by Laura Lee P. Huttenbach

To obtain permission to quote, reprint, or otherwise reproduce or distribute
material from Ohio University Press publications, please contact our rights and
permissions department at (740) 593-1154 or (740) 593-4536 (fax).

Printed in the United States of America
Ohio University Press books are printed on acid-free paper ⊗ ™

25 24 23 22 21 20 19 18 17 16 15   5 4 3 2 1

Library of Congress Cataloging-in-Publication Data
Huttenbach, Laura Lee P., 1982– author.
 The boy is gone : conversations with a Mau Mau general / Laura Lee P.
Huttenbach.
    pages cm. — (Africa in world history)
 ISBN 978-0-89680-290-2 (hc : alk. paper) — ISBN 978-0-89680-291-9 (pb : alk.
paper) — ISBN 978-0-89680-488-3 (pdf)
 1. Thambu, Japhlet, 1922–2014. 2. Mau Mau—Biography. 3. Generals—Kenya—
Biography. 4. Kenya—History—20th century. 5. Kenya—History—Mau Mau
Emergency, 1952–1960. I. Title. II. Series: Africa in world history.
 DT433.576.T43H88 2015
 967.62'03092—dc23
 [B]
                              2015007874

To Muriel Patterson Huttenbach,
John Mason, Dr. Ted, and Dale

CONTENTS

ILLUSTRATIONS

Maps

Photographs

(following page 68)

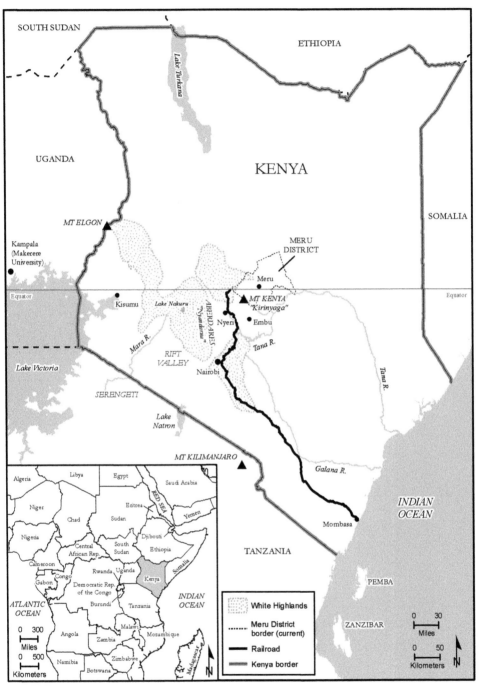

Kenya and its highlands. *(Map by Brian Edward Balsley, GISP)*

SERIES EDITORS' PREFACE

In this selection for the Africa in World History series we focus on one person in one country. We do it through his own account recorded in interviews with Laura Lee Huttenbach, a young college graduate from the United States. Japhlet Thambu, also known as the General and by several other names, was born in Kenya in 1922. He grew up in a rural community, fought in a resistance movement, participated in the Kenyan independence movement, and moved back into farming in the area of his boyhood home, where he succeeded in the radically changed circumstances of the late twentieth and early twenty-first centuries. His narrative weaves in and out of present-day Kenya's story, providing a wonderful way to understand and reveal an experience of colonial rule, resistance, and its ambiguities, as well as the opportunities and perils of political independence.

The country where Japhlet Thambu grew up was something of an East African backwater for Indian Ocean traders who traveled through it in the nineteenth century and for the British and Germans who competed for control of it. The British "won" control and called the area British East Africa. For them at first it was a territory between the Indian Ocean and their prized colony of Uganda, which lay at the origins of the Nile River. Their ignorance of its cultures and inhabitants was total.

In the first decade of the twentieth century, the British began to call this land "the last frontier of white settlement" for those who had missed the boat for settlement packages in Australia, New Zealand, and South Africa. The British colonial government transferred their administrative capital from coastal Mombasa to the rapidly growing interior town of Nairobi, brought in white settlers who received large amounts of fertile land at the expense of the indigenous inhabitants, and designated the cash crops of tea, tobacco, and coffee for their exclusive cultivation. They recruited indentured laborers from their Indian empire to build a railroad up to Uganda, and when the rail line was completed, many of those workers moved into the commercial sector of the colony. By the time Japhlet Thambu was born, there was a clearly demarcated hierarchy: Europeans at the top, Asians in the middle, and Africans at the bottom.

The European settlers managed their new estates but depended on African labor to do the hard work of farming. The newly alienated lands given to the settlers were called the White Highlands, shown on the maps in this book; these areas were not far from Nairobi and the Meru people of Japhlet Thambu. The settlers' reliance on low-paid African workers living on their lands bore great similarities to the agricultural labor practices in the very segregated and white-dominated South Africa, from which some of the settlers came. In his conversations with Laura Lee, Japhlet refers to the similarity. Reserves were created adjacent to the highlands for the Africans removed from what were now white "farms." In the reserves, Kenyan families tended small farms but had to send some of their members to work the settlers' estates. These workers became squatters on the European estates and raised their own families there. Most of the squatters and inhabitants of the reserves were Gikuyu, the farmers and pastoralists who today form the largest ethnic group in Kenya.

In Meru, where Japhlet Thambu grew up, the disruption was less brutal and slower to take hold. His people were able to work their own lands and raise animals without being forced into a crowded reserve. Japhlet came from a poor but closely knit family, where the traditions of sharing and solidarity made poverty a little more bearable. The roles for boys and girls, men and women, young and old were clearly demarcated. Japhlet spent his early years herding goats and cows and learned the importance of having land—a *shamba,* or farm. He lived close to his parents, siblings, and age-mates and drew on all of their wisdom as he grew up. He learned to endure pain without complaint, and at age sixteen he went through the male rite of passage culminating in circumcision. After completing this transition to adulthood, Thambu became a young man, a *murani,* and declared, "The boy is gone." Eight years later he courted Jesca, a young woman in his neighborhood whose family he knew well. They married and formed a partnership they shared until Japhlet's death in April 2014. Japhlet's ties to the custom and culture of Meru in the 1920s and 1930s served him well. Later in his story he expresses regret that the present generation, his grandchildren, cannot draw on a similar experience of the security of extended family and community.

But Meru was not isolated from colonial rule. Meru men were recruited for service in British armies in both twentieth-century world wars. At the end of World War I, Japhlet's father was called up for the Carrier Corps, which, in the absence of roads and mechanized equipment, transported goods and war materiel for the British army in eastern Africa as they engaged in a long struggle with the Germans in nearby Tanganyika—then German East Africa, today Tanzania. During World War II, many of Japhlet's age-mates were recruited for service in Burma against the Japanese. As veterans of a harsh struggle alongside units of the regular British army, they came back with a strong sense of equality with their British rulers, and they resented the strictures of colonial rule. Many turned this military experience into armed struggle and "went into the forest," the vernacular term for the Mau Mau Rebellion.

The colonial regime intruded into Meru in other ways. All families had to pay tax, in the British colonial currency, and this meant finding waged employment with the Europeans. Japhlet recounts how his father earned his tax payments by working on a coffee plantation and in a soda ash factory. The most bitter memory of colonial rule was the *kipande*, a passbook or passport that Africans had to carry on their person and in which work and personal information and European employers' certifications were recorded. It was very similar to the "pass" that black South Africans had to carry at all times, which produced equally bitter memories. With a single negative notation, a European employer could easily sabotage the future of an African worker.

One of the most lasting legacies of colonial rule was the missionary movement, including the Christian schools, churches, and convents that European and American missionaries created. Meru was no exception. At his father's urging, and while also learning in the traditional mode, Japhlet went to mission schools in Chogoria and other towns for eight years. It was in the mission schools that Japhlet acquired literacy in English, donned a uniform, and was baptized a Christian. He learned, among other things, the mission perspective on "civilizing" Africans and that his country's history began only when the Arabs came to the coast and when Europeans took over the country. It was in that setting that Japhlet met, and we meet, Dr. Irvine, a medical missionary and director of the school. Irvine appears frequently in this recollection and judges the behavior of his young Christian client. At the end of the eight years, Japhlet acquired a Certificate of Primary Education, enrolled in Kahuhia Teachers College, and began teaching elementary students.

Missionaries dominated the educational system. The British government largely relinquished this responsibility to them in the early decades of colonial rule. British colonial officials supported the missionary enterprise to spread Christianity to the "natives" and to instill European values, including hard work for others, particularly the settlers and themselves. Administrators, settlers, and missionaries shared a sense of superiority and a duty to spread British "civilization" to Africans, whose cultures and standards they ignored or, alternatively, condemned as backward and even evil. Japhlet's discussion of what the Meru meant and understood of God, religion, and culture, as compared to what the missionaries meant, reveals the gulf that yawned between the two.

In the missionary and European universe Japhlet Thambu could have felt grateful for the opportunity to learn and then teach the culture and values of his white mentors. But he felt constrained by it and struck out on his own to earn an independent income by harvesting timber and selling it to Indian merchants in the towns. This, of course, was illegal for Africans, who were not supposed to be entrepreneurs. Japhlet spent a few days in jail as a consequence, but he returned to the timber trade, where he enjoyed his first taste of prosperity.

The system of pressures on Kenyans that British colonial administrators, settlers, and missionaries had constructed unraveled after World War II. Additional land grabs by new settlers, increasing demands on African workers, the determination of returning African veterans to assert themselves against British rule, the increasing impoverishment of Kenyans everywhere—all these forces led to a resistance movement built around recovering the land by whatever means. The soldiers organized themselves in the forests on the slopes of Mount Kenya adjacent to the settler estates of the White Highlands. Given his missionary training, Japhlet could easily have chosen the "loyalist" side, the Homeguards, who joined forces with the administration and settlers, but he opted for resistance. He took the oaths of allegiance to the struggle, entered the forest, and started on the career that earned him the name General.

Though resisters sometimes called their movement the Land Freedom Army, the British labeled what they saw as an insurrection, Mau Mau, and that is the name that stuck. The colonial governor declared an emergency in 1952. The declaration allowed the British to arrest and detain anyone they suspected of anything less than complete loyalty to the fragile edifice on which colonial rule was built. They quickly arrested some of the African leaders, such as Jomo Kenyatta, future president of the country. They brought in thousands of troops, planes, and an apparatus of repression to subdue the resisters. They poured their prisoners into a system of "rehabilitation." The "Pipeline," as it was known, was designed to bring "natives" back from "savagery" to "civilization" by whatever methods. In the process, the British created a mythology of African barbarism and a glorified view of their own civilization that they came to believe and that they exported the world over. This story has long been the prevailing perception of the Mau Mau struggle. The success and durability of this can be seen in the right-wing allusions to this "myth of Mau Mau" to vilify President Obama's background as son of a Kenyan during the 2012 campaign.

Only recently has the fuller record of the British Emergency come to light, including the torture inflicted on thousands in the Pipeline. Fully sixty years after the declaration of emergency the British apologized for atrocities committed during this period and provided millions of pounds of compensation to some of the victims of the brutality and their descendants.

And only recently in independent Kenya, in the past decade, has it become permissible to talk about Mau Mau and the crucible of violence the country endured through the 1950s. A violent civil war is not a desirable history for building unity in a newly independent country or for securing international support for a modern economy. Many Kenyans feel that the "forest fighters" have not been accorded recognition for their role in winning the country's independence, nor have they received their land back. Toward the end of the book Japhlet tells a poignant contemporary story about Safari, an elderly fighter wandering around Meru country, waiting for compensation. Japhlet reflects on the injustice but also the impossibility of returning the land—part of his ambivalence toward the whole struggle. He does not fully share the determination of President Kenyatta to "forget the past."

Japhlet's experiences of "going into the forest" and fighting against the colonial system form some of the most moving passages of the memoir, and some of the most vivid. Taking the oaths of allegiance. Slipping through the forest. Shielding anything that might reflect light and give away their position to the planes above. Hiding the identities of comrades. Ensuring the confidentiality of communications against government infiltration and informants. It was during this time that Japhlet acquired the name General, or General Nkungi, as he directed his group of recruits in guerrilla warfare. Japhlet kept control of many of the men he took into the forest, but he could not control all of them. The area of Meru was distributed among three generals: Martin, Simba, and Nkungi.

Japhlet remains torn by the struggle in Kenya in the 1950s. Mau Mau fighters on the one hand, Homeguards on the other—they fought with equal violence and high casualties, civilian as well as military, women and children, as well as male fighters. Despite the perception of "savagery" directed at "civilized" settlers, not many Europeans were killed. It was a civil war. The British planes and bombs together with their repressive apparatus tipped the balance of the struggle early on.

By 1955 Thambu saw that the fighters in the "forest" would never win and prepared himself and his followers for surrender. He gave himself up, and while he seemed to receive a good reception from the district officer and district commissioner, he ran afoul of the government-appointed chief, a former pupil of his, and was soon thrown into the Pipeline system of detention camps along with thousands of suspected Mau Mau. He was placed at the notorious prison camp at Manyani, in the dry plains inland from the coast. Detainees held at Manyani were violently abused by the guards and all but starved. Note how many of his memories of detention deal with food, or the absence of food. But he did meet Peter Kenyatta, the son of Jomo, who was already being touted as a future president, and J. M. Kariuki, future author and national politician of considerable note, who was an inspiration to the General and others in the camp. We will come back to Kariuki below.

At the end of 1956, the General advanced to another camp on the Pipeline of so-called rehabilitation with less harsh conditions. A little later he was able to spend some weekends at home with Jesca, help her with the construction of a house and the restoration of the *shamba,* and prepare to become a free man again. His European friends arranged for him to go to an agricultural college, where he learned more about modern techniques of farming, and he began to plant coffee trees again. Soon he got back into the timber business and began to prosper. With these successes he was ready to put most of the past behind him, to move on.

In 1960, the British ended the Emergency, which had given a cover of legality to the brutal assault on the fighters in the forest and the prisoners in the Pipeline. As Britain began to withdraw from its colonies, colonial authorities authorized a small political arena for Africans, and the General cautiously entered it. The decolonization movement started with the political independence of Ghana (formerly the Gold Coast) in 1957 and accelerated; 1960 became known as Africa's year of independence. The General became secretary for the Meru branch of the Kenya African Democratic Union (KADU), the principal opposition party to the Kenya African National Union (KANU) of Jomo Kenyatta. It was as a representative of KADU that he flew to Accra in 1962, where Kwame Nkrumah presided over the first sub-Saharan nation to achieve independence. This trip was a moving experience for Japhlet and broadened his horizons to the national, continental, and international implications of his nation's independence. He accepted the victory of KANU and Kenyatta in the elections that provided Kenya's first national government and joined in the celebrations that accompanied Independence in 1963. He had no problem accepting the pluralism of the new country, including the presence of whites as well as blacks in government; he had no problem with being in the opposition and not part of the majority. But he was concerned about the widespread corruption in the country as well as the growing tendency toward authoritarian single-party rule, tinged with violence. His old friend Kariuki was assassinated in 1977, after becoming a harsh critic of the Kenyatta regime, which further reinforced this concern.

Most of Japhlet's attention in the latter chapters revolves around his private life, earning a living, and securing his family. He went back to teaching, and he tried growing coffee again. By the late 1960s he had consolidated scattered holdings and had enough contiguous land to grow tea, an even larger industry in Kenya, on a significant scale. He and Jesca opened a shop that sold beer, but they realized that they were drinking up their profits. Recognizing that their behavior was also a bad influence on their children, Japhlet poetically expressed his decision to reform their ways: "I will stop dancing when I see my child coming to dance."

By the late 1970s he had helped form a tea cooperative, which became the South Imenti Tea Growers Cooperative, or SACCO, and he began to take on the identity and responsibilities of a large and successful farmer. His fellow farmers wanted him to keep leading them, well into his nineties. Together, the General and Jesca have raised ten children. They tried to treat them equally and to instill the traditional values of community responsibility as the new generations moved into new worlds. But they have not been able to protect them from health issues, losing one child to HIV/AIDS, which has played a major destructive role in numerous African countries. Nor have they escaped the violence of the city, which laid claim to another daughter; Nairobi has become a much larger and more dangerous place than in the 1940s and 1950s. But other children survive and thrive; some have joined their parents in the cultivation of tea and play roles in Laura Lee's conversations with the General and the creation of this book.

In the 1950s the United States became a significant player in the old colonial empires of France and Great Britain, which had been seriously weakened by World War II. Kenya was no exception, being one of the significant centers of this attention. We get a few glimpses of the growing presence of the United States late in Japhlet's story. He mentions Tom Mboya, an important labor leader and Luo politician from western Kenya, who helped bring the Emergency and the pernicious Pipeline to an end. Mboya went on to play a significant role in the negotiations leading to Independence in 1963. Before Independence, Mboya also organized the Airlift Africa Project, which took eighty-one Kenyan students to the United States for study. One of them was Barack Obama Sr., who met and married Ann Dunham at the University of Hawaii and fathered their only child, the forty-fourth president of the United States.

In the late twentieth century, American investments poured into Kenya, and Nairobi became a base for international journalists, foundations, academic research, and aid projects. Tourism flourished, featuring game parks, alongside well-publicized archaeological research that traced the origins of humankind back to the grasslands of East Africa two to three million years ago. Kenyan students continue to attend American universities, often on scholarships. It was in part because of Kenya's close ties with the United States that Al Qaeda operatives chose in 1998 to bomb the American embassy in Nairobi, along with the one in Tanzania. Another cell chose an upscale Nairobi mall for their attack in 2013, to protest Kenyan and American involvement in opposing radical movements in neighboring Somalia.

Violence and corruption in Kenyan politics continued under Presidents Moi (1979–2002) and Mwai Kibaki (2002–2013). Tensions in Kenya reached a climax during the elections of 2007, when Raila Odinga, son of the country's first vice president, Oginga Odinga, won the elections by a small margin—or at least appeared to. When Mwai Kibaki was nonetheless declared the official winner, Uhuru Kenyatta, Jomo Kenyatta's son, and others, on both sides of the electoral struggle, turned a blind eye to or at times provoked open violence. Hundreds of Kenyans were killed, and the International Criminal Court based in The Hague in the Netherlands issued warrants for the arrest of Uhuru Kenyatta and five other Kenyan politicians. At the time of this writing, the indictments are still outstanding, while the accused continue to resist and challenge the legitimacy of the court. Uhuru Kenyatta was confirmed as the winner of the following round of elections, held in 2013, and in April of that year became president of Kenya.

One of the General's journeys abroad was to the United States, to visit Wilson Mugambi, a Kenyan friend who would introduce Laura Lee and the General later that year. Wilson had settled in Atlanta and attended the same church as Laura Lee's neighbors. Wilson and the General went to a monument to the battle of Kennesaw Mountain, when General William Sherman was closing in on Atlanta in the final stages of the Civil War in 1864. "When misunderstanding comes, people fight," the General said. This was the "American . . . Mau Mau." With these phrases Japhlet Thambu brings the Kenyan experience to bear on US history in a striking way, to the conflict that produced hundreds of thousands of casualties and still ripples through American emotions and politics.

Laura Lee Huttenbach here presents the General's mature and highly personal reflections on the violence that people are ready to undertake to defend their land and livelihood. The General understands what drove the fighters in the forests of Mount Kenya, the Homeguards, and British colonial authorities. He carries this insight over to the commitments of Union and Confederate troops in America. He understands how important it is to move beyond these bitter conflicts but also how difficult it is to do so. His story is a treasure of reflections—on human tragedy, division, and reconciliation.

David Robinson
Okemos, Michigan

Joseph C. Miller
Ivy, Virginia

INTRODUCTION

On a tea farm in the central highlands of Kenya, Japhlet Thambu told me his life story. Called the "General" by friends and associates, Thambu once led fifty-eight men to the forest to fight against British colonial rule in a struggle that came to be known as the Mau Mau Rebellion. Armed with machetes and a few old rifles, these warriors fought to take back land Europeans had stolen and to kick them out of the country. That is how Mr. Thambu saw it. But much of the world saw their struggle as less justified.

I first met the General in October 2006 while I was on a backpacking trip through Africa. After graduating from the University of Virginia with a degree in history, I had wanted to know the African countries behind the pages of the *New York Times* or *National Geographic*. For six months, I traveled by public transport more than four thousand miles up the African east coast.

The General and I had a mutual friend, a Kenyan man named Wilson Mugambi. He was living in my hometown of Atlanta, Georgia, and went to church with my neighbors. Wilson sent word to his family and friends in Equator, a village named for its location on the equatorial line in the high, hilly country that forms the populous backbone of Kenya, that a young American ambassador would be coming to visit.

Wilson had said the General was a "big man"—a beloved teacher, respected elder, successful farmer, and sharp businessman. He was indeed "big." We met for dinner at Texas, a restaurant boasting the best *nyama choma*—barbequed goat—in town. The General's imposing six-and-a-half-foot frame commanded deference, yet his smile was warm and somehow familiar. At eighty-five, he had not one wrinkle in his dark skin. "Welcome to Texas," he announced, shaking my hand. "How was your journey from Nairobi?"

I told him about the bus breaking down four times along the 150 miles from Kenya's bustling urban capital and finding myself carrying a crate of baby chickens on my lap for the last leg. He clutched his belly and laughed until tears came to his eyes. "I can only imagine what the other passengers thought when they saw a *mzungu* [white person] carrying that man's chickens," he said. "That's wonderful. You are getting to know the people." We enjoyed a delicious meal of goat and *ugali*—a starchy paste like grits. Toward the end of dinner, he announced, "Tomorrow, I will teach you how to pick tea."

At sunrise the General collected me from Wilson's family home in his jeep and drove us to his tea farm, eight miles off the paved road at an elevation of six thousand feet. Jesca, his wife of sixty years, was waiting for us outside their one-story stone house. From their front yard on this clear morning, I could see the snow-covered peak of Mount Kenya, Africa's second-tallest mountain.

Jesca passed me a bulky wicker basket and motioned for me to place its leather strap on my forehead. Forty years of picking and carrying full baskets had carved a permanent indention across her scalp, which was hidden under an orange headscarf. The General went inside for a moment and came back clutching a brown felt cowboy hat. He placed it on my head. "You shall be called 'Captain,'" he said. "I am the General, and you are my captain. Now, you will learn to pluck tea. You must select the stems with two leaves and a bud. The bud is to ensure soft, fresh leaves that are the highest grade."

We walked out to his seven acres of lush green terraced slopes that cascaded toward the valley below. Still wet from the night's rainfall, leaves glistened as the sun took its place in the bright blue sky. Jesca demonstrated how to "pluck" tea, slowly at first and then picking up speed until her hands moved in a blur from plant to basket. Then she pointed to me.

I snapped off my first stem of two leaves and a bud. The General and Jesca nodded their approval, and I carefully placed it in my basket. The farmhands gathered to watch. "Ah, you are the best white worker we have ever seen!" said the General.

"Thank you," I said, feeling flattered. "And how many other white workers have you seen?"

"None. But you are very good."

I spent the next two days by the General's side. At every step, he told me stories. I came to feel that the history of Kenya was entwined with his life story. I wanted—I needed—to hear everything. And he needed a young person to listen.

Until the British arrived, he explained, African children learned generations of history while sitting at the feet of their elders. The legacy they transmitted included instruction in morals and expectations of behavior. But when missionaries introduced the Western system of education, converts were told that true education takes place in the classroom. The General lamented that children these days seemed to care about things only as they related to Western civilization. "You never see my grandchildren coming to visit me and benefit from me," he said. "We never knew that not all the education people get is valuable. Now they have got good TVs, but when they are given responsibility they don't perform because they never acquired the culture."

At our last dinner together, we were joined by the General's youngest son, Murithi. They decided that I should have a traditional Meru name. "You shall be called 'Nkirote' [N-keer-OH-tay]," said Murithi. "Nkirote is the name for an independent, generous lady. She can make a home anywhere and really manages her things well. You are no longer *mzungu*. You are Nkirote."

Back in the United States, I announced my desire to return as soon as possible to Kenya and record the General's life story. My parents flinched at the words *Mau Mau*. "Our daughter has gone crazy," they thought. In the 1960s, years before I was born, they had read articles in newspapers and *Time* magazine that described how Mau Mau murdered their victims "by methods ranging from merciful garroting to having their heads bashed in and their brains removed, dried, and ritually eaten."[1]

Other pictures of barbarism came from books like Robert Ruark's *Something of Value*. On the front cover of the novel, a fair-skinned woman clings to her strong, rifle-bearing husband as a bare-chested black man with blood-splattered pants burns down their settler home. Ruark, a North Carolinian who had gone on a hunting safari in Kenya, cautioned readers in his foreword that "to understand Mau Mau it is first necessary to understand Africa"—and to do this, "you must understand a basic impulsive savagery that is greater than anything we 'civilized' people have encountered in two centuries."[2] This is a stunning judgment, considering that it came barely a decade after the civilized world gave us Auschwitz, Dresden, and Nanking.

I had trouble reconciling this portrayal of Mau Mau with the kind man who had taught me how to pick tea. In 2009, I arranged to go back to Kenya and hear the General's side of events. Who better to tell the story of a revolution, I thought, than a soldier who fought in it?

That spring, I lived with the General's son Kinyua and his family on their coffee farm and, every morning, commuted up the hills to the tea farm on the back of a *boda-boda*, a two-wheeled motorcycle taxi. In the Thambus' living room, I would sit on a couch next to the General in his armchair, which we called our "classroom." Over a period of three months, I recorded more than one hundred hours of audiotape about his life.

On our first day together, the General asked me how we should begin. I suggested that he say his whole name and his approximate date of birth and "just go, we want your personal story," I said.

"My own personal story. Yes. I was born in 1922 in a family of five . . ." He spoke uninterrupted for the next few hours as he outlined his life, highlighting the most important events with dates, down to the day. The detail with which he recalled his eight and a half decades suggested a cultural past preserved by oral tradition. He spoke from memory; he had never kept a written journal. When he finished speaking, he looked up and said, "Yes, Nkirote, that's how I managed to survive, myself. I'm a man of that kind. See whether I've got it right—anyway, I think you can ask me questions."

I had come to the tea farm with notebooks full of questions, and the General answered many of them before I had the opportunity to ask. Questions became interruptions or distractions, and after a moment of silence he often gave his most vivid recollections. On days when I was not interviewing the General, I met with his colleagues, family, former Mau Mau fighters, and community leaders. I also reviewed tapes from earlier sessions and made notes where I needed more information, then followed up with further interviews. Every few weeks I visited friends in Nairobi, where I would transcribe select interviews and e-mail copies home using high-speed Internet.

"I have learned a lot from the countries where I have walked," the General told me when discussing his trips to India, Israel, and America. "I didn't bother to go because of politics. I wanted to see the people. And the way of the place and how they live and where they get their food." Articulating his motivations, he saw that they were a lot like mine for traveling in Africa. "I like the way you are learning," he said. "If you want to say anything concerning people—stay with them, live with them. It is the only right way of understanding if they are either good or bad."

We often joked that I was a student at "the General's University," and from his years of teaching, the General noticed immediately if my attention drifted during a session. "Nkirote, why don't you sit up straight?" he ordered. Or, "Is it time for a soda? I see you are tired. I think we can take a break." When I did not understand something, the General patiently explained what I needed to know to navigate his stories. He never scolded me for my ignorance but instead commended my desire to learn. "You are getting your history from the people who can tell an event from memory, and that is good. You can write a very unique book to the Americans. You are the only one who came to Kenya and who talked to General Nkungi, so get the information, and the way that you put it depends on you."

That "way," the General warned, should always give truth precedence over entertainment. "Trying to see whether you can put it better than the way I have put it, then you spoil it, and it becomes irrelevant," he said. In the books he had read on Mau Mau, he found "a lot of things that were not Mau Mau business. Some people are saying that Mau Mau were the people who were eating other people, which was not true. Mau Mau were killing other people but not eating. That's the author trying to put stories in a way that will strike somebody to buy the book—that's all."

His awareness of how Mau Mau had been portrayed made him suspicious of how the rest of the world perceived his country. "When people hear you are in Kenya, they wonder which Kenya you are in. They think you are in the bush." He told me a story about a business colleague who attended a conference in Mauritius, a tiny Indian Ocean island country off Africa's southeastern coast. "He was sitting next to a fellow from a developed country, and the fellow asked him, 'I have heard that in Kenya, people live in trees. Is it true in your country that everyone lives in the forest, on top of trees?'"

The General's friend took a moment to collect his thoughts. "True!" he answered. "That is quite true. And it is from a tree that I boarded the airplane, which brought me here. We have wonderful trees, with airports. And even your ambassador lives in a tree—that is where his embassy is." The General dabbed his forehead with a white handkerchief, then adjusted his tie. "Kenya would be a wonderful place if planes could land on trees. But I think that is the picture that goes to the mind of foreigners—that we are wearing skins and living in trees."

One day the General asked me, "What was it that the Americans said when they fought against the British to separate?"

"No taxation without representation," I said.

"Correct," he said. "We had that, too." When the British arrived in the early twentieth century, the General explained, they rapidly occupied the most fertile parts of the Kenyan highlands. "The Europeans chased the Gikuyu away from all the good areas and took the best land," he said.[3] "We were lucky in Meru. We didn't lose the land." British settlers and their African workers planted coffee, tea, and tobacco but denied Africans the seeds. "That was for Europeans only. We Africans had nothing of the cash crops." The British imposed heavy taxes, but "we had no money," as he explained, so African men in the community, including his father, were forced to leave home to labor on settler farms far away.

Unaware of the political resistance to these exclusions that was brewing in Gikuyu lands, Japhlet was growing up in Meru, 150 miles northeast of Nairobi. He fondly recalled palling around with boys his age and learning from his elders how to behave. His memories were tempered with recollections of disease and hunger, but all in all, he "grew in a very good manner."

A medical missionary from Liverpool, Dr. Clive Irvine, had taken charge of the mission station and opened the region's first school in the nearby town of Chogoria. At first Japhlet had no interest in sitting in a classroom and wanted freedom to "roam about" with his friends. But his father, who never learned to read or write, insisted that he attend school. "Europeans were the ones who educated the people who turned against them," reflected the General. "And that is natural."

Japhlet was the first in his family to be baptized as he struggled to balance his cultural values with the religion of the Europeans, a faith that demeaned indigenous practices and beliefs, calling them "witchcraft."

"Before the missionaries came, what religion did the Wameru practice?" I asked.

"We had no religion in Meru," he told me. "Only the culture."

At first I took this to mean that missionaries brought the notion of God to the Meru people. But what the General meant was that their God, Ngai, was so ingrained in daily life that people never thought to confine faith into an institution like religion or the church. Culture wholly embodied spirituality. "The Meru always believed in only one single God," said the General. "But the difference between Meru and the Israelites is that the Meru believed their God lived on top of Mount Kenya, and the Israelites believed their God lived in Heaven and didn't have a specific place where you can visit Him."

In 1942, at age twenty, Japhlet graduated from eighth grade and decided to become a teacher. That same year, the British conscripted tens of thousands of Africans to fight against the Japanese in the Far East. "Most of my age-mates were warriors by then and went to join the military," said the General. "It is from that time those who were in the army became more brave."

I confessed to the General that I had studied World War II largely in the context of Pearl Harbor, Japan, and Europe. "When things of history are spoken, be careful," he said. "You are telling me how you and your people heard the story of the Second World War, and you never knew whether the Africans were involved. But we were seriously involved." I felt like a piece of my understanding of world history had been missing before I met the General. He put it in its place.

While Japhlet was busy teaching, he did not lose sight of the life he dreamed of leading as a farmer. He was determined to marry someone who could help him manage the *shamba* (fields), and seventeen-year-old Jesca Mukwanjeru seemed perfect. I asked the General what first drew him to Jesca. He thought for a moment. "The character of her father," he said. "He was a good Christian, and a very good farmer. Her mother, too, was a hard worker—a very good lady." Later, he added that it did not hurt that Jesca was beautiful.

Jesca knew Japhlet from participating in an after-school "football" (soccer) program. "He was very popular in the community," recalled Jesca. "When he took over leadership of the school, everyone was happy. Students were finally passing primary school and getting an opportunity to study further." She admitted that she did not know why he was coming to visit so often. The first time, she hid from him and busied herself taking care of her younger brother. The next time, she greeted him and went on with her chores. On the fourth visit, she recalled, the General finally announced his intentions. It surprised her that the highly regarded teacher was pursuing her, a girl who had left school in fifth grade. To this day, sixty-three years later, Jesca calls her husband Mwalimu ("Teacher").

In 1951, while teaching, Japhlet discovered that the real money was to be found in dealing timber on the black market. This illegal work brought him into contact with individuals from other ethnic groups, newly returned war veterans, and future revolutionaries. It also took him to Nairobi, a "hot" place for politics.

On one trip from Meru to Nairobi, the General and I rode in the car with a few of his colleagues. Someone had to make a quick stop at a hardware store on the outskirts of the capital. To dodge the scorching Kenyan sun, the General and I got out of the car and squeezed under the store's awning as we waited. "I could never go to that hotel," he said, pointing to a building across the street. "That was for whites. Only Europeans like you could enter. We Africans were not allowed." He made the statement as if he were reporting Kenya's average rainfall or per capita GDP. "In Kenya it was like in South Africa, from what we hear. There were places for Europeans and those for Africans." He shook his head and looked at me. "History, huh?" was all he said.

In 1952, he was initiated into the underground organization called Mau Mau. "The way Europeans treated me, the way they were treating the whole [all] Africans—I became annoyed," explained the General. "I said 'I'll join this movement of Mau Mau,' and I was pleased to do it." Initiation was by oath, a traditional practice and the most serious way to pledge allegiance to a cause. If anyone went against an oath, terrible things would happen to their past (ancestors), present (family), and future (descendants).

To combat the rising revolutionary faction, the British "divided people—you know that's what they do." They aggressively recruited Africans to remain loyal and employed them to fight as Homeguards in their colonial army. On the other side, Mau Mau *askari* (soldiers) targeted colonial sympathizers and picked them off one by one. The overwhelming majority of killing occurred between these two sides—Mau Mau and the Homeguards, all of them African. From 1952 until 1956, more white settlers in Kenya were killed in automobile accidents than died at the hands of Mau Mau.[4] The General observed, "In fighting the Europeans, we killed ourselves."

"Do you ever regret joining Mau Mau?" I asked the General.

He took two minutes to form an answer. He stared out the window, and his eyes watered. Clicking his tongue against the roof of his mouth, he shook his head. "No," he said, then repeated the word four times. He looked at me. "Any other question?" I was silent. He leaned back in his armchair and rested his hands behind his head. "Nkirote, it was a horrible time," he said. "God is good that we survived and forgot it."

But the General had not forgotten his time in the forest. Mau Mau, for him, was a means to an end. And the end, they gambled, would be Uhuru—Freedom.

One morning, his son Murithi came to visit, and the General took us on a field trip. "I want to show you the path we took when going to the forest," he said. Although we visited on a bright, clear day, the General remembered the forest as dense bush—cold, wet, and foggy under a thick canopy. "The bamboo parts were the best because you couldn't leave footmarks there," he said. "There were very many elephants, and when they move, they clear each and every thing, so we could follow in their paths."

He pointed to mountains in the distance. "On days like today when the sun is strong, we had to be very careful when carrying our *panga*s [machetes] and going around the mountains." If sun rays hit the machete's blade, the glint drew unwanted attention. "The Homeguards and Europeans were watching to see where and when we were crossing, so we held our *panga*s in a way that never reflected the sun." Airplanes were waiting to drop bombs on anyone careless enough to reveal himself.

Murithi asked to visit a nearby village where he was interested in buying land for a mango farm. As we got out of the car, an old man waved and shouted in the distance. All I could understand was "Nkungi." Hobbling over to greet us, the man stood at least a head shorter than me and three heads below the General. I asked Murithi what was going on.

"The man is saying that he fought under the General's command, that he was not in the forest, but a collaborator in the village. He's very happy to see the General." Indeed, he was giving him a hero's welcome. The General did not recognize the gentleman but thanked him for the introduction and complimented his farm. Looking me up and down, the man chattered nervously. I knew he was talking about me, and I asked if I should put my camera away.

Finally, Murithi translated. "He's just noting how times have changed. He's saying that before Independence, he could never talk to someone like you. During the [Mau Mau] Emergency if someone like him or the General was caught with a white lady—even just talking—he could be shot. And now he's looking at us working together, riding in the same car, and enjoying each other's company. It's surprising."

"Ah, yes—times are different now," said the General. "Independence is good." The man's eyes shifted back and forth between me and the General. Curling his tongue over the few teeth that remained in his mouth, he tilted his head back and laughed. Then, clasping hands once more with the General, he said goodbye.

On September 17, 1955, after two years of dodging bullets, turncoats, and wild animals in the forest, the General surrendered to the British, who promised that he would not be punished if he cooperated and helped bring other fighters out of the forest. But rather than freeing him, his captors took him to Manyani Detention Camp. For three years, he followed "the

Pipeline," a system of detention and "rehabilitation" designed to reintroduce former Mau Mau gradually to their home communities. At each stop, colonial intelligence teams extracted confessions from the detainees, often after torturing them.

One day, while the General was talking about his time at Manyani, his cell phone rang. It was his close friend and business colleague, John Mwiti. The General spoke first in Kimeru, the language of Meru, and then switched to English. "No, no—we are still here at home with Nkirote," he told Mwiti. "I'm being screened. She has become my screening team." He started laughing so hard that he slapped my knee. "Mm, okay—let me stay here a while with Nkirote, and, if we feel to relax [like relaxing], we will come."

The General hung up the phone. "It was Mwiti. I told him it is you who is screening me," he said, still chuckling. "If you care to, when we finish here, we can go to Texas and say hello. Now let us continue." I marveled at the General's humor and his ability to separate himself from the trauma of Manyani.

When I told the General I wanted to visit Manyani, he said he had just driven through the site on his way to a conference in the coastal city of Mombasa. "It is not as it was when we were there," he said. "Where we were detained is bush. Now you can only see monkeys. That's the name of baboons: *manyani*. Most everything has been taken down. Maybe the next time you come we can try and go to the coast—then we can pass through Tsavo [National Park], and you can see some lions." I thought of Alcatraz in San Francisco and the Confederate Prison in Andersonville, Georgia, where I had taken tours and studied history where it happened. Today, Manyani—a site where thousands of Kenyans were detained against their will and suffered unbelievable cruelty—is a skeleton of what it used to be. The only attraction the General could offer was a nearby game park.

When he was released from the Pipeline and allowed to go home to his wife and three children in 1959, the General was scared to get involved in politics, but an opportunity to visit West Africa as delegate of a Kenyan political party changed his mind. On December 12, 1963, the General celebrated at the State House in Nairobi, the presidential residence, as the Kenyan national flag replaced the British Union Jack.

Mau Mau veterans, expecting to be honored and rewarded for their sacrifices, were shocked when President Jomo Kenyatta instructed the new nation to "erase from our minds all the hatreds and difficulties of those years which now belong to history." He would not allow "hooligans to rule Kenya." He called Mau Mau "a disease which has been eradicated, and must never be remembered again."[5]

The General was more ambivalent.

For more than fifty years the Kenyan government declared Mau Mau an illegal terrorist society. Then in 2007, at a public ceremony in Nairobi, President Mwai Kibaki unveiled a life-size bronze statue of Dedan Kimathi, field marshal and supreme commander of the Mau Mau Rebellion who was hanged by the British. At the fiftieth anniversary of Kimathi's death on the gallows, President Kibaki noted, "My government has over the last four years, made deliberate efforts to redress the historical injustices of the British colonial government." One step it took was to reverse the colonial ban imposed on the Mau Mau in 1950. Today the Mau Mau Veterans Association is a legally registered organization.[6]

On a lunch break between interview sessions one day, the General pointed outside. "We do expect rain," he said. "Today is the 14th [of March] and tomorrow begins the short rain." If it did not start raining the next day, he explained, it would surely come before the twenty-fifth. "It rains here in March up until the end of April. Then it rains again in October to the end of November. In America, you don't know when it rains because you use irrigation."

Our interviews were often interrupted by matters of the farm. When his bull came down with east coast fever, the General excused himself every hour to feed the bull salt as we waited for the veterinarian to arrive. Tea laborers would come to collect payment. *Mbolea*—manure—would be delivered from Tharaka. His cell phone rang more than that of anyone else I know, and most often calls were from the South Imenti Tea Growers SACCO (Savings and Credit Cooperative Organization) office.

The General loved to talk about anything related to farming. He could talk about it all day. When he traveled to America in 2005, one priority was to visit a farm. "We were driving from Minnesota to the state of Obama, and we went to a farm of corn and soya beans—wonderful! It was wonderful." The General told me he was almost speechless by the time he met the *shamba*'s manager. "He took us to the place where he kept his cattle, and I could never imagine how many cattle he kept. Ah! I could not talk to him."

Just recalling the experience brightened him. "I saw this railway running all through the maize, with supporters underneath, as far as the eyes could see. It was a spray, for irrigating! You find the maize being of one size, like one garden—the same color, the same height." He kept waiting for an appropriate reaction from me—like Hallelujah!—but it never came, and he was a little disappointed. Where I would see monotony in row upon row of corn, he saw rational use of land, advanced technology, and abundance. "That's beautiful country," he said. "I like the way you used your country. Leave the farmers to farm, and they farm for their own and the nation." His only regret was that he did not see the West. "I wanted to go on the other side of America to know the desert, where I hear they have petrol [gasoline]."

When he talked about his trip to Israel in 2001, though he said he went there "to see the biblical Israel, where Maria got pregnant from the Lord and where Jesus was born in Bethlehem," most of his recollections from the journey were about land and farming. Flying into Tel Aviv, he said, he "saw nothing but red stones. People were living in desert, an area of stones." On the ground, he got surprised. "I saw something wonderful and different—a beautiful, green airport with trees. I wondered, 'How did it change from the stone I saw to this beautiful place?'"

He posed this question to his *matatu* [public minibus] driver, who answered, "God promised us that this is wonderful, good country where we will live on honey and milk. That's why we are getting potatoes from the sand and stone." Irrigation provided another explanation. "You find these wonderful, big orange trees," said the General. "You never believe they are real, but when you look deeper, you see there is a pipe around the trunk which gives drops of water. Through the technology that they have, because of the promise, they have made gardens."

The General saw the world from the ground up. When describing people, he would often differentiate character from farming ability. For instance, when describing one neighbor, he clarified, "He was not a good man, but he was a very good farmer." To understand why the General fought in Mau Mau, I had to understand how important it was to have control over the soil.

The General's first hands-on experience with coffee was in 1937, when he dug holes for Dr. Irvine and the missionaries at Chogoria to cover his boarding school fees. Chogoria was one of the first missions outside the White Highlands to plant coffee. The General planted his first coffee crop in 1948, one year after he married Jesca. "I planted 750 trees," he said. "In '49, '50, '51, it grew very nicely. Before the Emergency we had a good number of coffee factories, with two in Chogoria, one in Kaaga, and another one at Igoji. My coffee was giving a lot of beans."

But when the General went to fight in Mau Mau, the British and the Homeguards ransacked and demolished his timber house. They destroyed his farm. "When I returned, I met nothing," he said. "Nothing." The General was still shaken by the memory. "All my coffee I had was uprooted," he said, making sure I understood this point. "Not cutting, but completely uprooted. And burned. Seven hundred fifty trees." He grabbed his car keys that were sitting on the table, and as he spoke, he tapped them against his armrest. "We had to start again from the very roots."

In 1958, the General got a lucky break in his Pipeline. Instead of going to the chief's camp to perform manual labor like most ex–Mau Mau, the General was sent to Kaguru Agriculture Camp. "In every district, there was one of these agricultural training centers, headed by Europeans employed by the Ministry of Agriculture, to teach people the method of small-scale farming," the General explained. "I was the only detainee at Kaguru. The rest [of my classmates] were earning money to take the course, from the ministry." At Kaguru, he was allowed to visit his family on weekends, and the family started rebuilding their *shamba*.

"The training we had at Kaguru helped us," said the General. "I completed the course in general agriculture, and I learned a lot in farm management." The next year, a British district commissioner helped the General get a job as marketing assistant at the cereal board, where he saw firsthand that Europeans were still controlling markets. "All produce was controlled. We [small-scale farmers] had to sell it to the cereal board, and the cereal board sold it to the brokers. The market was for the Europeans because they pay you for the produce, but they never let you know the price they are selling it. That was very direct corruption." The General believed that those colonial practices carried over to what is happening in today's Kenyan market. "Exactly what they [Europeans] were doing, they [Kenyan inspectors] are still doing it. It turned to the other side, to our coffee. Nowadays you never know the price that they are selling it. They are terrible—stealing, sucking other people's blood."

After he got fired from the cereal board, the General returned to dealing timber illegally, whereby he honed his entrepreneurial skills. "I never regretted to leave the job of teaching and join timber because I learned a lot during that time," he said. Every shilling he earned he put in the soil. "People thought I was mad," he said. "They never knew what was ahead of me. You know what they said? They said, 'Mwalimu, now, instead of helping and buying clothes for the family, he is clearing the bush with the shillings he gets.' But I knew unless I got back again to the position where I was, when I had nice coffee and vegetables, I could not survive. And I didn't want to cry about it. No, I meant to work."

In 1961, he planted a thousand coffee trees and added a thousand more in 1962. That same year, an agricultural officer offered the General three thousand shillings to plant two acres of Napier grass, feed for cows. "I did it very quickly. Within one rain, I had two acres." The General used the money to buy three cattle and fence his property. "That's how I started earning again from my *shamba*. Those three cattle gave calves, and I was even selling milk."

Following Independence, "it was Kenyatta's approach that we planted tea," said the General. "He formed a body called KTDA, for small farmers to plant tea." Before Kenyans were issued permits, KTDA (Kenya Tea Development Authority) officers had to approve terracing, sizing, and spacing of the holes. For this to be done, districts first had to establish ownership of land. The General took charge of "gathering" and demarcating lands when he was elected district chairman. "That was the time I added to my *shamba*," he recalled. "I used all the money that I had to buy land."

In 1966, he planted his first five thousand tea stems, with another four thousand the following year. "In 1969, I started plucking," he said, nodding. "The work that I did surprised everybody. They wondered where I got that money. Ah, we worked. We helped ourselves, and people know that."

After our first round of interviews, I had a good sense of his chronology except for two decades: he had said almost nothing about the 1970s and 1980s—only that he returned to teaching, and he was focused on rebuilding his family and his *shamba*.

One afternoon, Murithi and the General were in the living room, looking at a photograph taken in the 1970s. In it, the General was thin, almost gaunt. "Pictures never lie," said Murithi, chuckling. He let me in on the joke, that around this time his parents were "taking a lot of beer" and arguing almost every night.

A decade after Independence, at age fifty-six, Mr. Thambu faced one of the greatest challenges of his life. He and Jesca had opened a bar but found that they were drinking up the proceeds. When I broached the subject with the General, he was candid that the 1970s were a rough decade for him. In 1978, he had outstanding loans, and his farm was unproductive. "Have we forgotten the way we came?" the General had asked Jesca. "It is beer that has made us to forget?" They decided it was time for reform. They turned to the church for redemption and poured their energy into the farm.

In 1983, the General retired from teaching at age sixty-one with a final salary of 1,560 Kenyan shillings per month, which at the time amounted to approximately 150 dollars. Having put ten children through school and receiving a next-to-nothing teaching pension, the General looked to coffee and tea to build his retirement. When the coffee sector collapsed, the General planted more tea. "Coffee was giving nothing. You could never pay even the laborers, so I left it *kabisa* [completely]. I turned to tea."

Though he had served on various district tea committees, retirement gave him time to learn more about the industry. Commercial banks in the area were of no use to rural communities, in which small-scale farmers could not afford to meet the minimum loan requirements. Farmers received payments for their harvests once or twice a year; with no safe place to keep their money, they would "eat their profits in one day." Without access to facilities to save money or take out loans to improve their lands, acquire better agricultural technology, or put their children through school, families struggled.

In 1990, the General, along with three tea farming colleagues, organized a tour—a "feasibility study"—of the nearby town of Kirinyaga to learn about the agricultural cooperative industry. The next year, the four men officially registered the South Imenti Tea Growers SACCO. In the first executive board election and in every election since, the General was voted chairman of the cooperative.

Farmers today are able to accumulate savings and access credit for up to three times their account balances. They can invest in agricultural technologies and get loans to cover their children's school fees. They are investing in universities and buildings. At the Kinoro tea factory, where the General has his tea processed, the local primary schools have accounts. If a farmer cares to, he can designate a number of kilograms of his tea to be deposited into the account of a school. Thus, a farmer can pay his child's school fees in kilos of tea—the rural equivalent of "direct deposit."

When the General took me on a tour of the SACCO's headquarters, farmers crowded the building to get advances from tea sales, and everyone respectfully addressed the General as "Chairman." The SACCO's general manager, John Mwiti, explained how the industry had enabled the rural population. "We are here to assist the small man," he said. "Because if you reduce poverty with the small man, then even the big man will live well."

The General agreed. "We have changed greatly through the cooperative movement," he said. In other parts of the country, he conceded, "the question that still needs to be answered is about the land. That's why people are fighting in the Rift Valley."[7]

When I returned to America, I transcribed my conversations with the General. From 1,500 single-spaced pages, this book has emerged. Our talks ranged widely but invariably returned to common themes, and I have arranged the material to connect related topics and to reflect chronology. Most stories I heard more than once, some three or four times. The content did not change, though his delivery depended on the point he was trying to get across, my question, or an addition to our audience. In editing the transcripts, I pulled every version of the same story and placed them next to one another. Sometimes I chose a single version; at other times I combined parts of one with another for the sake of clarity and thoroughness. In making selections for this book, I gave priority to stories with historical interest but could not let go of passages that were just plain beautiful. Though impressions from his travels in Israel and America are charming and enlightening, his narrative is centered in Kenya. In my editing and in my subsequent review of the manuscript while sitting next to the General, I have faith that I have not misrepresented him.

About modern Kenya, the General avoided lengthy debates. He liked to talk about the old days—his childhood, teaching, Mau Mau, and Independence. When I asked about current politics, he resisted. "Ah, I think you can get that from Murithi or other people who are better than me. I don't like that thing very much," he would say. "Refer me to the old things." He and I agreed that modern Kenyan politics should not be included in this work.

The General told me that many people had suggested that he write a book, but he had little time and never thought of himself as a writer. "Even my children do not know the stories I've shared with you," he said. "You're writing for me. There will be a time when my grandchildren want to know something, and they will have to read what you write." The General's mother tongue was Kimeru. His second language, Swahili, is the lingua franca of Kenya. Our common language was English. The General's vocabulary was charming and resourceful, enhanced occasionally by words not found in standard English dictionaries. Context usually makes the meaning clear. Where it does not, I have offered definitions.

One day, I asked the General how to say the word *relax* in Kimeru. He told me there was no such word in their language. "English has a lot of vocabulary. That language is rich in vocabulary, also Swahili. But some of our Kenyan languages have very little." Speaking English, he depended frequently on modifiers, especially the word *very*, to intensify words or feelings. He used the word *wonderful* in the most literal sense, meaning "full of wonder." It can also mean good, strange, or shocking. *Serious*, in the General's usage, means severe, desperate, dangerous, or brutal. In many scenes, he quoted extensive dialogues to dramatize the narrative. Often these conversations took place in Kimeru or Kiswahili, but he reported them in English.

Because the General wore many hats in his community, he was known by many names: Mwalimu (teacher), Chairman, and General Nkungi (or just "General") are the most common titles. His full name is Japhlet Kithinji King'ua Thambu.

Japhlet is his Christian name, necessary in the mission community. Before being baptized, he had to select a name that appears in the Bible. He chose Japhlet from the book of Chronicles.

Kithinji is his birth name. "My mother called me Kithinji," the General explained. "I'm named after my grandfather's brother.[8] *Kithinji* means a butcher, a man who always has meat. He doesn't buy meat, but he has his own cattle and goats. He's a rich man. So I'm called Kithinji, and we have meat."

King'ua was his father's nickname, meaning "a fellow who likes to joke around." While he was growing up, this was his surname.

Thambu became his "manhood" name. His father chose it when Kithinji turned sixteen and was circumcised, a critical rite of passage for Meru adolescents. Thambu replaced Kithinji and means "a man who does not like to waste time."

———

Jesca and the General were the hardest-working people I have ever met. At eighty-one, Jesca spent her days out in the fields planting, weeding, picking tea, or managing farmworkers. Even when she came down with malaria, she refused to stay inside. Jesca does not speak English, so Murithi translated my sessions with her. I hoped she would talk about the hardships she had lived through—her time in prison, sicknesses, arthritis that is inhibiting her tea plucking, raising a family of ten—but she said she has lived a good life.

Jesca was raised to believe that life is hard. Life could be rewarding and fulfilling and have its share of love and happiness, but at its most basic level, life is hard. The times and troubles that I considered unjust and insurmountable, she considered normal. Even Murithi threw up his hands when he tried to elicit some iota of self-pity or bitterness. "She is saying she's lived a very good life," Murithi told me. "She has nothing to complain about. I think maybe things that appear too hard to you, to her did not make such a big impression."

One morning, the General's oldest son, Kirimi, stopped by for a visit. The General and I followed our normal routine until Jesca interrupted us. They spoke briefly in Kimeru, and the General laughed. "Ah-hah. She is selling vegetables," he said. "She sold some to Kirimi. She is selling them to our children even. Local people are coming to buy from us, and it is good. She is making money. She has got her own account. Although she did not go to pluck [tea], she has got money for today, a dollar for today. That's what we say—we're told if you manage to make a dollar a day, you can survive. But now the costs have gone up beyond a dollar, so we need more."[9]

"She can sit down now," I said. "She doesn't have to go to the fields to pluck."

"Uh-huh! You are correct. She has done today's work, today's earning. Anything else is additional. Another sale, another dollar. That's what I say—we have water, we have land, why should we be poor?"

When I asked the General what he considered to be his greatest accomplishment, I thought he might say the tea cooperative, his Mau Mau leadership, or his success as a teacher. But he surprised me. "I praise God that He gave me good knowledge to marry well," he said.

In August 2009, Jesca and the General celebrated their sixty-second wedding anniversary. As husband and wife, they were partners—as fighters during the Mau Mau Rebellion, comanagers of the *shamba*, and heads of the family.

In his classic study of African autobiographies, James Olney noted, "Africa and the West go on meeting one another all the time and at all sorts of contact points. And, as many people have observed, they go on not understanding one another very well."[10] One aim of this book is for readers to understand the life of Mr. Japhlet Thambu, a wise and generous man who spoke of the double-edged sword of colonialism not as a scholar but as someone sculpted by it.

Japhlet Thambu grew up wearing goatskin loincloths. At the end of his life, he donned a business suit most mornings and headed a highly successful, multimillion-dollar tea farmers' SACCO. On March 8, 2009, the Kenyan government recognized Mr. Thambu for his pioneering work in the agricultural cooperative field. He received a "Head of State" commendation from the minister of cooperatives and a certificate signed by President Kibaki.

The General long pleaded with his SACCO members to allow him to retire, but they continued to elect him chairman. "I think I finally found the way," the General, at ninety-one years old, wrote to me. "This year we've put a change in our bylaws that any person serving on the executive board must have at least a secondary school education. And you know I'm only a man of class eight."

In December 2013, when I visited the General, I learned that his ploy had not worked, and he remained a very active chairman. I had returned to the tea farm to deliver a near-final copy of the manuscript and to take pictures for this book with photographer Mary Beth Koeth. During our visit, the SACCO was in the middle of an audit, and the General's phone rang off the hook with questions from headquarters. "Also we are organizing a study tour of Bangkok. If my health allows me, I will go next year," he told me.

We were together when we heard the news that at age ninety-five, Nelson Mandela had died. I asked the General what he thought about it. "That is the way of all of us," he said. "But he used his time. He can go now, peacefully." Because, the General continued, Mandela fought every moment he was alive.

Four months later, back in the United States, I opened an e-mail from Murithi with the subject line "News From Home." The General was dead. In a few short months, Africa had lost two giants: one who is known to the world, and the other who is not yet known. Through his life story, however, the General will not be forgotten.

"I got the call from Nyagah at 01:48 that they had just arrived at the hospital by which time the General had passed on," Murithi wrote from his iPad. "He had arrived home earlier in the day (on Sunday) from a trip to India and I understand he was all jovial and strong then." It was the General's second trip to India, where he traveled with the Yetu SACCO Society Board of Directors to "benchmark and to form partnership."[11]

On Tuesday, April 15, 2014, the General was buried at Mutunguru Presbyterian Church of East Africa, on land he had donated. The service lasted four hours. More than 2,500 people showed up.

During one of our last conversations, I had asked the General what I now realize was a stupid question. "Do you think you're representative of Africans?"

He gave his answer. "You know, you are American," said the General. "I am African. Do you think all American ladies are like you? No. Not all Africans are like me. Not everyone comes to the extent of knowing that these are all ladies, and these are all men. You take somebody as he is."

Meru District and environs of Mount Kenya. *(Map by Brian Edward Balsley, GISP)*

PART I

HOW I GREW

WE WERE WEARING SKINS

From the very beginning, I grew in a communal way, in a group culture. My time was not of individualism. Let's say we had a bull, and we decide we are going to kill it. In my family, we cannot eat the whole big animal, so the father tells his sons, "Get your friends. We want to eat that bull." It would be known that we were going to kill a big bull, so if anybody wanted to come and join the family, they could bring a goat. If they didn't have a goat at present, they can contribute later. You can tell them, "Keep your goat, and when your family kills another bull, then I will call on you, and we can eat that meat." Others could bring bananas or porridge.

The soft meats of the bull, the liver and tongue, were prohibited to the young people. That meat is reserved for old people because they cannot chew. When the *murani* [circumcised young men] kill the cattle, they know that old people are at home, and they cannot come to collect the meat, so the *murani* carry soup for them.

There's also meat for women. The marrow and some other meat, the fat, is for mothers. When a woman gets a baby, she could be helped to have animal's blood. You mix it with millet, or with milk, or drink it as it is, and it helps the woman after delivery of the baby. Any woman could get blood. Whoever has the cattle could do it for any woman. Although somebody owned the cows, they serve the community. So everything was shared in a very beautiful, wonderful way. There was enough meat for us all.

In Kimeru we say a child does not belong to one. A child is for the community. If the mother dies when she is delivering the child, and the family has no cattle, but the surrounding community has cattle—we must feed that child. Whoever is left with the child will come for milk, and they will take it freely without charge because the baby has nowhere to feed.

My *juju* [great-aunt] used to say that if somebody keeps away from corruption, he can live longer. But if somebody is naughty, and he beats someone who is weak or takes somebody's things, he will die earlier. Nobody will say a good word for you, and they will be cursing you to get lost because of your actions. But if somebody says you are good, and that's followed by another person, and another person—all those goodnesses will follow you and give you a longer time to live. You will have blessings.

We were taught that you could never demand somebody's things, and you should get satisfied with what we have. Never give false witness. Speak the truth. Help the poor if you can, and never count the cost. Have strength and never let anybody curse you. My *juju* taught that in our family. We had this legacy of learning from the old people. The younger children had to learn stories from their grands. I had to visit *juju* all the time. She was very kind and respected my father terribly [very much].

When my *juju* became sick, my mother was telling me how to put fire in her home and cover her with whatever she had. In the morning, I had to check on her in the house. When I went one day and saw her, I thought she was just sleeping. I opened the house very quickly. I knew that she was sick because I had been caring for her, but she had some saliva coming off her bottom lip. I had never seen somebody dead.

I ran to my Mom and told her, "*Juju* has died. She's not talking, and saliva is coming from her mouth." I was crying, but she told me, "She was old. Don't worry, she was old." I think that was sometime between 1926 and 1928. We buried her. You know, we were not burying people before the Europeans came with Christianity. When somebody died, there were no hospitals, so he was to die in the house. The body was taken to the bush in the evening and thrown there. Then the whole family shut their houses and cried. Do you know the animal, hyena? They were very many. When the hyenas heard the sound of people crying, they knew somebody died. They would come at night in the bush to do the job. In the morning you never find any body.

But we had a fellow from our clan who had gone to the mission [converted to Christianity]. He reported it to the subchief and arranged for my *juju* to be buried. She was a great friend of me, teaching me many things.

When I grew to an age of five, I think that is when I started my memory. My elder sister was laughing at me because I was telling her, "I want you to carry me." And she would say, "No, I cannot carry you. I carried you for long, but you are trained to walk now." We were to joke with one another. She was called Mercy Ncugune and was somehow like my mother. She was looking after me when my mother had to go look for food or firewood. My sister fed me with bananas, chewing it for me and putting it in my mouth with her finger. I loved her very much. She was calling me "Kauyo Ku," which means "the man who has known very many things in his youth." I think I grew in mind before I grew physically.

In Africa or Kenya, when somebody says he is rich, he might have cows or goats, animals to keep the family. But our family was very poor. I was brought up in a wonderful, poor family. Before the First World War, people were not many. If you tried to put anything in the ground, the wild pigs would come at night and eat it. Having something from the *shamba* [farm] was very difficult. My father put a house next to where he planted yams and just watched these animals, guarding our vegetables at night. But the animals were more than ourselves, so the life was terrible.

We had no clothes like what we have today. We were wearing skins, from the goat. We brought the fire in the house where we people lived and slept next to it. My mother used to cover us with skins to warm ourselves. Some families had no good covering. Children were dying of pneumonia, whooping cough, and the measles—you could hardly see a family of five. Most families had two or one or were without children. I was born in a family of five. I don't know how we survived.

My parents worked hard for us, especially my mother was working every day. She had to go and look for this sweet water [spring water], we call it *mwonyo*, down in the lower area, from our place here. *Mwonyo* has a special thing in it that makes it sweet, and if you put something hard in the sweet water to cook it, then it will become soft. If you cook maize, it will become ready quickly because of that water. It was not salty but sweet and differs from other water. We call it the wonderful, sweet water that comes from the God. My mother was selling *mwonyo* to exchange for bananas or whatever she could get for us to eat. One day she was at home, and the following day she was taking that *mwonyo* to look for food, then back again. I knew the way that my mother worked for us, so I respected her widely. Although my father was trying, my mother did a lot for us to survive.

My father was working for the tax. Europeans were taxing people who were grown and mature. They were calling it a "hut tax." It was difficult for Africans to pay because by then [back then] we had no money, so my father had to look for employment from the Europeans. You could work for two to three months to pay the government. When the Europeans came, they were to look for which cash crops can grow where. In Gikuyu land, they found that place was good for coffee. That is where our fathers went to work. In Meru we Africans had nothing of the cash crops. Those were strictly for Europeans.

In 1920, before I was born, my father went to Limuru, where Europeans had made settlement with coffee farms. He walked for seven days and left my mother with young twins—two boys. My father came back in the middle of 1921, and he learned that unfortunately the twins had died.[1] He stayed with my mother and left her pregnant. He returned again to work on the European farms at Limuru, and that is when he had to get *kipande. Kipande* was an ID card.

You could not get employment without *kipande.* It was a big paper with all your personal details and employment information. It was put in a hard-covered metal thing so it would not get dirty. You were to carry them [around your neck] where you could not lose it. When you go to work in the farm of a European, he had to write down that you are in his *shamba.* The European could write, "So-and-so is within my *shamba* working for me, from this date to this date." The *shamba* employers could write anything—where you came from, how you worked, what your character was. If he didn't like you or if it was incomplete, then you could never get employment. It was not a good system because the white settlers could put anything on your *kipande,* and you wouldn't know what it said.

You could never go from a *shamba* unless the owner released you. If you go to another *shamba* without getting stamped, it will be seen that you were not cleared to leave the first one. You have to go back again. You could never move without *kipande.* It was that way.

Now we have *kipande* only to know identification. Kenyatta got rid of those cards. "No, no, no," he said. "We are no longer slaves. We get ID cards only to know whom you are, but not for anybody to sign."

My father's *kipande* was stamped August 1921. He worked for some months on the European coffee farm and came home in early 1922. When he came back, he met my mother with another baby—that's myself!

I was very young, only two months or so, and my father could not enter my mother's home. That's Kimeru tradition. The mother and the baby stayed alone with the old women helping her in the house. They wanted no contamination of any sort—just the clean baby and clean mother. So my father, when he returned, could not take food from my mother's home. He had to eat from the community.

I was the last one in my family, born after the First World War. My father used to tell me that I was his only son who was with him during the army. My father joined the First World War in 1917 to fight the Germans in Tanzania. The chief appointed him from our clan to go to the war and said, "He is a good *murani* [warrior] to go to fight." He joined the Carrier Corps, the company to carry the luggage for the army.[2] They were the company of carrying, the Carrier Corps. In Nairobi there is a place called Carrier Corps, except the Africans spell it Kariokor.

When my father joined Carrier Corps, I was in his loins. His other sons were at home, but I was with him. But my father did not fight, because the war was almost over. The Germans were cleared out by then, so he went to work for money in the company of Magadi Soda.[3] My father joked with me that when I left for Mau Mau [in 1953], he was not surprised, because I had war in my blood.

When my elder brother grew, he started working, and then the other one followed him. They helped my father to buy a goat, the first one I saw. My father sold a big sack of finger millet, and the man gave him a goat as payment. My father and brothers bred it, and it grew to a herd of ten—that's when I started looking after them. My father sold five goats and bought a cow. We were breeding that cow, and now the family changes. I had work to do. I was looking after those goats and cows. Also I was helping another woman who had no son, and I looked after her goats together with ours. My brothers had no work to do in their youth because we had nothing—we had no cattle, no goats, and farming was terrible because of these wild animals. I think my time was a bit better than the time of my elder brothers, because I was a herd boy. Their youths were idle.

The *murithi* [boy who tended the cattle] was highly respected. We had no shelter, no umbrella—you had to go with the animals, wildly. It was a hard duty. No matter what, even when it rains, you go with the cattle. You grazed them anywhere because all the lands were common lands. Only you could not graze in somebody's field in front of their home. That is for them to keep their own cattle.

There were old men who went with us. They could not work in the *shamba* anymore, so they would go back again to the animals and help these younger, little kids to look after the goats properly. These old people were to guide us and make sure we were safe. My mother knew that I would go with them and could not come back at lunchtime, so I carried food from the night before. The old man would ask, "Did your mother give you anything to eat during lunchtime?" If she did, then he keeps it for you until lunchtime. He knew the time to eat. Also, the old men could carry some little treats in their bags. They cut sugarcane into pieces and then gave them to each of us looking after the animals.

As a herd boy until the age of five, I lived with my mother. Then I was told by the grown-up boys, "Do not go back to your mother's house. Do you know why your father comes there? He does not come to get sleep, because it is one bed. It would be bad for you to see what is happening there, so don't go there."

I was taught in that way, and I left my mother's house and joined the group of small boys, and we grew together. We ate together, and we would sleep together in the houses where the women stored their maize or millet. If somebody lost his mother, he could never feel it because we were to feed together. You were never to let your mother know that you were not with the group or go home to ask for food from her. When a group comes to her home, she will give them food because she knows that you will eat from another home.

If you feed yourself alone, away from the group, you will be seriously beaten. There was no private feeding. In Kimeru, we have a saying: "He who never moves doesn't know whether the women cook well, because he eats only his mother's food." I was taught a lot from the older boys how to behave in the community and care for yourself. It was a nice school. I grew in a very good manner.

We had to do very many traditional trainings between the age of five and ten, when we were herding these goats. Boys were shown that certain things in life should not be shared with anyone. Men were secretive, so we were trained not to be afraid and how to deal with secrets. We were even given tests. If we told our parents or other boys the secret, then we were powerfully punished by these older boys.

Then we were trained on pain. Pain is a big problem, because once you get pain, you can say anything you weren't supposed to say. We were not to give information because of pain, and that's a big training. You see? I have many scars on my arms, also my legs. These are burns. Some old people make a stick hot, rubbing it, and then put it in your skin to burn you. You dare not pull up. If you *sema* [say] anything, you will be laughed at because you were scared. When one heals, they put another one. And also it looked very nice! It is known that you are a brave gentleman. When you are young, dancing, you are not to cover the scars.

For the girls, they were cut underneath the eyes, twice or thrice, so when you look to her, you will find those marks.[4] When you cut some people, the blood would come. Ah, it was terrible. Anyway, we were doing it.

Also they had to take two teeth here [*pointing to a gap in his bottom front teeth*]. As soon as you lose your first teeth, and the new ones shoot up, then those are the ones to be taken because they weren't recovered. You remain without the teeth. We were told that if those teeth were not taken, and you get sick, then you will die because nobody can give you water. If you get lockjaw, then the water can't go in. But if you have removed the teeth, you have an entrance.

The teeth were plucked off by an old man—one of my *jujus* was doing it. My sister took me to him. I did not want to go, but she said, "You must keep up with these things." There was no anesthesia or anything of the sort. You have to feel it. They take the teeth with a knife [chisel]. Our knives had one flat end where you could handle it. So, they put it that way, wedged it under the teeth, knocked it with another rock, and then the tooth comes out the other side. Then, the same thing happens to the other tooth. I did not want the other one to be taken in the same day, but my sister said I must. Then they burned the branch of a banana tree and put it on the gum to stop the blood, but it made more blood to come.

Losing the teeth was very painful, but, ah—you could never cry, never. You must be brave enough. Now, when you are done—good! They clap. They say, "Come and show the others that you have done it so the rest will follow." We were trained to become brave so during circumcision time, we will be used to the pain. There will be nothing to stop it then, but you keep quiet. They are doing it even today, the Maasai and Nandi [ethnic groups]. When you look at the people of my age, everybody is missing the two teeth. We know ourselves when we look at one another because of that sign.

We also learned how to fight. We played games that taught us how to throw spears with accuracy. One game was called *kamunta thigu*. *Kamunta* means "throw" [pierce], and *thigu* is "hoop." We had two teams, facing opposite each other. One team threw a hoop, and the [other] team tried to throw their spears through the hoop as it rolled past them. It was difficult but good training. If the stick goes through the hoop, if it stops and falls down there, then they will call a person from the other side. That person is given a number of steps. You say, "Now look, you are going to throw your spear in such a way that it goes right in the center of this hoop." And many times that person will not. If he can't, he is taken captive. He is now detained. Boys will be trained to be accurate in that way, just like in shooting.

We played these games after we took the goats or the sheep in until it was too dark to see. People had all these communal things, and they were good because we were to know one another.

My brothers appreciated my work looking after goats and cattle because I began it in the very youth. That gave my father time to go out in

Nairobi or Limuru to look for money, so we changed from skins to what we call *amerikani shuka* or *gitambaa,* a white sheet [like a toga or loincloth] that we were buying from the Indians.[5] I think that was 1926 or 1927—my father came back from working, and he had these new clothes. My brothers were calling him Padre [Catholic Father] because he was wearing this blanket, a sheet, like how the white men dressed. Even we were to tell my mother, "Mommy, the Padre has come."

I think I was favored in a special way because I was the last-born. I don't recall any times when I got in trouble. Only there was the time when we had hunger, when we had the shortage of food and could not feed everybody. That was the only time I noticed we quarreled. Laws did not allow children to have differences with their parents. It was prohibited seriously. If it is reported to the Council of Elders, Njuri Ncheke, that you have gone against your parents, you are charged to say sorry, bring a goat to your father and mother, and take an oath to say that you will never repeat.[6]

OUR GOOD THINGS WERE CALLED EVIL

Long ago we had prophets here called *aroria.* Gacuria was [the name of] a very famous one. He was telling people to be careful. He was seeing a big dangerous beetle which made a wonderful noise. When it went up [in the air], people ran into the forest. People never knew what he was talking about. He was also seeing a long, black snake which people could never find the head of to kill it, neither could they see the end. People were running away fearing that snake. After so many years there came an airplane. And people said, "Uh-huh, this is the beetle that Gacuria was seeing." Then came the tarmac road, and people said, "Uh-huh, this is the snake that Gacuria was seeing many years ago." We had these stories from our fathers.

We believed that our God lives on top of Mount Kenya in the white [snowy] place. If you go to see Him, before you reach, the clouds cover. It was the God of blessings. If something goes wrong, people will know that we have done something bad. We will know by no rain or too heavy rain, where we will have hunger. So we had to give a sacrifice. We kill a goat of one color, all white for the God who lives in the white place.

The *wazee* [old men] kill the goat in a very sacred area, with special trees that we could never cut down. These trees were like our churches. You could never fight there, and if you got hurt in that place, then you had to be cleansed, so it would not be contaminated. The *wazee* were from a special clan, the family who gets blessings from God. They were the people to do the ceremonial functions. I am born in that clan. We are the family of the clan called Nyaga, which is related to the God. The oldest were the ones to perform the cleansing ceremony. They say, "We are sorry. We have mistaken you. Please hear us. We have gotten too much rain, so now can you please stop it?"

My mother was the one to tell the local women when to plant. She got permission from the God, and then she planted. She knew when it will be the time of rain. Women would never plant before she planted.

When the missionaries came, they said this was an evil thing. All our good things were called evil. Oh—they cut down our lovely trees, our sacred churches. The Christian people spoiled our wonderful environment. They said, "There is no God there. Don't believe in that tree or whatever it is. We will clear each and everywhere."

Our sacred place was changed by the new religion. Instead of studying and knowing what we were doing, missionaries imposed completely everything. They didn't want to know.[7] They said we had to turn away and leave everything. We had to follow them. Everything of ours was dirty and evil. We lost our connectivity—the traditions—that gathered and joined us together. We got mixed up.

We had our old doctors who could cure illness with plants. We called them *mugo*. They knew a lot about the herbal. They knew the roots and leaves of trees that mix together to make medicine, even to cure meningitis. They were healing our people. But the Athome, the Christians, did not like the *mugo*s. The Christians were fearing them and did not want to mingle. They called it witchcraft.

There was a time when I had a lot of trouble, a lot of pain, in my stomach. I was crying every morning. I had worms, and they were moving all around. My stomach was sticking out, and I could hardly eat. It was much better during the daytime, but at night they didn't have anything to eat. They were eating me.

I don't know if my mother realized what it was, but she took me to a *mugo* named Kabuuri. We were somehow related to him, and he knew what to do. He took out this quill, this stick from the porcupine, and dipped it into a very small bottle of castor oil. The quill filled with castor oil, and he put it on my tongue. I had to lick it and to swallow. Then he repeated, and I took it one other time. I took only two times from that quill, and everything came out before I reached home. I had diarrhea everywhere and gave a lot of worms. Castor oil is the best medicine for worms. We plant trees here for the castor seed, and that oil killed each and every worm in my stomach. I've never had any more from that time. Kabuuri helped me very much. I regretted the long time that I had suffered while Kabuuri was there to treat me.

Now the opposite of *muga* is *murogi*. They were the ones who knew the poisonous trees. *Murogi* could mix poisonous trees with animals or snakes and use it to kill people. *Murogi* were hated and hid themselves. They were not allowed to attend ceremonies, because they might poison the drinks at these parties.

I don't know how somebody becomes a *murogi*. Life to him looks very hard, and he knows that if he kills you, he can take your property. I knew one *murogi* during my youth time. He was called Soro, and it was widely known that he was *murogi*. One day, a very brave young girl followed Soro into the forest. We were calling her Sareena. Soro went to a tree and hid a pot there, and Sareena saw it and knew what that thing was. She ran and reported it to the police.

Soro was caught and brought to Meru Town, together with his *urogi* [pot of poison]. They asked him questions, but he refused. He said, "It is not *urogi*."

They said, "If it is not *urogi*, will you eat it?"

"Why not?" He was given some to eat, and he died. Soro took his *urogi*, and he died for it. The girl who caught him was very brave, and she was widely honored.

In our tradition, crime was not common. The community would not live in fear because of the actions of one person. A lot of things changed during our time. With chiefs being employed by the European government and all—it encouraged a lot of thieves. Before that, we were ruled entirely by the Council of Elders, by Njuri Ncheke. They were regulating all things. We knew that if you committed this, then the punishment was that. Life was orderly. If you become a prominent thief or *murogi*, and the people have revealed that you are the one who is killing other people, then you will be accused.

You could never be called a thief unless you were caught red-handed with the thing you have stolen. When you fail to prove otherwise, the young people tie you. Someone from your family will throw the first stone. That's to say that you are no longer in their family. You no longer belong to them. They throw a stone to you, and now you'll be killed, like what was happening in the Bible.[8] After killing, there was a cleansing ceremony by the *mwiriga* [clan] who is connected to the God, the Nyaga clan. They sacrifice a goat, and you are finished.

Now, if people do not want to kill you with a stone, neither they don't want to burn you, then your head is put in a beehive, and then they roll you down a hill into a valley. Nobody has killed you, but unfortunately you entered the wrong place, and you die that way. You call this a kind of vigilante justice. I never knew anyone punished like that.

During my father's time, there were very limited cases of crime, and they were treated right away. No court of appeals, but when you are proven guilty by a group of people, honorably, then you'll be treated in that way. That's the thing in Meru—people were fearing enmity. They want to live social lives, liking one another.

Somebody accused my father that he committed adultery. When accused, a person can choose between two things. He can take oath, saying, "I did not do this act that I am accused of, and if I did or if I meant to, then let this oath kill me." We believed it seriously. An oath could not only affect the individual, but if you go against it, it might also affect your family and your ancestors [and descendants]. It might upset your entire family. Almost nobody chose to take oath. Even if you did not do it, maybe you had a thought to do it, and that was enough to go against the oath.[9]

The other option was to take *gikama,* a ceremony where many people are observing. First the iron head of an axe was put into the fire until it becomes red hot. The Council of Elders says a special blessing over the fire, "He who fears the truth, let this *gikama* burn him. He who is innocent and speaks the truth, let it not burn him."

My father did this. I was not allowed at the ceremony because I was too young at that time, but we were waiting at the house to hear the results. My father put his hands out, and somebody spread lard on the insides. The axe was red enough from the fire. They put it in his hands, and my father walked some meters and brought it back again. His hands had only this white ash on them, from the lard I think, but they were not scalded or boiled. That proved my father was not guilty.

The man who accused him created enmity because it was proven that my father did not commit [adultery] with that man's wife. People took that man as a horrible person because he gave false information and made my father take *gikama*. That man was not believable any longer.

Some people said they were going to take *gikama*, but they had committed the things, so they knew it will burn them. In the end, they refused. Everybody knew, "Uh-huh! You don't have to take it—that's okay now, but you have committed the crime." Then you are judged and follow the same channels of those who are burnt. You have to pay whatever is decided. And then contribute a goat for cleansing.

Now we old people like myself have gone through all of this. We were Meru from the very beginning. It was only myself who became a Christian. My father was not. I know both sides. With everything, there is a cost.

MY MESSAGE CAME THROUGH MEASLES

Before the missionaries, we had no schools. I had never seen one. Nobody from this area knew how to read or write. A Scottish fellow called Dr. Irvine came and built the Chogoria mission in 1922. He got married to a very good Christian lady, the daughter of Ernest Carr.[10]

One of our relatives, Charles, joined the mission when it began. He went to school in Chogoria and settled there with other people of the same background. I never knew him, because once somebody became a Christian, he pretended to be completely different from other people.

The missionaries wanted their African mission people to become role models of the church, so they had to leave our culture—*kabisa* [wholly, absolutely]. That was very difficult. If you belonged to the mission, you were not carried as anybody in our community. Charles didn't attend most of our custom functions. To us, he was a lost man.

Those who were trained up to class five in Chogoria were sent back to teach in their home areas,[11] and the missionaries put up some outposts there. When Charles learned up to class five, he was posted back to his own country—that's Kiangua now. He was a teacher there for a time before I knew anything about it.

My father wanted me to go to school because he was a friend of that man. I don't know how, but my father differed greatly from his age-mates. He was not so deep with these traditional things. He tried to convince my first brother to go to school, but he didn't. The second one went for two days and then left. He refused. I had no interest to go to school, because I was a herd boy, and none of the boys in my area went. But my father wanted me to go, so that fellow from our clan, Charles, hired me to look after his goats, which were next to the school. My father wanted me to see other children of my age schooling. They thought by seeing the boys in school it would attract me to go to school, and of course it did.

There was a time that I felt that I wanted to be a man. I told my father, "I don't want to look after these animals at the school anymore. I don't want to go to the school."

He said, "Okay, if you don't want to go to school, then come back to your duty at home. Take your stick, and tend to our animals." Ah—I tell you, I did not like what my father said to me. I knew that I would never have the time that I wanted to roam about. I would be tied up with the animals from morning up to evening every day. I was only released from that when I went to school. My father was serious. He said, "If you don't go to school, follow the cattle. They are there." So I thought to go back to school.

I stayed with Charles looking after his goats for three months in 1934. Very unfortunately, which was [later to prove] fortunate to me, I got measles. Measles was a very spreading disease, so my relative didn't want me to stay at his school. I had to go back again to my home. It was so serious that I had to be taken to Chogoria Hospital. I could not walk, so my brothers were to carry me on a homemade bed of sacks. I was shivering, feeling a lot of cold, with all these very painful spots around the body and a very high temperature. It was like smallpox but bigger.

I had never gone to a big place where I could see the streets and the electricity. I'd been in rural areas [for]ever. Also, I saw my first *mzungu* there. I don't know the name of the woman—the white woman whom I saw—but she was a nurse. I was not so surprised, because I had seen an Indian before. At that stage we could never see the difference between Indian and European.

I was kept in a timber-roofed house, just alone because of this measles. I was to dip in warm water with I don't know what medicine, and all the sores that I had became somehow open. They were very painful, but within two to three days, I got healed. I was moved from that place to another where we were two boys, sleeping in one room. I don't know what the other boy had, but he had not the measles. He was called Njema.

On Sunday, we were told to go to church, Sunday school, wearing these hospital clothes. We had our own separate room, and we were shown where to sit on a bench so we did not mix with others. We listened to the service and saw young people of our age answering questions. We watched them. We didn't know the questions they were answering. Even we admired.

We said, this is a good thing. On the way going back to the hospital, I was talking with Njema. I said, "Njema, how do you see these people from Sunday school?"

"Me, I have never gone to school," he said.

"Would you like to? Let us promise that when you go back, and I go back, we go to school." We said, yes, we are going to do it. "Now, there is a time when the schools call all the students together. We must not miss this. We will meet there."

When I arrived home, I said I would go to school, and my father was very happy. On my way the first day, an old man from my area followed me. I never knew where he was going. When I entered school, he came in too. The teacher [Charles] was very happy to see both of us—a grown-up fellow and a boy. He said, "You have come!"

"Yes," I said.

He wanted me to stay with him. "Are you going to stay here?"

"No. I will be coming back and forth from my home. You did not like me when I was sick. You said your children will get measles, so I had to go home. You couldn't help me, so my mother told me never to depend on you."

I think the measles were a message calling for me to go to school. When I was looking after his goats, I did not want to go to the classroom. But when I became sick, I was taken to the hospital and met Njema. That's the Bible speaking. My message came through measles.

In 1935, I attended nursery school in the morning and then in the afternoon I went back home again. I did that for a term. I was older, a boy of thirteen by then, and finished nursery in one term. The next term I went to class one. I left the *mzee* [the old man who followed me to school] there. He couldn't write. I could read and write.

We were poorly taught in the beginning. Students from one class ahead were teaching us. And for two years I had terrible sores on my legs. Even now, I have scars. I was swollen above my ankle on my legs. It was not painful unless you touched it, but it gave a horrible smell. I went to Chogoria Hospital many times. I got a weekly dressing, but none of the medicines could stay because all of the pus inside. It was blackish all around on one leg—and then after some months, it showed reddish on the other side.[12]

I was very, very unhappy because everywhere I went, I knew people were smelling me. Ah, I suffered. Even when I shared a room with another boy, his mother was telling him, "Don't worry. Don't tease him. You're in good company. He will get better."

In 1936, the missionaries organized the event for all the boys in primary schools to gather at Chogoria. The promise that I made with Njema was in my memory, so I went and met my good friend there at the camp. We were sleeping in one house. We asked each other, "Can you write?" And we showed one another how we could write our names in little books. We enjoyed it very much. We said that we are going to continue.

For class one and two, there was no charge to go to school. Only at Chogoria for class three I had to pay fifty cents, a half-shilling, for each term. Grown-ups were paying one-fifty [one shilling and fifty cents]. My mom paid for the first term. Indians had brought tobacco to our area and gave seeds to people to plant, so my mother picked some tobacco from a bush on her way to sell *mwonyo* and gave it to the Indian at Igoji. "This is very poor grade, but I will pay you a little money," he said and paid her a shilling—two fifty-cent pieces. She gave me fifty cents, and I paid to go to school for one term.

In class two I was wearing this *shuka,* a white sheet, that my brother bought me. My father had planted tobacco, and my brother went to sell it to the Indian at Igoji, and he bought it for a rupiah [Indian currency worth two shillings]. Indians were the ones to bring money to this country [Meru].

Class three was a half day. We were starting school around noon and ended sometime around four thirty, so I had time to go back and forth to school from my home, and it was an easy thing to get food. It was a distance of eight kilometers, and *thigu** helped me to run. You want to keep the movement of that *thigu* not to let it fall, so no matter whether you want to run or not, you run. The more it runs, the more you run, and you never get tired, because you have work to do. Go to school—running, running, running—back to school—running, running, running. Everybody was to look at me and say, "What is this boy doing? Where does he go all the time? Why, he doesn't even care when it rains. Hmm."

In 1938, before class four, I met Njema at another field trip. "I can speak Kiswahili," I said. "I can write even Kiswahili."

"Very unfortunately, I failed," he said. "I'm repeating class three."

"You keep on," I said.

Thigu is a game in which a child fits a pronged stick over a tire or the rim of a tire and runs behind it, pushing the tire and trying to keep it upright.

That year, school was the whole day. From the morning you start at seven, you break up in the afternoon, and then return until the evening at four thirty. The first term was a very hard time for me because I had nowhere to eat. We were eating in communal groups, and I could not eat with my [circumcised] classmates at their house. Also, I could not carry anything with me to eat in the afternoon—that was somehow shameful in our culture. There was no money to buy food for lunch. I stayed only with the food we had eaten the night before with my group of boys. I made it twenty-four hours relying on that. So I went to Chogoria to do the morning session, came out during the afternoon break—nowhere to eat—back again to school, up to the night.

During that time, a man called Ernest had a business. He was the first one to do a hotel in this area. One afternoon, when he came from Chogoria, he saw me sleeping near his hotel. I was very hungry. He called me and gave me a cup of black coffee and a *mandazi* [fried dough]. I became strong, and I was very grateful to the *mzee*. That afternoon, I was happy to go back to school. I did not forget that.

It was a difficult time. I don't think I could do a second term if it continued like the first.

NO LONGER A BOY

In Kimeru, to pass from boyhood to become *murani*, you were to be circumcised. It was April fourth, 1938, during the school holiday. I was circumcised at age sixteen. Preparations had already been going on and local people were celebrating, but the school was not yet closed, so we, the people of the school, could only join during the very week of the event. It was a very cultural thing. People were singing songs, doing a lot of rituals to make sure that you are ready to be circumcised. The younger people honored you because you were going to separate from the boys.

Two days before the time came of circumcision, everyone was shaved. During school time, my hair was a natural, medium length—not long, not short, but we were not allowed to part the hair as gentlemen do.

We had a very honored traditional lady who my mother chose for our family with the advice of my grandmother. She was our ceremonial lady for all occasions. She was supposed to shave me, but she was too old and could not do it. So my sister took the typical Kimeru knife and did it. It was painful and cut you a little, but you couldn't mind.

The week before, you stayed with the *murani*, the older circumcised boys. You learned a lot, preparing to become a man. We were with those gentlemen, moving from one home to another, going wherever they wanted to eat. The night before circumcision you could hardly sleep. Very early in the morning, you were forced to take cold porridge of millet from your father's home. The porridge was supposed to help the blood clot quickly. You were to take as much as you could, not what you wanted, but until they see that you are filled up so that you will not shake. No matter whether you vomit, you drink. You are in a hurry. You have to follow each and every thing you are told, speedily. You get mixed up, but you followed whatever system you were given because you were projected to be *murani*. You are not your own by then.

From your father's home, you begin the journey to the river. On the way, you meet others on the road doing the same thing. After moving a certain distance, your clothes will be taken off, and you run to the place where you will wash. It will be very early, before six. Every locality had its own place for the boys to go and wash. Our river was called Maara. We had none of this anesthetic medicine, so the water was cold, and it was good for the blood and to reduce some of the pain, but it was not so good. There was an honored lady, a young one from a holy marriage, who could dip her leg into the water before, to say that the water is now free for the young to wash. Then, you could go to bathe.

From the water, you go to a field surrounded by bushes where you could not see inside. You are arranged according to the age of your father. I was number four. I was to be three, but the boy next to me was somehow related, and they didn't like blood to go to your brother [from one relative to another]. So we were separated, and I became number four. On that day we were thirteen in all, but you could find up to twenty in other groups. The group was called your *nthuki*.

You were not supposed to look at the circumciser. Everyone was looking one way. Somebody sat behind you to support you and make sure you sat properly. The old man was properly trained, and he didn't take time. Once it happened, everyone screams "heyyyyyy," and you are covered with a *shuka*. Then you can turn and look to see what has happened with the others. You were properly trained not to cry or make any noise or movements—not one. If you did, you would be laughed at, and it would be difficult for you to marry.

The mothers, all the women, were to gather around, but they were not allowed to see. They were very clever. They knew the arrangement, who was to go in what order, so they would listen to the shouting, the "heeeeeyyyyy!" and know if their son had finished. When they hear those shouts, they could never wait—they went home to say to everyone that it is done and their boy had gone through without fear. He was strong and brave, no longer a boy but a *murani*. They prepared many things to eat. It was a precious, wonderful ceremony, very enjoyable to the women. They would be very happy, jumping and dancing.

Supposing somebody had no mother, he will be treated in a wonderful kind of sympathy. The community will feed him. Someone well up in the community will take charge and take care for him. People will make sure he is well looked after. Nobody would know if you didn't have a mother.

If something happened in the family of someone hoping to be circumcised, if a child or anyone dies, that fellow could not go to the ceremony. We cannot mix two things—loss and happiness. You must give it time. I knew somebody that it happened to. He was called Mainda. The child of his brother died just two days before circumcision, so he could not mix with our group. Neither could he go back to mix with the younger boys, because he knows a lot of information which is only for people ready for circumcision. So Mainda went with his brother to Nairobi, and he stayed there with other *murani* for almost a year. He was circumcised in another group of people. We were praying that nothing should happen during the times of circumcision.

After circumcision, you walk back to your place with the group. You were not carried but walk yourself. You are in the middle, *murani* are behind you, and they follow you to the home which was built for you that day, called the *gicee*. People were singing. There was no hurry by then. You go to your *kibanda* [hut] very quietly, and the other *murani* will continue to their place. Even your mother will not know you have arrived.

Your *mugwati* [mentor] will tell your mother, "We have come. If you have any food, give [it to] us now." And my mother will prepare soup, and my father will give us meat. The *mugwati* had a very important role. He was the one to build your *gicee* on the very day of circumcision. He was in charge of everything during the healing time. He had to get water for bathing—everything was upon him to make sure that you were not bothered, so you could heal properly. Mine was chosen by my older brother, and I honored him. You stayed in seclusion being cared for by your *mugwati* and fed by your mother.

During this time of healing, you were trained how to be a man. You have to respect women because they can respect you only when you respect them. You never quarrel with your older family members, especially your older brother—you have to behave before them. They are married and have women who give you food.

After one to three months, you will come out of your *gicee*. The *murani* come to burn the house where you were staying. They burn it in a fire at night to say that whoever has been there is no longer there. The boy is gone. He has gone with the men. They sing songs that you have left and no more food should go to that place. You will be fat and healthy. Everyone will see that you were well looked after.

You are called a new name. You move up to "Mto" something. *Mto* is the title [like "mister"], to show that you are a man, a grown-up fellow. My father was asked what I should be called. According to my actions, he gave me the name "Thambu," "M'Thambu [Mr. Thambu]." "Thambu" means somebody who doesn't delay. If he means to go, he goes straight away. He doesn't waste time. I don't know where my father got it, but I knew the meaning, and I liked it. When I became M'Thambu, I did away with "Kithinji." Young fellows or age-mates could never call me by the name my mother gave me as a boy. Only the people of my mom and father's age could call me by my birth name, Kithinji.[13]

If you misbehaved, your whole *riika* [age group] will suffer. Someone would say, "We cannot keep *murani* of this kind. Now because of him, come on, gentlemen—you will be beaten." People were fearing.

One day, we were together waiting for meat to be prepared. Somebody said, "Before we take this meat, let us talk about the way that you are moving." One of my friends reported that he saw a fellow from our group taking snuff from a lady. The lady did not give him the tobacco, but he took it himself.* My friend was serious. He said, "You did not see me, but I was hiding, watching you. Why did you do so?"

We were worried because it was during the daytime, and women were passing along this big road. We did not want to be beaten in front of them. We looked down to the ground, and without our notice, that gentleman took off. We could only see the back of him running away. He ran away like a boy, but he was circumcised. He did not turn back

---

*To "take tobacco" from a lady was code for "have sexual relations."

up. He went to live in Chogoria forever until he became a Christian and got married.

Ah, we were beaten. And we did not eat any of the meat. They sympathized with me a little, but I had to take two or three canes. It was terribly shameful—we were beaten in front of women. I regretted going to that meeting. It was during the school holiday, and I thought, *Why did I come to this meeting?* I told my friend, "Please, don't report like that again. Report it during the nighttime. We were terribly ashamed."

"I meant you to be ashamed!" said my friend. "Why did that man take snuff from the lady?" Your age group was seriously watching you to make sure you were not sexually playing or anything. It was believed that you will curse the entire age group if you were reckless. You were to keep friendship with a lady until you were married. When we had dances with women, no matter whether someone is your girlfriend, we were to take the girls home in groups. You could never go home alone. We wanted these young ladies to love us, but *murani* kept us away from them. If something happened, you suffered consequences seriously. It will be known by everyone that you have messed and spoiled yourself. You will not be invited to any traditional event. It would be hard for you to marry because you are known by that thing, and it was everlasting.

A TIME WHEN HITLER LAUGHED

Around the fifth of May [1938], I was okay and went back to school. Without being told what happened during the holiday, the teachers could know, "Uh-huh, these are *murani* now." Some of the teachers respected those who have done it. After circumcision, you were to leave each and every childish thing behind. Even you were not allowed to go with *thigu*, which helped me to go to school. I asked my age-mates, "Please, allow me to do this. I'm not doing what uncircumcised boys are doing, but please, for this situation, I'm going very far to school, and I need to use it." I couldn't make it without *thigu*.

They couldn't argue. "Let him do it," they said. So I continued.

After circumcision, I was part of a larger community of circumcised boys, and it helped me very much. I became great friends with Francis, who was circumcised before me. Francis had a grandmother within [near] the place [school], and we used to go and get something to eat from her in the afternoon and then go back again to school.

We had to pay fifty cents, a half shilling, to attend school, and it was difficult to get a shilling, so we used to dig holes for the missionaries for planting coffee. We were paid two cents a hole. I dug six holes, and I got twelve cents. That bought me twelve long sugarcanes. I went to sell them far away, down past the market, for two cents each. I had twenty-four cents. That twenty-four could buy me twenty-four mugs of millet. Then, with that millet, I went to exchange it with maize in Kithunguri, far away, past Meru Town. I got a bushel of maize. Then I took that bushel of maize to an Indian and sold it for one shilling. With that I could buy shorts and pay for one term. You have to work for it, but there was no alternative if you wanted to wear shorts. Otherwise, I was a big boy, wearing *shuka*.

My teacher in class four was an awkward fellow. He was mixed up. We performed poorly in his class, and I missed the chance to go directly to boarding school. From his class, only two fellows passed well and were taken to Chogoria Boarding. I was number three.

Very luckily, because I was very good at doing high jump, the teachers favored me. I defeated one of the Chogoria fellows of my age in a competition. They wanted me to come to boarding. I was called to do an interview, the "general examination," with a lot of tests identifying animals and pictures and things. I passed and was taken to boarding in 1939, and that is where the problem arose because the fees were higher.

I had to pay ten shillings per term. My elder brother helped me to pay the first term, but I couldn't get money for the second term. I had to join the people doing carpentry during the holidays for the missionaries. I was a good carpenter and could make wonderful desks and tables. We had to remain in school for three extra weeks and do whatever was needed. We were given one week to go home for the holiday, and the missionaries paid my fees because of my carpentry work. That's how I managed to get through primary education.

When I entered into boarding in class five, I was given a uniform. Now I was a gentleman, a boarding *murani*. All the problems that I had of traveling from my place to Chogoria ended. I was very happy. My friend Njema got lost in class four. He couldn't pass. When I was taken to boarding school, I could see him, but I was a gentleman wearing a good uniform. He was still wearing *shuka*. I told Njema, "I'm not speaking Kiswahili now, I can write even English!" We were ever friends.

That year I had another poor fellow for my teacher who failed from the teaching college. He taught us English and math. We had to work very hard to pass the common entrance exam, which you had to pass or else you couldn't go to intermediate school. Luckily in boarding we were staying with other fellows in higher classes, of class six, seven, and eight, and I learned a lot from them. I nicely passed the common entrance on my first try. Everyone else had to repeat.

We took many subjects in intermediate [grades six, seven, and eight]. We were to do math, English, Swahili, geography, nature studies, hygiene, history, agriculture, and handicrafts. Math and English were compulsory. [In] hygiene [class] we learned about dressing, cleanliness, and the animals that cause disease—that we should keep away from fleas and all these things—and also that drinking water should be boiled. Nature study was the study of birds, flies, insects, but not animals. Animals were a part of agriculture. History was when the Arabs came to the coast, how the Europeans came, how we people lived, and where did we come from. Also we learned our local African geography—the altitudes, where it rains, the seasons, the latitudes, the deserts. I liked math the most. Everyone in this family is good in math.

In class six, there was a very serious hunger in our locality. There was no food in 1940. The mission could not keep us in the boarding, because they could not feed us. [The] only [ones who could remain were] the Embu people, because they were able to pay more money than ourselves.[14] I was sent home. The school was closed in April for holiday. We were told that when it opened in May, boarding would be closed. Whoever wanted to attend school had to come from home. Most of the people went to a Catholic school at Mujwa, but I could not go, because I could not afford the school fees. I was getting my fees through carpentry.

It was terribly wet and raining when the school opened in May. I arrived at eight ten in the morning.* The headmaster of the school was a Gikuyu fellow named James Kaberee Kahuho, "Mwalimu [i.e., Teacher] James."

Mwalimu James saw me coming that morning. I was covering myself with a banana leaf, but still I was soaking [wet]. He called me to speak with him. "Do you mean that you are coming from your home?" I said yes. Then he took me to a room inside. When we used to stay in the dormitories, we were given two pairs of shorts and shirts yearly. In the middle of the year,

---

* Heavy rains make the hilly dirt roads nearly impossible to traverse.

24   HOW I GREW

we could return a pair and get a new one. So, in the room inside, there were very many returned shorts and shirts. "Try to see whether you can find a good one there and take off this wet one," said Mwalimu. "Wear it, and then put yours to dry."

So I went and changed my clothes. They were good clothes. In the afternoon at four, Mwalimu James called me again and asked, "Have your clothes dried?" I said yes. "You can use either. Come tomorrow. If it rains, you will change into them." I took off the old one that I had and wore mine going home.

The following morning it rained again. Mwalimu James was waiting to see me. "Now, are you going to continue like this?" he asked. I told him yes. "Then I'm going to pay your fees. You go and pay your class master." He gave me ten shillings.

There was another boy who was doing the same thing, coming from home. Mwalimu James negotiated with Dr. Irvine. "There are two chaps, one from Makerero and the other one is Thambu coming from upper Kiangua. They do come very wet in the morning. Can we squeeze them in with the chaps from Embu?"

Dr. Irvine agreed. So in the evening Mwalimu called me and the other fellow. "Now, today you will go back to the dormitory. Eat the little food that those Embu people are eating."

"Thank you very much, Mwalimu." So we joined them. My fees were cleared, and the problem of coming from home ended. At the end of June, there was plenty of food, and we continued. Some of those who went away came back, but some didn't turn up.

I was very grateful to that *mwalimu*. When the time came of baptism, I needed a Christian name. Dr. Irvine was very strict that you could not be baptized without copying a name from the Bible. It is because of that *mwalimu* that I chose the name Japhlet. In the issues of signing things, he had put "JKK" for his initials. I wanted to sign like my teacher, and I already had "Kithinji King'ua," so I needed a name to start with "J." I went to a book of the Bible called Chronicles, and I met [found] the word "Japhlet." Then I could sign my initials like my teacher, Mr. James.

I took two years to learn the catechism and all the rules of the church. Then you had to take a test from the catechist teacher. If you pass, you got baptized. I was the first in my family. My mother didn't want me to do so, because in our traditional Kimeru, especially in our clan of the God, Nyaga, we never ate wild animals. Never. We had similarities with the Israelites for the food we ate.[15] But when you become a Christian, you have to eat any of the animals, the pigs or whatever. My mother was very worried for me to be Christian. She did not want the pig to touch any of the plates or utensils that my family was using. She said, "You will be using your own plate, and your cup will be assigned for you. We will never mix with somebody who eats wild animals."

But I had my good sister, Mercy, and she helped me. "I will cook for Japhlet and eat food with him," she said to our mom. "We shall have our own cooking because we are Christian, and we can eat any animals. Give us our plates and pots to cook for ourselves, and you cook for the rest of us." So my mother was not complicated, because my sister supported me. And my dad was supporting my sister, so it was not serious. I could continue.

Now also the war was very serious here. It was called the Second World War—"World," because everybody was touched by it. We never knew how it was that Germans came to fight against certain Europeans, but the Germans started with Poland and Holland and also France. When they beat France, the Italians joined. Italy joined the Germans. They were almost to win against London when the Americans joined. Britons were fearing that if America joined, that Russia will join the other side. But luckily, the Russians joined the British side.

In Africa we had colonies of these people. The Britons had more colonies in Africa than other European countries. The British were to fight against the Italians in Ethiopia and Somalia, so our people, the King's Rifles as it was called,[16] were to join. When we speak of Europeans, we usually speak of British, but this war was with the whole continent.

All the Italians in our country were taken captive by the Europeans [British]. In Nyeri, there was a big prison for Italians. One day, some escaped and came along through the forest to Chogoria. They went to a hotel here where they were trying to get food. People reported that there were Italian prisoners from Nyeri, and Dr. Hill and Dr. Irvine came to see them. Dr. Hill was a doctor in Meru, and he spoke Italian. They took the five Italians to Dr. Irvine's home. They were given chapatis [Indian pancakes], and at night they were given water to take baths. It is at this time that one man revealed he had a pistol and gave it to Dr. Irvine. Dr. Irvine said, "God is good. We prayed with these people. We treated them nicely. And after all, instead of killing us, one surrendered a pistol." The following morning, they were taken to the DC's [district commissioner's] office in Meru and then went back to prison.

The government used the Italians jailed during the Second World War to build the road going from Nairobi to the Rift Valley. There was an escarpment there, and the road was built on a very steep cliff. We heard that many people died falling from that escarpment down to the ground. So they made a church, and it is still there, where the Italian prisoners could pray before going to start their work. The British took great advantage to use Italian labor.

We lived in fear. We had to cover our houses in Chogoria with grass [banana leaves] because we were fearing bombing. We were not allowed to have light on during the evening time. Dr. Irvine told us to put off all our lights because of the Italian planes from Somalia. They bombed [the city of] Isiolo in 1941.

We were to pray in Chogoria. We went to the church one day, and Dr. Irvine started crying before he got to the prayers. The priest had to take over. We were worried. "Why has Dr. Irvine cried?" Dr. Irvine told us that when some French people were fighting on one side in the English Channel, the Germans came another way around. The French thought that it was the British coming from the other side. But they were the Germans. Instead of taking the French captives, the Germans shot each and every French *askari*. They told us that you could never see the sea—it was all blood running on the top. We could never understand what he meant. We prayed and cried. The whole English Channel was nothing but blood.

According to how people fight, if you get people who surrender, you're supposed to get them [as] captives. All the Britons, all over their country and all over Kenya, they had camps for Italians and other enemies. They were put in prisons. In Germany, they didn't do it. We Kenyans never knew the hatred that Hitler had. We were fearing him because we thought he was a very powerful warrior, but we never knew that he had an animal mind. It was when I went to Israel that I realized.[17] He was a killer. He was not fighting people to conquer but to finish [them].

The way that he killed Israelites—he was beyond a human being, beyond an animal—he was neither. He was evil. He killed children. I don't know whether anybody would like to be called "Hitler." No. I tell you, when that sea was blood, it is a time Hitler laughed.

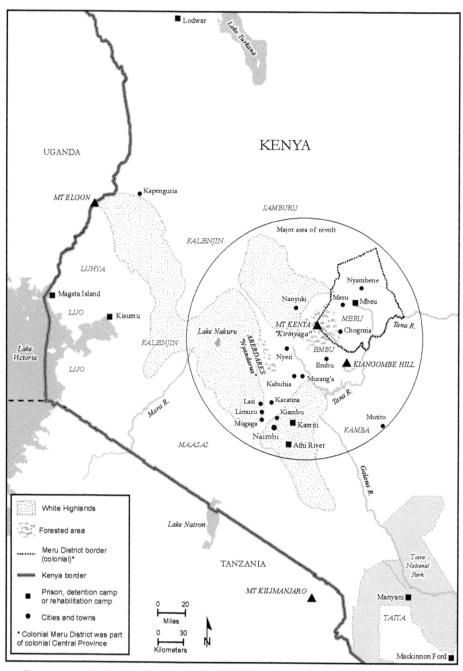

Regions involved with the Mau Mau Rebellion, 1952–63. *(Map by Brian Edward Balsley, GISP)*

PART II

BLACK MARKET

PAID FROM THE CENTER

In class eight, I was again the only student who came [direct] from class seven. The rest were repeaters. From class eight you have to sit for the Kenya African Primary Examination. We were not doing the same education as the Europeans or Indians—ours was for Africans. There was only one secondary school [for Africans] for the Central Province, that's Alliance High School.[1] If you could pass the exam with an A or B+, you could go to Alliance High School. The best students were taken there. This was an alliance of the Church of Scotland (that's the PCEA [Presbyterian Church of East Africa]), the Church of England (that's Anglican), and the Methodist. There were no Catholics allowed to go to Alliance High School.

I did not score well enough to go to Alliance. But I was fearing that I might fail, and if I failed, I didn't know where I could go. If you didn't pass in English, you had to do agriculture, veterinary, or carpentry. But I was lucky that I passed in math and English. We were very few in the class by then—I think we were only thirteen. Five passed, eight failed. I got my Kenya Certificate of Primary Education and graduated in 1942. I could continue to study in a higher grade, called P-3, and join either nursing or teaching.

In 1943, I went to Meru General Hospital and did my first year of nursing practice to see whether I liked it or not. You take a year of observation—if you like it, you enroll in the full program. I stayed for seven months, and I didn't like it. I could have gone to Nairobi and completed the course, but I decided not to continue with nursing. I saw that it won't help me in the future. Why? Because there were no hospitals or dispensaries within a district which would allow me to farm. I decided that I wanted to teach in my own area, where I could develop myself and have a farm. I knew that's what would help me make my living. I thought that if I got married and had to live in a city, then what would my wife be doing? She might not be educated. She could not do something for the family living in a city, so after all what would our life be?

I came back and reported to the European education officer at Chogoria, Bwana Watt, "I would like to go to Kahuhia Teaching College." Kahuhia was a big, national teaching college with people from all over the Central Province, the Coast Province, and parts of the Rift Valley. The European officer laughed at me. "Didn't I tell you to do that the first time?" he said. I studied at Kahuhia Teaching College for two years—1944 and 1945.

Kahuhia was the college that had good teachers. We had a *mzungu* lady called Miss Oakley. She was a wonderful woman and a good teacher. Later, she went to teach at Alliance High School. We had English, nature studies, and hygiene with Miss Oakley. She also taught us PE, with very hard exercises to perform. She could do exercises that we could never do. Ah, she could jump like the Akamba.[2] I knew [learned] women could play sports, and I respected her very much, and I learned how to deal with the girls [in the classroom].

"The problem you are going to face, especially as a young fellow, is that you have young and grown-up fellows in the same class," she told me. "When you have to teach a class with grown-up men of your age together with grown-up girls, it will be hard because all of them are naughty. The girls will not like to perform together with the boys, and we have no school for only girls. So what we are going to do is treat them serious. If you go and laugh with them, they will learn nothing from you. Never, never separate them from the groups. Make sure you don't discriminate them from the boys, old or young. They are your age-mates, so you can make friends, but with integrity that you are the teacher."

We also had Mr. Hooper. He was a hardworking fellow. I remember he could sweat and change his color to red. He did the teaching methods. We liked Mr. Hooper and Miss Oakley very, very much. They were active, and we could play football [soccer] and netball with them. Both were not married, so we were all young fellows. Mr. Kentle was the principal. He taught drawing and the principles of teaching. Those were three good European teachers. Mr. Nyaga was an African, from Makerere [University, in Uganda], and he was to teach us the vernacular method,[3] Kimeru and Gikuyu, and also math.

I was appointed the head of students. I could attend even the staff meetings of the teachers. For my last two terms in 1945, a teacher of class six fell sick in an intermediate school where Mr. Nyaga was teaching, and I was appointed to take his class. I did that for the rest of the year until I was called to do the government exam for teaching, the P-3. I got the certificate of P-3, which was a good certificate to have.

The teachers at Kahuhia liked me, and they wanted me to teach at the primary school where all the trainees had to do their practice teaching. "I'm sorry," I said, "I am needed at Chogoria. My people want me back at my place." But if Dr. Irvine gave me trouble, I could come [back] to Kahuhia because the Europeans there were my friends.

I began teaching at a school called Kimucia in Chogoria, the biggest primary school within the locality. When I came there, the teachers were fearing me because they knew I was going to perform, and some had failed from the place where I got my certificate of teaching.

I taught class five. Some students were even older than me and had repeated three times, trying to take the common entrance exam but failing. The uncircumcised students were easy to teach, because I could talk to them or beat them, and they would cry. They always listened. But with the ladies and gentlemen, we had to negotiate.

On the first day, we had a nice meeting. First, I talked to the *murani*. I said, "Gentlemen, do you know why you are repeating here?"

"No, Mwalimu."

"One thing: it's because you are *murani*," I said. "You are circumcised fellows, and you never mix with the uncircumcised boys. Because of that, you are failing. You must lower yourself to that status of the boys who are not circumcised. If you lower yourself, I can assure you [that you] are going to pass. So will you do the same PE or whatever I tell you to do, just like the others in your class?" They agreed.

Then I talked to the girls and used the teaching of Miss Oakley. I told them that if they are girls, then they have to go and marry. But if they are students, then they are going to follow what I say and do exactly the same as what is being done by the other students. Later, many became teachers, and they told me, "Mwalimu, you helped us to know many things. You were open to tell us that it was not the time to marry."

Just recently we had a nice woman, an ambassador from America, visit us during a meeting of Njuri Ncheke. She was called Aurelia Brazeal—a big, strong, colored woman. She said that she had enjoyed Kenya but asked us if we [Meru] were like the Maasai or the Turkana. She wanted to know how we thought about the education of women. We told her that in Meru, we differ from those people. We declared that we were not going to strictly follow some of the traditions of our culture. There is no circumcision of women, and we equally educate our girls.

"I am very happy to hear that," she told us. "I have two sisters but no brother. My father told us that all his wealth, all the money that he had together with my mother's, was going to make sure that we could compete in the world. He wanted us to become a member of the world through education. So educate girls, educate boys—they are the children of the country."

I think that lady was happy with us. "Also teach other people, the Turkana and the Maasai, that a vehicle cannot go with a punctured wheel. It will be clicking to one side because it will never be balanced. If you leave women out of education, one side of the vehicle will not work. No matter how beautiful, the vehicle won't run smoothly," she said. "Fill that side with air, and you will run in a wonderful car." With education we must go together.

At Kimucia, we changed the school. Every schoolteacher was to look at me doing the PE of Miss Oakley, with girls jumping and whatever, and nobody could laugh. I introduced sports competitions to Chogoria like we had in Kahuhia. I had four football teams—two teams of girls and two teams of boys, junior and senior. We competed with schools locally and got a lot of trophies. Within a short time many youth came from the reserve [rural areas] to play. They heard there was a good teacher doing good work with big girls, and many who had left school came back to do the PE in the evening and play football. *Kina* [people like] Jesca came to play football. She had left school in class five but enjoyed playing sports.

In 1946, I sent twenty-one students to Chogoria Intermediate. Before that, no students had passed. Mr. Bernard Mate was principal at Chogoria, and he was very happy to see me sending so many students to his school.[4] "Now you have filled one class," he said. Other teachers wondered whether their children would have a chance to go to school, because all of class six was filled with my Kimucia boys and girls.

Even I had to quarrel with Mr. Mate, [though,] because he did not want old people in the school. One of our age-mates, Mr. Dobe, was from a poor family, and his legs were full of *jiga* [chiggers].[5] He wanted to study in our school, but Mr. Mate said no. I said, "Mr. Dobe is a local fellow and has performed very well. Even myself—I went to school at an age of thirteen, and I was lucky to mix with small boys. So give Mr. Dobe only the four years he has to do the primary education, and I think you will find him useful later on." Mr. Mate took Mr. Dobe as a student but was not happy [about doing so]. Mr. Dobe passed both English and math and went into nursing at Chogoria. Many years later, I met Mr. Dobe caring for Mr. Mate's wife at Chogoria Hospital. I was very happy. I went and told Mr. Mate, "The nurse of your wife is Dobe, and he's doing a very good job."

I knew the places where I got mixed up in school because I had poor teachers, so I cleared the problems for my students. The most important thing about teaching is knowing the person who is learning from you. When you go to young children, you have to remember the understanding you had at their age. You will see people enjoy learning because the information is clear, and they can respond. You get very good friends.

Teachers are not rich people—that we know. The people working in the government have money. The poorly paid people are teachers, and they are doing great things, but it's not a business. That's the thing. Teaching is not a business. It is a body-building—a culture-building, whatever-building—it is a building of some sort, but it is not a business. What you build—they can become the business people and run hotels or rule the country or do anything, but you are the builder. So our work will be paid, but not in money. The work gets paid from the center.

Students and parents loved me. The problem was that I was not "saved," according to the missionaries. It was very early that I began quarrelling with them.

Dr. Irvine and I exchanged some bad words when I started teaching. When I had gone to the college, I had no money for transport, so Dr. Irvine gave me nine shillings for each way to Kahuhia. I told him I would pay his money back when I became a teacher. Now when I received my very first teaching salary, Dr. Irvine had cut the money that I used for transport. He told the clerk to only give me half of my first salary—instead of forty shillings, I was brought twenty.

I had barely started teaching, and I did not even have anything to cook with. I was annoyed. I put the twenty shillings in the envelope and sent it back to them. "Why have you taken my first salary?" I asked.

Dr. Irvine said, "Because you have taken money when you went to Kahuhia. You promised to pay when you came back to teach."

"But why not give me time to settle? Why did you take my very first salary?" We started quarreling there. "Now Japhlet, you know the way the mission has helped you to grow," he told me. "I took you in as my boy, and I helped you more than others so that you could pursue teaching."

I was very serious. "Do you know the difference between a slave boy and a boy of somebody?" I said. "The time that I stayed with you I was in a very slavery situation. Do you know that I couldn't go home when all the other children were going home? I stayed there making your desks and chairs. I never even received the money. You paid nothing back to me for my labor, only ten shillings for the fees. Do you know I completed school with one [pair of] shorts and one shirt, and I was wearing a blanket on Saturday when I had to wash these? Is that how you helped me? Is that what you mean by calling me your boy? Ah—to hell with your money and even your teaching."

I wrote a letter to Dr. Irvine: "I will never teach in this school. Now that I have started this thing with you, I don't want your money. I can go back to the teaching college, or I will go to an Independent school and teach there."

By that time we had our African schools that were not run by the missionaries. There was a good one at Kiambu founded by a man called Johnson. Dr. Irvine did not write to me, so I said "That's it" and gave him back his money. I took my books from my father-in-law's house; although I was not engaged to Jesca by then, I was keeping my books at their house because they lived close to the school. I went to meet with Mzee Johnson, who ran the Independent schools.

Dr. Irvine went to see Jesca's father and asked him, "Do you know anything about Japhlet going to the Independent school? Is it true he has left our school?"

"We don't know," he said. "He used to keep his books at my home, and he took his books." Dr. Irvine gave him a letter and asked if he could try and give it to me. I went to the Independent school, but it was not open. I had to pass my father-in-law's home on the way. He gave me the letter from Dr. Irvine on a Saturday. The letter said, "Japhlet, when you get this letter, please forget all what was written and come and see me."

I went to see him on Monday. I was quite prepared to visit him. I had my good Kimeru knife with me. Dr. Irvine was somehow wild. Once he became annoyed, he could give anyone a blow. I knew: *If this man tries to beat me as he beats other people, I will strike with a knife.*

Dr. Irvine saw me through the window, and he came to the door. "Come, Mr. Japhlet," he said. I was happy to hear him calling me "Mister." He never called any of the teachers "Mister." Never. That was the first time I heard "Mr. Japhlet." Dr. Irvine talked very friendly, and then his wife came. The wife of Dr. Irvine was a wonderful, good lady. We called her "Mom," and she was calling us "my boys."

"How are you, Japhlet?" she said.

"Thank you, Mom. I'm okay, Mom."

"Let us pray." She prayed, and after that, she brought me a cup of tea. I wanted to hear what Dr. Irvine had to tell me, but he didn't speak any words. "Why have I come?" I said.

"Mom wanted to pray with you. That's all," he said.

We honored that woman very much. She built the nice building for Chogoria Boys, the school I attended. She did that with her own money. And she was teaching us English in class eight. She never liked to see anybody suffering. Even she could not pass through certain roads going to school, because if she met somebody who was sick, she would come back and tell me, "Japhlet, oh, Japhlet. Somebody's sick. You have to go see him." She had her own way of coming to school, and we escorted her. We were very attentive to see whether she's coming and open the door for her.

It is through her that Dr. Irvine became converted. If he beat or abused anybody, his wife would cry. She was the opposite of Dr. Irvine. She knew that she could solve any problem, so she didn't want to involve him. She tamed the brutality of Dr. Irvine, and he finally cooled down. Later he changed completely and became a priest.

That afternoon, after listening to her, I said, "Okay. Thank you very much, Mom," and I left. I went again to the Independent school, but Mzee Johnson was in Nairobi, so I could not make any arrangements. Coming home, I passed the house of Jesca's father and met [got] an envelope. There was a letter from Mom. "Thank you very much, my boy. You came, we prayed together—now leave what you are talking with Dr. Irvine. Go back to school." All my money was there, the full salary. I did not speak to Dr. Irvine, and I did not speak to Mom, but I honored that lady. That was all. I went back to teaching at Kimucia.

Still, the problem that I had was that I was not saved. There was a European education officer called Mr. Graeves. He was a good Scottish fellow, older than Dr. Irvine, and he wanted me to become an inspector. But Dr. Irvine and the missionaries told him, "This man Japhlet, although he's a good teacher, he's not converted. He's not saved." Mr. Graeves came and told me they didn't want anybody to join the inspectors' team unless he's saved.

"Ah, leave it," I said. "I'm satisfied with my teaching." Missionaries had very tight rules, and some were kinds of hypocrites. I learned from my friend Ernicio that he was only getting three-quarters of his salary from the Catholic mission. We went to find out [why] in the church. Eh-eh-eh.

That father was almost to hit me. He said that Ernicio had to pay the Catholic church that money.

"Do you accommodate this teacher in your house?" I asked. The father said no. "So what are you doing with the twenty shillings of his?" He could not say who took the other quarter of his salary. It was something like offering. "Ah, never, never," I said. "If you want him to pay something for room and board to the mission, okay. He pays it back to you. But for any church business or whatever—give him his full salary." We were lowly paid already—why would they only pay their teachers some of their salary? They paid Ernicio his money back, and he was happy to know that he was being paid rightly.

We had a union to represent the teachers—the Meru African Teachers Union. We wanted Mr. Mate to be chairman, but he feared Dr. Irvine because he was principal of Chogoria Boys. So I said, "I will be chairman. You, Mr. Mate, will be our advisor. We don't fear these people."

SOMEBODY TO HELP ME

One of the teachers at Kahuhia told me that the longer you stay not married, the more mistakes you make. "If you want to start nicely, get married," he said. "I stayed for four years before I did, and I know the mess I made. I tried to make everything right so that when my wife comes, she will meet a good home—but I didn't make a good home until I got married."

I taught for only two years before I got married. I felt that without having somebody to help me, I couldn't make it. Now I'm not shy to tell you that I had a girlfriend before Jesca. We stayed together for over a year, but I never understood her in the way that I wanted, and she never understood me. I was in the teaching college by then, and I spent one night at her home. We talked throughout the night, and she was very surprised that sexually I did not touch her. *Why should I hurry?* I thought. If I committed anything [sexually], then rightly I'd have to marry her because the missionaries could sack me from the college, so I was fearing.

I went home for a three-month holiday. When I was due to come back, I got a letter from a close friend of that girl. I think it was December 1944. The letter told me that the girl was suffering from tuberculosis and had been admitted in the hospital.

When I came back, I met the girl being very sick. She was isolated in her own room in the hospital. When she saw me, tears ran down her face.

I said, "*Pole* [sorry]. Don't worry. You will be healed." But the girl died. She didn't survive, and I said okay—God is good because I was never understanding her in the way that I wanted.

From there I had very many friends. You know, I was a friendly fellow with everybody. I was a good dancer, a good talker—very social. I taught with a few teachers who had good educations, but I never liked their character. They were very much after me, but I knew: *Ah, these are very dangerous people.* Those with good CVs don't always do the best job. During my time of marrying, I did not want papers. I did not want somebody who had degrees and a good CV. I wanted somebody whom I could talk to, whom I can reconcile with when one does a mistake, and whom I know the character [of]. I observed those ladies [at school] and said, "No. I don't want this. I don't want somebody who will give me difficulty with farming." God helped me to know that I didn't want to end up poorly. I knew whatever little I got from teaching I could invest in the soil.

The school at Kimucia was very close to Jesca's home, where I kept my books. I had known her father because he was a cook employed in Dr. Irvine's home in Chogoria. He began working there as a young fellow before he was married. He was one of the first missionaries, and he was a good Christian and a very good farmer. I also met her brother, a good boy, in class two when I was teaching.

Jesca had left school very early, and now she was working with her mother. I started watching Jesca, farming with her mother, following one another to church and coming back again. I took time to study her and learn her character. I knew the father was very, very good, and so was the mother. She [Jesca] was brought up in a wonderful way, and her father had wonderful cattle, and although he was employed, he relied on his farm to feed the family since the beginning. I thought, *This girl has never gone anywhere. If she follows what I tell her and strictly adheres to it, according to her work ethic, we will make a very good shamba.* I decided to approach her.

One evening, when I was writing my notes at her father's home, we ate together. I asked her, "Would you like me to become a friend of yours?" She thought that I was okay, but she never knew what I meant. She was afraid to say anything, so I wrote her a letter. I called her to come to the place where I used to have lunch, and we talked a lot. "Me, I'm a teacher," I said, "and I know your education is very low. I like you because of the way you were brought up. I want to be a farmer and live the life as your father lived.

Will you follow my teachings? If I want you to go and learn something, will you do it?"

"Yes," she said.

"Don't just say 'yes' because you don't know what to say. Don't joke. I know you are from a very good family. You are going to a poor family, but forget the poor family of my mother and father—you will be of me. I will try to keep you as you have been living, but your mother and father didn't start in that life. They started down below, where we will start, and then we will try to see whether we can come up to the standard you have been living. Now, I'll give you time to think. Please don't speak to your mother. I don't want your parents to know what we have talked about until you take time to reason [it out] yourself."

The very same evening she revealed it to her mother. When I went there the next time, I saw a lot of changes. I said to Jesca, "Did you reveal this to your mother?" Then we repeated the same conversation that we had earlier. I said, "Now you can reveal. But if we have a disagreement, I want us to reconcile our things. I don't want you coming to your parents. If you feel that you don't like something, please never let it go on. I will give you good time to think and prepare, so you can know me. Let's understand one another, as friends."

We meant to live, and we talked of our life. We stayed talking nicely but keeping away from anything sexual. We had no method of condoms, and I didn't want anything sexually that would make us to love one another. That's the thing that will end within the first week. I wanted to see something that is endless.

After six months' time, I said, "Can I approach your father now?"

"If you wish to," she said. I approached the family.

By that time, teachers were very honored. Everybody wondered why I was leaving the teachers, the learned ladies, to marry a girl of class five, but I was so impressed [with her]. "This is my choice," I said, "and [at least] I did not marry a student."

On the sixteenth of August in 1947, we married in the church. There were no cars by then, but we were carried on a lorry [truck]. It was only myself from our age group who carried his wife on a lorry. And the people danced and sang good songs—ah, we were very proud.

When we married, I wanted to start my *shamba*. But I was told, "This is not your family's land. Do you know where your land is?" I said no. "It's there at Kinoro, a place called Mutunguru. That is your *shamba*." You could only plant crops in your original family's land. At that time, I was living in Ikumbo. That's where I was born, but it was not the place of our very original family land. During the hunger in 1919,[6] all the people left our land and went to live together there and try to survive. Some others went to Embu and never returned to their original places.

I came to this place, Mutunguru, where we are living now, and my father showed me our land. Jesca and I moved here together. We were the first to resettle on our family land, and my brothers followed. We wanted to plant coffee, but this area, beyond the river Mutonga, was not planting coffee. I had to approach Dr. Irvine to see whether we can plant coffee.

When the Europeans came to Kenya, they brought coffee and planted tea, but that was for Europeans only. They didn't allow any Africans to cultivate it. We Africans had nothing of the cash crops. The white settlers had a union, the Kenyan Planters or Farmers Association—the KPA, I think. It was a combined association for the European farmers that had coffee, tea, and pyrethrum.[7] Pyrethrum is used to kill insects and was doing very well in the Limuru areas, bringing a lot of money. Dr. Irvine was appointed to attend the union's meetings in Nairobi on behalf of the church. He, together with a missionary from Kaaga and an Italian from Mujwa, complained that when their local people became Christians they were very poor.

He said to the Europeans, "In the places where we work in Meru, those people are good Christians. They want to be missionaries, but their poverty is beyond [bad]. It is a long way for them to go and work in those plantations [near Nairobi]. There's no means of transport. They cannot even pay tax because they don't have any cash crops. So could you kindly please allow us to plant coffee with these people, which we will bring to you, and you sell it? Just give a little help to them."

The Europeans were very aware of how it could affect their *shamba*s. They were getting their laborers from the Central Province, and Meru was of the Central Province. There was an argument between the white settlers, saying, "If you want to introduce coffee in Meru, Gikuyu will do the same, and once they have money from their own *shamba*s, they won't come to work in ours."

Dr. Irvine said, "We are very far from where you are, so you will never lose people. Gikuyu will not come to work in Meru. Our coffee will never interfere with your farms in Limuru or Kiambu." The missionaries fought for us to plant coffee. The Europeans [in the union] asked, "And who is going to do the research?"

"We are," said Dr. Irvine. "We will see whether coffee can do well in our areas." They were allowed to do the experiment, and Dr. Irvine planted a little *shamba* of coffee in Chogoria. That was early 1930s. When it gave beans, Dr. Irvine put a little machine in the mission to take off the *maganda* [husks]. Then he went back again to the European coffee board and took a sample. They tasted the coffee and saw it was good. "Come and see our experiment," said Dr. Irvine. "The coffee is doing very well within the areas that we are [farming]. Can you please give coffee to the people who have agreed to become missionaries?" They said yes.

So the people like Jesca's father who were baptized and working in the mission were allowed to plant. They were given a few coffee trees and made a nursery for growing coffee. It is we who dug the holes in the *shamba*s of those missionaries. When the coffee did very well in Chogoria, Kaaga adopted it late in 1942 and also in the Igoji Mission there. So coffee was planted in Meru, where it didn't interfere with the laboring of those European *shamba*s because Gikuyu were to work there. Chogoria was the first mission outside [the White Highlands] to have people with coffee. I think most of the Gikuyu planted only after the Emergency. We were ahead of them to plant coffee, ten or fifteen years ahead.

Soon the coffee became more than what the one machine could do. So, the first society [cooperative] began. A group of people put up another machine just two or three kilometers from Chogoria Mission. All the coffee was dried and taken back again to Dr. Irvine who directed some Indians to take it to the board for sale. The growers, of course, got a little money, and many, many people were interested. Even people who were not with the missionaries approached Dr. Irvine to plant coffee.

By 1945, people had built another factory to process the coffee. But the chief of this area, in Mutunguru, was arrogant and refused completely. He did not allow people to plant coffee. "This is the way, the approach of the Europeans coming to our land, to take it as they did with the Gikuyu," he said. The chief knew that the coffee was an experiment of the Europeans to see whether it could do well in this country. So there was a tug-of-war, very slow moving, for us to plant coffee in this area with that chief.

By the time I got married, that chief had died, so I asked Dr. Irvine if we could plant coffee. "And how many are you?" Dr. Irvine asked me. I counted very few people here when I did the census. We were eight, but we added some other names. I gave the number twenty-two people. Dr. Irvine said we could plant. I planted my coffee in 1948. I planted 750 trees—that's a lot of coffee. We were not allowed to plant more than an acre, but I used my name, my father's name, my mother's name, Jesca's name—so I got their tickets and planted more. I knew the way. Jesca and I worked, and we did very well with our coffee. In '49, '50, '51, it grew very nicely.

In 1948, we were blessed with a baby—a girl baby, our firstborn, called Beatrice Muiti. That's how we started building our *shamba*. Now the problem that I had was that I could not agree with the church.

THESE AFRICANS ARE NOT FEARING NOW

The Second World War gave a lot of changes in Kenya. When it started in 1939, I was a schoolboy of seventeen in class five. I was almost to join the military, but it was when the war was toward the end, so I didn't go, but my age-mates were warriors by then. Most went and joined the military—not "carriers" now but *askari*. They went to the [Far] East to fight the Japanese in a place called Burma.[8] It was near India, and there was a big forest where the Japanese were hiding. The Japanese were also against the Europeans. The war was spread from Europe to the other side of the [Far] East.

It was from that time that my age-mates who were in the army became more brave. We had big people there who were majors and sergeants. They learned to use guns. When my age-mates came back, they said, "The Europeans are cowards. We fought with them against the Japanese. The Japanese feared Africans, the black people, but not Europeans. They were furious to see the Europeans. So the *wazungu* said, 'If these people are fearing Africans, why should we not color ourselves to become Africans? We will put color—black color—on the skin to show we are not white.' They were coloring themselves black! And when we were there fighting with them, they were calling us 'Mister,' not 'Boy.'"

The military did not discriminate. When people are fighting on one side, they don't have discrimination. So they could live together, they could cook together and eat together. There's friendship in war. When the war ended in 1945, people reasoned, "Why—we were very good friends with these people. We helped them to fight and to chase the Italians and Germans. What do we ourselves earn from them? How do they reward us? Still they are in our land."

When Europeans [originally] came, they scattered all over, and they found the Rift Valley being important for the cattle and for the farming, [especially] wheat, because the Rift Valley has very fertile, black volcanic soil. They took that land by force. The first people took the best places from Rift Valley up to Mount Elgon [next to the Ugandan border]. So the Maasai were separated—one toward the north and the other toward the south—mixed with the Samburu as far as to Tanzania, where they mix with animals and wildlife.

Also, around Gikuyu [lands], Europeans possessed places like Limuru and Muguga—the best highlands—and were calling the settlement the "White Highlands." They moved the Gikuyu to the poor areas. Also around Mount Kenya, near Meru—Timau. The highland is very good for animals because there's no trees but grass. They chased the Gikuyu away from all the good areas that produced coffee.

We have one problem in Kenya which you don't have in America or other states. In America, if you don't own any land, you [can] live happy. Here, if you don't have land, you will be the poorest man because you won't get even something to eat. You'll be living in the towns helplessly. People without land are without anything. They are nomads. Here, once you have water and property—just an acre or two—you survive. You live—simply, properly. We don't forget work, but you never complicate. It only gets difficult when you depend on buying.

So Europeans brought coffee, they planted tea—but they didn't allow any Africans to cultivate cash crops. And they taxed people with no money. Also that suppressed people. Once you were circumcised and grown-up with a house, you have to pay the hut tax of eight shillings. The chiefs were very serious about it, going from house to house recording the information for the DO [district officer]: "How many *murani* did you get this time?"

Even myself, I was initiated in 1938, and I had to pay eight shillings when I was in class five. But I couldn't get eight shillings—from where? I had nothing to sell. My brother who was working in a European *shamba* in Kiambu paid for me, and I had to give the receipt to Dr. Irvine, and I was permitted to keep schooling. Africans were working in European farms, almost slavery, because they were paid very little. People were serious.

Now, also, when the missionaries came, they educated people. They started schools, and people learned a little. Alliance High School was opened in 1926, so from 1926 to 1930, many Gikuyu had good education. From the learning, the Gikuyu demanded wealth. They came to reason, "Our best lands were taken by these people forcefully, and we can fight for it."

They began the politics in the very early time, in the 1920s. It started with a man called Harry Thuku. Women wanted to fight. Women were telling men, "You are fearing these people. Why can't we fight them? If you are fearing, let us change the clothes. You can have the dresses, and let us have the *shuka*."

Askari [police] tried to force people to move, and very many were shot. I think 150 were shot, in the group of Harry Thuku.[9] That's where things went wrong. The association was banned. The members of the movement were imprisoned. This stirred the politics. Thuku formed a political party, the KCA—the Kikuyu Central Association. That's the old organization of Harry Thuku, the KCA—only for Gikuyu. They were preparing for war against the Europeans.

People contributed for Kenyatta to go to London,[10] to see the colonial secretary. Kenyatta had a little education—up to standard six, and he was a fellow who could speak English. He was a politician. So KCA sent Kenyatta to the Colonial Office, where they could accuse white people who were in Kenya. He wanted to see why Gikuyu were being killed and Thuku was imprisoned.[11] The head of the Colonial Office in London noticed it was very bad—killing [the] people of Harry Thuku, for nothing.

"Europeans are planting coffee within our *shamba*s, but we are not allowed to plant it," Kenyatta said. "Why are people planting in other areas, but we Gikuyu, whose land was taken, cannot plant coffee?" Remember, we Meru planted coffee earlier than the Muranga and Kiambu people, because those were servants to the Europeans.

Even the big [Gikuyu] senior chief Koinange made a nursery where he could plant coffee. But it was uprooted. And burned. He was a senior chief! So the struggle started.[12] Africans said, "Unless we get rid of these people, our children will remain slaves." That was a difficult time because they were not paid properly. They could not get something to eat. Everyone was feeling the same because we were lowly paid.

Gikuyu thought, *Should we strike and not do the work in the shambas of the wazungu?* There was a lot of underground moving, and they organized a strike. The [approach of the] strike was "go slow." KCA said, "Work slowly, and make sure that these people do not benefit from our labor." So it was difficult for the crop. The KPCU (Kenya Planters Cooperative Union), the Kenya Planters Association, declined because the Gikuyu laborers were working in a strike of "go slow." This movement went as far as the colonial secretary, and some [British] people were sent to survey. They found that the Europeans have seriously suppressed the people, in the land and also the payment.

In Kenya it was like in South Africa. It was not so serious, but it was serious. An African was not allowed to speak English with an English woman. No, no, no—if you were caught, it could be bad. We had to call her Memsahib and no other name.[13] You could never even say "Morning" to a lady. Never. You could be charged criminally. And the young *mzungu* boys had to be called Bwana Mdogo, not Tom or John but Bwana Mdogo ["Little Master"]. And every *mzungu* was *bwana*. You had to salute them in this way. I think when the younger people came—forget the people who first made settlement—when their sons came, they came in a very proud manner. Not all the Europeans were bad to Africans, but there were some who thought that Africans are animals. Even in the *shamba*s where people used to work, they were terribly mistreated, as they were animals.

In Meru, there was a place called [the] Pig and Whistle. In Embu, there was a hotel called Isaak Walton, and another in Nanyuki.[14] They were for Europeans only. They were very discriminative. Even big people, big Africans, could never enter those hotels. Indians also were not allowed to go. Indians were fearing the white man. I think they had something before, from the very country of the Indians. There was a very great enmity. It was a colony for [the] British. Indians also fought with [against] Britons for independence. They [the British] never leave in peace.

I remember only one Indian who could enter in [the] Pig and Whistle [Hotel]. He was rich. He was dealing in timber, and he could speak English. So he was not counted as an Indian. He could go and take beer in that hotel. The big hotels in Nairobi were the New Stanley and the Norfolk, but we called it "No-Folk" because none of the "folk" could enter into it. No Africans or Indians—"No folks"—allowed. Europeans said, "Never go where folks are."

Dr. Irvine was telling us a story about when he tried to go to the Norfolk with his [adopted] son. Dr. Irvine had an [African] man working in his small flower gardens, but unfortunately that man died and left three children. I don't know what the arrangement was, but Dr. Irvine took over the care for those children. He paid for their education and school fees.

One of the boys was very intelligent. He went to Alliance High School. He passed form four [high school] very well and wanted to become a doctor. To do the medicine, Dr. Irvine had to take that boy to Britain. The day before leaving they went to Nairobi together. When Dr. Irvine tried to go and eat at the Norfolk Hotel, the Europeans said, "No. Unless you buy food for that boy, and he goes to eat it elsewhere, I'm afraid he cannot come in."

Dr. Irvine became annoyed. "Why?" he said.

"This hotel is for whites and not for Africans. That is the law. If you don't want to eat, then you can go together with your boy. Even yourself, we cannot sell you food." Dr. Irvine was told by the Norfolk in a very horrible manner that even [he] himself could not be allowed because he was serving an African.

He said to that boy, "When you go to London, you go and eat in any hotel. Leave these Europeans in Kenya. They are very proud. But when you go there—there is no discrimination." When Dr. Irvine came back to Chogoria, he was telling us, "Although I had money, my son couldn't get anything to eat because of the color. So I think those are the hotels where idiots eat, not people."

Also, Africans could not get beer or wine. That was taken by Europeans only, and we did not have African breweries. I think the drinks were coming from Holland and South Africa. There were shops, but nobody could be allowed to sell it to Africans. If I were employed by a European as a garden or a kitchen man, I had to take a letter from the European and bring it to the shop where the beer is sold. Then, you get the bottle that you want and go and bring it back for the European. Without that, as an African, you could never get it. But those who fought in the war said, "The military came with beer. We have drunk this—now, come on."

In Meru we had a DC called Bwana Johnston, but we called him Bithumbi because he had floppy bangs [that] hung over his face. Bwana Johnston had been in the army. Before the war, an African could never ask a question in a meeting. But after, people started asking questions in Bwana Johnston's meetings. When somebody wanted to ask a question, the DC would say, "Have you been in the military?" If the person said yes, then Bwana Johnston would say, "No. Sit down. Somebody else who was not in the army can ask a question, but not you. You are *mbaya sana*." He had known those words in Swahili: *mbaya sana* [very bad].

Bwana Johnston could not accept a question from someone who was in the military. Because of that *mzungu*, our whole age group name was changed. The name which our fathers gave to us was Gwantai. But because it was our group who fought in the war, it got changed to Mbaya. Our old name got lost, and we were Mbaya. We liked being called *mbaya sana*. We were proud because we knew what it meant. Even our fathers' age set changed from Miriti to Kaaria because they were in the Carrier Corps. We were the very sons of the Kaaria age set.

It was my age-mates from the Second World War, returning from the [Far] East—that was the time that people believed we can fight the Europeans. By then, very many people were educated within the Gikuyu and Luo. They could write and complain to the governor, and even to the colonial secretary. They were working in the offices of Nairobi, with a lot of people being employed by Indians. Most of the businesses in Nairobi belonged to Indians. Europeans were the rulers, Indians were business-men—above the African status but not so much.

In the parliament, there were Indian representatives and the Arabs and the Europeans but nobody of us. We had no African representatives. The parliament was for white and red. A good *mzungu* man—Beecher, a missionary, was to represent Africans. In 1944, we had a man called Eliud Mathu who had finished form four at Alliance High School and was very learned.[15] "Now, we are tired [of this]," said Mathu. "Why should we re-main represented by Europeans?" He could hear Mr. Beecher representing us, but he asked, "Why not me, representing my own people?" Europeans did not listen. We fought wonderful.

Our people said, "Why can't we have Mathu in parliament instead of being represented by somebody who doesn't understand our problems?" The *wazungu* knew, "Now, this is the way, of [Africans] coming to politics." Mathu was appointed to replace a European in parliament, but you know, Mathu was one man among the lot. Even he claimed that he could never say a word. "We must call Beecher," Mathu said. "He was doing better than myself because I don't have words to speak to these people."

By then, Kenyatta had stayed in Britain for a long time [since 1929]. He got lost there. He married a European, had a family, and that is where he wrote the book, *Facing Mount Kenya*. We said, "Kenyatta, you've been in London for so long—what have you learned?" So he came back in 1946, when our things were hot but somehow harmonized. Our people were edu-cated, and we had the Independent schools. With Kenyatta, we believed that our king has come. And the movement grew. Kenyatta founded an-other party—not only Gikuyu now. It was called the Kenya African Union, KAU. It was for all of us—only *mzungu* and *muindi* [Indians] could not become a member because it was for Africans. Kenyatta told us, "Now don't fear these people. If they want to be *bwana mkubwa* [the "big man"], let them go to their own country. But they are within our country." All of us who were in politics joined KAU. Very many people registered for the party. They had branches all over—even our younger people were joining KAU. Kenyatta was moving all around, especially in Central Province.

He spoke with Eliud Mathu, our MP. "Now, if you find these people cannot listen to you, leave them. They have been here for a while," said Kenyatta. "Let them continue to talk whatever they want to talk of their own [issues] but not of Africans, not about ourselves. We are people who can make our own parliament." He was serious, so we became very strong. Europeans began to listen to Mr. Mathu.

In 1948, Kenyatta came to our place here in Chogoria to have a big meeting. There were very many Indians from Chuka and Muthambi and very many Africans. Dr. Irvine and the other missionaries came to hear what Kenyatta was saying, and they could not understand Gikuyu. They needed someone to translate Kenyatta's speech from Gikuyu to Swahili, and Mate was nervous. "I will do it," I said. "I will translate."

Kenyatta was very dictative [authoritative]. "We have been very friendly with our Europeans," said Kenyatta. "We fought for you in the wars, and we helped you to get whatever these people, Italians and Germans, have taken from you. Why should we remain like this? You have stayed a long time now, and I think it's the best time you can leave and say thank you to us."

It was me who was translating. Instead of listening to Kenyatta, Dr. Irvine and the people turned to me! That was the impression that they got. Each and every European thought it was me who was putting these words to them. Kenyatta said, "I have been to their country and spoken to the colonial secretary, and they have said they are going to leave our country. Now, when I come back here, they don't do what they say. These people, Europeans and Indians, are foreigners, and this is the time for them to agree with us, or else they go."

After the speech, we spent some time with Kenyatta. It was my first time I tasted Tusker [beer]. We drank it with Kenyatta that day at a house. We couldn't drink in public, because if a teacher was found drinking, you could be dismissed from work completely. Ah, I liked Kenyatta very much. Everybody liked Kenyatta. He was a good man, and we believed that he would lead us.

From interpreting his speech, I got a very bad reputation. Dr. Irvine knew I was the very same person from when we'd quarreled before. They thought I am one of the people who invited Kenyatta, and I was not. But from that meeting, they thought, *Uh-huh, that man sides with Kenyatta. Japhlet is no longer with us.*

With the long history that we had [of suppression]—ah. After conquering the Japanese, that was the sort of beginning of a revolution. They [Europeans] knew people changed. They knew there will be war.

TIMBER

In 1949, I went to lunch with a lady I was teaching with at Kamucia. She did not have a bicycle, so I carried her on my bicycle. That evening I was called into the church court to meet with the disciplinary committee. "You made a mistake by carrying a woman on your bicycle," they told me. "Any person claiming to be a Christian should not give a ride to a lady on a bicycle. That is too close to adultery."

"What harm did I do?" I asked. "Am I not teaching with this lady? I was trying to help her so that she does not have to walk." I started to argue with these people.

"Now come on, Japhlet, this is the law. Are you telling us that you did not commit a sin?"

"Ah," I said. "If I wanted to do anything—commit adultery or whatever you say—could I do it on a bicycle?" Even one of the elders was to laugh. "I am a married man," I said. "I was not doing any of this business with my fellow teacher."

They told me that I could not take the holy sacrament because I had committed a sin. But I did not surrender. "I will do even more than that," I said. "If the bicycle is bad, then I will carry her on my shoulders! If this is the way of the church, I don't want to be involved in this business—to hell with your holy communion." They suspended me from the church and forced me to resign.

The priest who accused me of the bicycle story used to be a teacher. He was called Jerol and was trained at Kahuhia, but he could not teach. He tried for three years, but not one of his students could pass the common entrance exam. So he decided to become a *bwana* [priest] instead. This man could not take someone from class five to class six, yet now he was the best fellow to take people from earth to heaven? Ah—it was this *bwana* who said I was not converted and made me to resign.

I was transferred from Chogoria to another school, Gikurune School. That was 1950. All the children that I taught and the parents of Chogoria were depressed. I made a record there which has never been repeated.

At Gikurune, I was followed seriously. An inspector called Erasto did not like me. He had also been a teacher from Kahuhia, but his students could never pass. The European Mr. Graeves had warned me about him. He told me, "When this man comes to inspect you, remember he could not teach. Now he's the inspector to look after teachers who were doing better than what he could do. He will be seriously against you."

Erasto was a friend of the catechism teacher, Bwana Silas, at the mission. Silas was supposed to end his class at half past eight on Wednesdays, according to the school's timetable, but he prolonged it. I was annoyed because I started math at quarter to nine and couldn't do my class while some of his children were not in. One day, Bwana Silas kept his class until nine. "Why should we continue like this?" I said. "Let me have a direct fight." I went and took my students out of his class.

Silas reported to Inspector Erasto that I was taking students from the catechism class without requesting his permission. "Mwalimu Erasto," I said, "my timetable doesn't agree with what Bwana Silas is doing. I cannot teach my class while students are still in catechist. It is not me who has drawn up the timetable. Now, either you change the timetable for Wednesdays for math to start at nine, or we lose one of the subjects. Or can you please tell *mwalimu* to dismiss his students on time?"

He couldn't change the timetable. Bwana Silas was not happy, and the relationship went away. Erasto started reporting to the mission that I went to class being drunk. I asked for them to prove that somebody had seen it. No one had seen such things.

Now, during the school holiday that year in August, I was going to visit Nkubu [Town]. A friend of mine had opened a *duka* [store] in Kanyekine, which was on my way. I stopped by to have a beer with him at his *duka*. I remember it very well. When I entered, I met three men. We all knew one another because we were age-mates. They were involved in this business of dealing timber and had just sold a lorry [of timber]. They were counting the money, and when I saw the amount—ah, I was surprised. It was a miracle. They asked me to help them count because they were not able to read or write or do arithmetic. The three in the group were sharing seven thousand shillings. I had known there was a business of the sort with timber, but I didn't know it was giving such good money. For six years that I had been teaching, I'd never seen a thousand. I was getting a salary of fifty-five [per month], and after two years, [I got] five shillings more, which could never dress Jesca and myself. Even I worked for two years to get a bicycle of four hundred eighty shillings. Employment was very low. But I saw these people—illiterate!—sharing seven thousand shillings because of one lorry of timber.

This money was too much for an African by then. Europeans did not like anything that could make an African have money, so selling timber was prohibited. That's why we called it "black market"—we Africans were dealing timber like cocaine or heroin. If you were caught, they took it and arrested you. Even the timber which had fallen for many years and nobody cared for—we weren't allowed to touch it. It was better for it to be burned or neglected than split by anybody. It was terrible waste.

But I thought, *These people are illiterate, and they are getting money that I will never get in my life as a trained teacher. Why can't I do this job? Let me join this business.* I was a great friend of the chief by then, and I went to visit him. I told him, "I'm going to put up a *duka,* so I need timber to build it. I've seen some lying somewhere. Can you give me a permit to split and collect that timber? "

"Yes, why not?" he said. He gave me a letter, and we went to get a stamp from the local agricultural inspector who could give the permit to get this timber [for personal use]. I employed people to split the timber and put some of mine into a lorry with the chief's timber and [that of] these friends of mine who had their own permit, and I went with them to sell it in Nairobi.

You couldn't pass from one district to another without a permit, because there were checkpoints in between. They had inspectors at every crossing who look to see what you are passing with. One inspector at the check-point in Chuka used to be my pupil. Nathan was one of the older married men who came from very far and wanted to study with me. Although Mr. Mate did not want to admit him, I sympathized. Nathan passed my class, and I wanted him to go to intermediate school, but Mr. Mate said, "No, Japhlet, we cannot take these married people into boarding school." I felt bad, so when I saw an advertisement for an open position in the Ministry of Agriculture, I wrote that man a very good letter of recommendation to be employed. He got the job and became the produce inspector at the very Chuka barrier we were passing.

Nathan was not in that night we crossed the barrier, but we convinced his assistant that we had letters from the chief and divisional agricultural officer that allowed us to carry the timber. We signed our names in the book that we have passed, we got a permit, and continued to Nairobi and sold the timber. Mine gave me one thousand eighty shillings. One thousand and eighty shillings. Whew! I was surprised to see a thousand—I had never seen such money. I gave it to one of the tobacco sellers, my friend, so he could keep it for me, because I could not believe it. After working six years, I had never saved five hundred.

I reported back again to school during the September term. When Nathan read in the books that some people had passed there with timber, he saw my name. He reported that I am dealing in this black market of timber. Although I had gotten him his job, he turned away from me. On a Friday in the first week of September, I was in my class teaching when I saw an *askari* coming. He had a letter from the DO's [district officer's] office. "You are needed by the DO," it said.

I told the *askari*, "Go and tell the DO that I am in class. I will come tomorrow."

When I went to see the DO, he interrogated me. He said, "You passed Chuka with timber."

"The timber was not mine," I said. I [explained that I] was only helping people to transport the timber, to count for them and help them sell it because they did not know how to work the arithmetic. And these people had their own permit from the chief. I showed the DO my permit to collect timber to put up my *duka*.

"Oh, no," said the DO. "I don't trust you. You are dealing [in] the timbers." They put me in a cell, the main cell of the Meru police station. That was my first time in a prison, and I stayed for twelve days until I had a trial. Ah—if somebody was associated with money, and it could be proved that he gets it from black market, it was serious.

After twelve days, I had the case. I stated exactly how I had told the DO in my interview. My chief came and witnessed for me. He said that he gave me the permit, and my timber is still there because I'm putting up a building. I had selected some bad timber and stored it in a building to show that I am putting up my *duka* and still have my timber. I won the case. That's the time I realized, *Uh-huh, I'm going to leave this business of teaching and join these people. I've already started earning money.* I had my one thousand eighty shillings, and I was very, very happy. The friendship that

I had with Nathan disappeared and turned in the way of enmity. Later, he became a chief.

After the trial I went back to school to finish the term. Still, people were making false accusations, saying that I was going to class drunk and building *duka*s when I was to be in the classroom. I quarreled seriously with the missionaries. They did not want to pay me for the time I spent in prison and on trial. I wrote to the sponsors of the school: "You are following me and making accusations, and the government detained me for taking timber. But I was found not guilty. Now you do not want to pay me for teaching. What do you want me to do?"

Of course they argued, but they paid my money. I told Dr. Irvine, "These people are reporting false things, and they will keep on. Now, please—can I resign now?"

"You can decide whatever you want to decide, Japhlet."

I went back and wrote a letter to the mission: "Referring to our talk on the other day, I am here only to end the last term. I will never turn up for next year. This is my letter of resignation." And I signed it very seriously. I got somebody to take it to the inspector, and I handed over all the books and things from the mission. I knew what I had to do.

I went direct to Tigania—the whole December 1951 I was there. By January I was in Nairobi selling my timber. Meru oak—*muuru*[16]—was very valuable. If you burn it, it gave a wonderful white ash. Carpenters could make beautiful furniture from the *muuru* timber, also the camphor tree. The beds were very costly, and the Europeans liked it. Big people were buried in coffins made of Meru oak.

In Tigania I had a good Indian friend who was my age-mate and a businessman. We met in 1943 when I was doing the medical training, and we used to play football together. He had a *duka* at Meru and another in Tigania. He could speak nice Kimeru, as well as I, and was called Mr. Kassam. I made arrangements with Mr. Kassam to store my timber at his house. I would come in the evening and lock it inside. When I had enough timber to fill a lorry, I would tell Mr. Kassam, and he would say, "Can you clear the road?"

There were two ways of going with the timber to Nairobi. You could go direct with the lorry from Tigania to Nairobi, but you had to cross three very dangerous barriers. They were terrible. You could meet police even after the barriers. There was a time when these police were good. Once you meet the first group, you tip them, and you arrange for them to escort you to Nairobi. You will never be pulled over by any other group, because it looks like you have already been arrested. But that got stopped, so we had to take another way, the Nanyuki way.

Nanyuki was safer; you cross only one barrier, [though] you had to make arrangements with these inspectors at the border crossing. You tell him a time that you are going to pass, you give him something, and then you come at night, which you were not supposed to do. When you reach the barrier, you hoot at the gentleman with whom you made arrangements. He stamps you, and you go. In Nanyuki you load the timber on a train, and you take *matatu*, and you will meet the timber in Nairobi.

Mr. Kassam was going to Nanyuki to collect his things for the *duka*, so we would go together. I would load my timber on the train and collect my receipt, and Mr. Kassam collected his things for the *duka*. He was making double-profit because he made money carrying timber to Nanyuki and then could use that to pay the guard on the way back to Meru. That's a good double job.

In Nairobi, I sold the timber to Indians. I did very well. I was fully confident when I left teaching because I knew I was going to make my life better. I wanted the missionaries and school people in Chogoria to see me. They thought that if I leave teaching, I would be poor. But I had a wonderful suit and a tweed coat. That cost me eighty shillings. As a teacher, I could never afford a suit. But when I went to business—ah, I changed. I had money. I even had two shops. Jesca was wearing nice good clothes. She used to wear khaki dresses when I was a teacher, but now I managed to buy good materials. Whenever I passed by, I left Jesca with money.

One time, I went back to attend a function at the church in Chogoria with Jesca. I wore my nice suit to the meeting. I especially wanted Inspector Erasto to see me. It was reported to the missionaries, to Dr. Irvine, that I had put up two shops, so I must be getting money from the timber. "How could a teacher with very little pay build two shops?"

THE EMERGENCY

During my time of timber, people were fearing very much in Nairobi. We were fearing those who had already taken [the oath of] Mau Mau, because we heard they were killing people in the forest. KAU, the Kenya African Union, had branches all over the country. It is KAU, then, that was turned underground to become Mau Mau. It started when Kenyatta came from London, but only with a very few Gikuyu leaders from KAU.

In 1948, '49, '50, Mau Mau had good leaders, and they were training people to go out to other areas. They knew that unless we united together, we cannot fight these Europeans. What can unite us? Our natural oath, which people fear—that if you go against it, you'll die. So they started oathing.

People are trying to interpret "Mau Mau" in different ways, but, to us, it was "Get out." *Uma* is a Gikuyu word, also Kimeru, and it means, "Go, go—get out." If I tell you *"Uma,"* it means, "Get out." The group of Kenyatta twisted it, from Uma Uma to Mau Mau. People came together and said, "I'm going to join this movement, to send these foreigners out, out of our country. Mau Mau. Get out. They were telling Europeans that you people have to go. That's how I understood it.[17]

All the rogues in Nairobi were the first ones caught to be trained, because they knew the way—how to kill, how to run, how to steal, how to hide. The best place was in the slums around Nairobi city—below, in Kariobangi. Mau Mau started straight away from there. *Kina* Koinange and educated people used these thugs. They gave the thieves lots of support and money to kill those who did not believe in taking oath. They started eliminating people appointed by *kina* Kenyatta and *kina* Kaggia.[18] Gradually, gradually—it became known that there must be something going on. It was widely known that there is Mau Mau, but it wasn't a clear picture.

The office of KAU was called Kimuri House. *Kimuri* means a burning light that you can see from far [away]. The leaders of Kimuri House made up the war council [of Mau Mau] in Nairobi. It was a big machinery, and Kaggia was the head of Kimuri House.

In 1951 and 1952, Central Province, near the area where Kenyatta belonged, was the most serious area because the *shamba*s [European estates] which were occupied by *wazungu* used to be Gikuyu land.

If you refused to take Mau Mau, the thugs from Nairobi could kill you and hide your body in the forest. People were trained to do that business. Many people got lost. Also, big people were disappearing. The movement was doing a lot. It is within that time that the government knew. The government wondered, *Why are some people disappearing and nobody knows where they go? Where do they go and why?* Gradually, gradually—by 1952, it was thoroughly known that there was [an] oath being taken by Africans against Europeans, and it might be that Kenyatta was involved, because since he came, this movement started. There were CID [Criminal Investigation Department] Intelligence, these Special Branch people, who went deeper. They revealed that there was a movement, but none of the Europeans knew who was a Mau Mau and who was not [a] Mau Mau.

The Europeans divided us. You know that's what they do. They employed people to be trained as soldiers for the government. They were to guard the villages and fight the Mau Mau. Europeans called them "Homeguards."

Through my travels with timber, I made very many friends not of Meru but of Nanyuki, which is Gikuyu and Embu. I knew that some had already changed [taken the Mau Mau oath], but I didn't want to tell them, and neither did they want to reveal it to me. They took me as a very good man, a Mumeru, who could help to spread the Mau Mau.

In the end of April [1952], when I was dealing my timber, I was staying with my friend M'Arimi at his brother's house in Nanyuki. Some people invited us for a drink. I sensed something that night—from the moment that we went from the house. I knew it was most likely that we were going to take oath, because I had heard from the experience of Nairobi and Nanyuki people.

M'Arimi was a [well-respected] man of Nanyuki, and we were with him, so I didn't worry much. From the beer place we went to a house for *nyama choma*. There was a porch for eating *nyama choma* outside, but inside the room was guarded. You couldn't be let inside unless the guards knew who you were. It was there that the oaths were taken. We went inside a small, dark, single room and met people, and we knew—uh-huh, these are the Mau Mau people. There was a man sitting in a chair who was writing our names, and the only light was a little lamp plugged in next to him. We met four oath administrators including the one taking our names. I think we were six [in all]. We had to take off our clothes. I don't know where the rest were collected from, but they were Gikuyu.

At the ceremony there were many fearful things. They wanted you to understand this is a special thing—if you play with them, you can be killed. They show you a little pot—a gourd—with blood in it. They say, "This is the blood of somebody we killed, and this is the blood of the goat," and they mix it together in your presence. It was a very nasty, dirty thing. We were asked, "Do you know who we are?"

Each individual said, "No."

"Do you know the work of the Mau Mau?"

If you knew, you could tell. I said, "The Mau Mau are the organization of the Gikuyu, Embu, and Meru who are trying to chase off the Europeans from our country."

"Would you like to become a member of it?" We said yes because you could not say no. Everyone said yes. "Will you be brave enough to fight?" You agreed—if you played, you could be beaten by somebody holding a *panga* [machete]. He would smack his *panga*—ohhhhh. He could get you. If somebody was connected to the Homeguards—whew! Even there were some people to say, "No, no, no—don't kill him." They do it intentionally, so it is known that without that person, these people would have killed him. There was no sympathy. In many places, people were beaten.

With us, because we had demonstrated we were good people, they were told that we shouldn't be beaten: "Don't threaten them. They are not Homeguards." Although somebody had his *panga*, he did not hit anyone.

They asked us, "Do you know we are the people who kill?"

We said, "No." You could never say somebody is killing people.

Then they made an arch. It was made with local plants but tied together with animal skin of a goat. It had the parts of the goat swinging on each side. All this was to frighten us. We had to walk in a circle and go underneath that arch—seven times. We were not touching the arch, so we had to bend down. Seven times. After doing all that, you had to sit down and that is where you take oath in a very awkward way, using a stick. You drop to the knee, and he [the oath administrator] dips the stick in the pot of blood, and he will say, "Do you agree that you'll never reveal this to anybody who doesn't belong to this movement?" Then we say, "Yes."

It is like in the church after the ceremony when the priest takes something and reads to you. "Do you agree to one, two, three, four . . ." Then you say after each statement, "Yes, I do."

After, you are given blood to say that the oath can kill you if you go against it. "Do you agree that you can convert many people to follow the movement?"

"Yes."

"And is it true that any people who do not belong to our race—that's the European or Indian—is our enemy?"

"Yes, it is true."

You repeat, "If I go against my word, let this oath kill me." The first oath was very simple. You say that you agree to work in the movement, and you never reveal this Mau Mau to anybody. It was the uniting oath—very general, that we are uniting together. *Mwigwithania* was the first oath—that means uniting.

After finishing in the room, we got dressed and went out on the porch, to eat some *nyama choma* there that was for us, the Mau Mau. Then we went back into the bar. I said to M'Arimi now, "Oh, M'Arimi, where did you take me?"

We were very great friends, but he could never give me any hint that we were going to take oath. He revealed to me after[ward] that he had already taken oath before and knew what we were doing. He asked, "Did you fear it?"

"Ah, me? No, I was very brave," I said.

"I was fearing that some of these people are very arrogant and want to beat you. I wanted you to take it in my presence because these people have known me."

I told him I was happy. I had been fearing in Nairobi, but now I was more confident. You couldn't be comfortable unless you went to it. "I'm a Mau Mau now," I said. "So I will never fear the Mau Mau any longer." I was pleased because the way that Europeans treated me and the way they were treating the whole [all] Africans—I became annoyed. Now I could go to Nairobi and talk to anybody because I didn't fear. I learned the signal to tell somebody that I'm the Mau Mau. When I greet you, I do this. [*While shaking hands, fold the middle finger down so it rests on the palm of your hand. To say that the group is mixed with Mau Mau and non–Mau Mau, stroke the inside of the other person's palm with that finger.*]

I saw an old friend who was a watchman at the KAU office. He was from Mwimbi. I revealed to him that I am also a member of Mau Mau. He was telling me, "If you sell your timber to any of the Indians, and if he doesn't pay you immediately, you come and see me. We are not joking with them now."

Indians were fearing very much. If they played [around with you], you told him, "Let us go to the office of KAU here to report that you are not paying for my timber." And they paid you straight away. They did not want anything to be reported. Otherwise Mau Mau could take everything.

Then, the big senior chief Waruhiu was killed.[19] The governor declared a state of emergency. It was on [the] twentieth of October 1952. We had a big radio. He said [*doing an impression*], "By the powers that are conferred in me by her Majesty [the] Queen, I declare this state of emergency. I, Sir Evelyn Baring, the governor of Kenya, as commander, declare a state of emergency." Whether you have taken oath or not, you were detained. And you couldn't complain of being in detention—no. It was said that if you were not a man of Mau Mau, then you could be an informer. The Europeans inspected the Kimuri House, which was known as KAU's office, and it became known that it was a Mau Mau office. All the officers of Kimuri House, all the members running that office, were arrested. Kenyatta was arrested.

When you are known as Gikuyu, Embu, or Meru, and you are told "stand," and you run—chuuu—shot. Fired. State of emergency. No one tried to see whether you have taken Mau Mau or not: "The Gikuyu, Embu, and Meru are Mau Mau. Arrest them. And if one refuses to sit, when he runs— shoot! Piga! That's a Mau Mau." So, when you meet a European, you put up your hands to say that you have surrendered, and he can take you.

Mind you, the Gikuyu, Embu, and Meru were the people working in the ministries of government. None of them was trusted now. If you were Gikuyu, Embu, or Meru, you could no longer work in any office. You could never visit a European. No matter if you were educated, they knew you were hypocrites, that these were all Mau Mau people. The governor declared, "These people are murderers. Never keep them in the office. They are giving information to the other members of Mau Mau. He can organize for you to be killed, thinking he's a good man."

That is when the people from western Kenya, the Luo, took over, with kina Mboya.[20] The Luhya and others were termed as good people because they had not taken oath. They became replacements for all the offices where the Gikuyu were.

All the big and educated people were arrested and put in detention, but not all the people could be detained. Gikuyu, Embu, and Meru were swept from Nairobi [and] taken back to their home districts by train. Police were escorting these people on the railway going from Nairobi to Nanyuki. The mzungu did not know whether askari were Mau Mau or not, but most police of those areas had already taken oath. They helped Mau Mau to get home and continue the work. They were guiding who goes where, making sure they had enough weapons. Mau Mau had to share what they had stolen from Nairobi, pistols or whatever. Askari were saying, "Meru, come this way. Embu, this way. You go that way. And how many are going to Murang'a? Okay, you get two pistols. And Kirinyaga [Mount Kenya]? You get this"—so, it was done in that way. Places like Tigania or Karatina or Nyeri were big good places of Mau Mau, and the askari were sending people home with guns and weapons.

Only [Peter] Mbiyu Koinange, the founder of the Independent schools, was not detained. He went to Britain. Kenyatta was working hand in hand with him. They knew Kenyatta would be caught, so Kenyatta said, "You go to Britain and work with the Europeans from there. When I get arrested, you will be our spokesman. You represent us in the Colonial Office in London—tell them about the movement and how the people are mistreated." So Mbiyu went to Britain and stayed there during Mau Mau [until 1959].

The big leaders were put on trial at Kapenguria with Kenyatta.[21] Whether you have taken oath or not, the sharia of the governor now rules that anyone can be detained or, if it is proven [that] you have taken oath—imprisoned. There were terrible punishments if you were caught being Mau Mau. We had very many detention camps, and it is from there that screening was to go on. You could get beaten and made to answer questions. "Why were you arrested? Where did you take oath? Why did you do this? Who else do you know? Who is convincing people to go to the forest?" People could even give false information to make himself be released. If you don't like me, you can say that I took oath or that you know I killed somebody. So there was a lot of confusion. Kenya was horrible—people were trying to get jobs and money through spoiling other people's names.

After Kenyatta was arrested, things became much worse. After the Emergency, we could not move from one district to another, so that stopped the timber. In '52 and '53, people ran. Our people understood: "If I stay here, either I will be killed or screened, or I don't know where I'll be taken after all, so why can't I go join the gangs in the forest?[22] Uh-huh. These people are killing us, why can't we kill them?" A gang of thieves killed even Tom Mbotela, the brother of the very dynamic fellow Mambo Mbotela. Tom was giving information to the government. Mau Mau found out he went against them, and he was shot, immediately after the arrest of Kenyatta.[23]

I did not reveal to anyone in my village that I'd taken Mau Mau—not even to Jesca. When the government called a meeting for recruiting Homeguards, I volunteered. I was one of the first to be employed. Most of the lot who volunteered themselves were [already] Mau Mau. Our people were within. Here at Igoji, we had eight good Mau Mau youth. They were given guns and trained how to shoot and how to defend from the Mau Mau. We knew we were getting the whole story [from the government side] because they were our members. They reported what was going on in the training. And when things became known, we were going to rush in[to] the forest with those guns.

[Meanwhile,] I was directing people from the forest to recruit for Mau Mau. We knew the ones who had not taken oath. I got the people who were employed as Homeguards first. But we were taught by those in the forest, "You show us where they are—show us the house—but never come inside. We are new to them, and they do not know us. They cannot mention those whom they do not know." If two people mention that you are the one administering the oath—ah. You will be hanged. That was the punishment. If you administer the oath—hanged. But if you are only hiding outside or guarding the place, that was a different case.

So we led people from the forest to those who had not taken oath, and we were to guard outside the ceremony. Very many people took oath without knowing that we directed Mau Mau to them. If Mau Mau needed a goat, I would tell them where to go, and they would meet the man and say, "Give us a goat to take Mau Mau with." They would select one, and Mau Mau would use the blood to take oath and then go with the meat to the forest. The man was told, "We are going to hear if anybody mentions Mau Mau in the reserve, and we shall know it is you." They were beaten *kidogo* [a little], and they could not reveal it.

We tried to warn one of my relatives, Kabuuri, not to join the ceremony giving oath, but he did. When things were revealed, he was mentioned by all the people: "Kabuuri was with us, and he was giving us oath." Before we even went to the forest, he was at Nyeri Maximum Prison. Kabuuri, our brother, was hanged—direct, no trial. And we knew that could happen. That's why we didn't want the local people to see us.

I was known as a very fierce Homeguard. Mau Mau were telling me, "People honor you and say that you are a very good Homeguard. They don't want to be given oath because they don't want you to find out." People were reporting that if I see Mau Mau, I will get them. Even our chief was not worried, because I was there, guarding the village from up top. I was telling him, "We are protecting our things. If our cattle are taken, we cannot cry like women—no! Nobody will take our cattle."

By then, I was telling the Mau Mau from the forest, "Never do it. Don't take anything. All that you require, I can buy for you. We can give you food or whatever you want. But if you take things, people will notice and reveal that I am not guarding and must be a Mau Mau." They agreed. I was buying them whatever they needed from the market or the shops. Jesca knew that I was going and buying things, but she didn't bother much.

One night, some Mau Mau came to my home when I was here with Jesca. Some friends came and brought people of the forest to me. They said,

"Let's go and see Mwalimu because he's a good man and will accept the Mau Mau." They were coming to give me oath but did not know that I was already Mau Mau. I gave them the signal.

"What are you doing here with these friends of yours?" I said. "I have already gone that way. I took it long ago without your notice." They were surprised. "I am working very hard for Mau Mau. I have torches [flashlights] here that I bought for another group in the forest, you see? I am buying supplies." They were very pleased to see that I am active. "Take this [the supplies], and I will buy some more for them."

That is when Jesca took oath. I said they could give it to her but not me. She took it in my presence—very plain, with no violence. They asked her, "Had Mwalimu told you that he's taken oath?"

"Never," she said.

"We want you to be like Mwalimu was. Nobody had ever known whether he had taken Mau Mau, so also we want you to remain the same." Jesca was surprised. "How did they not know that you have taken oath?" she asked. I myself wondered, but they did not know. After Jesca took the first one, I took the second oath. That was the beginning of 1953, and it was serious. It was called the platoon oath, or *batuni* oath—the English word, where you can select people for war. That is for people whom you can tell any deep secret. People were chosen special because no matter if you are beaten or killed, you will not reveal the secret. And anybody who comes from the forest, I take him as my brother and keep him safe. If he dies under my protection, it is me who killed him.

To say that you are brothers, you can take blood of one another. We took this oath in [the] forest—seventeen [of us,] I think—separately from women. You prick the fingers, then the blood comes, and you touch it in a bucket—a gourd—of water with some other blood that was already inside. We mixed blood—so when you take it, I taste yours and mine—to say that we are brothers. And by all means, I will help anybody who is hiding from the Europeans and guard the people in the forest.

You say, "I swear before you and the Lord that I will never reveal this oath, even if I have to die. I agree, to you and to the other members of this oath, that if one proves that I've revealed it, I'm ready to die." If you go against the oath and are killed—you are not killed by the Mau Mau but have killed yourself. You are dangerous to the party.

Jesca only took the first oath. My mother and father didn't take oath. "Leave them alone," I said. "What is it for? Once my brothers and I have all taken oath, leave my mother and father." They were not given oath.

Also I saved my friend Francis, a schoolmate from class five, to whom I was very grateful because we used to eat together at his grandmother's house. He was working at the mission hospital with Dr. Irvine. I knew it would be very serious if it were known that Francis took oath because Dr. Irvine could be dangerous and dismiss him. We were giving oath in one room, and I told Francis not to go in. The other Mau Mau were telling me, "This is the man who can help us get medicine."

"Leave him alone," I said. "If you need medicine, send me. I can do it. But I don't want Francis to get involved. There's no need." I didn't want him to suffer at all, and anyways, I thought that he might reveal it. Later on, after many years, I told him the story, and he was very scared. "Ah, Mwalimu, you helped me," he said. And our friendship grew stronger. He worked in that hospital for more than forty years.

So it was me who led both sides, the government and the Mau Mau. We spread Mau Mau throughout this whole area, and we knew we had our youth getting trained at Igoji with the guns that we were going to take to the forest with us. That's what we were aiming at. We wanted our *askari* to easily kill government *askari* and supply us with rifles. But one of our Mau Mau brothers was killed before our things matured, and we had no time to waste and no regret.

THE SHOT YOU HAVE HEARD

I was telling the forest people not to rush with Mau Mau. "Unless you know that people will not reveal, please don't give oath," I said. Sometime in October 1953, somebody gave oath to a man called Muchiri, working in the agricultural ministry as assistant to an instructor. The next morning, Muchiri went to the police station and revealed that he had taken oath. He recognized someone who had been at the oathing ceremony, a man called M'Nyiri. M'Nyiri was one of our best Homeguards being trained at Igoji. Muchiri mentioned M'Nyiri.

The *askari* and the DO—a white man—went to Igoji camp to get M'Nyiri, but he wasn't there. M'Nyiri wasn't feeling well, and he went to Chogoria Hospital for treatment. The DO and *askari* found him there and took him to be screened. Later, Muchiri identified him as the man who was at the oathing. "Yeah, this is M'Nyiri, who gave us oath last night," he said. "He was with other people, but I didn't know them."

When the news broke, we were at Kiangua building a school here. We understood that M'Nyiri was caught, and he was at Igoji police station for screening. We knew the authorities were now watching. We had to pass information to one another. We spoke together, "Do you hear that M'Nyiri has been caught? He is our big man and knows all the Mau Mau. Now we should be very aware. It might be that he will be seriously beaten, and he will reveal and mention some of us. We ourselves may be arrested."

We decided that we should not wait for the news of M'Nyiri there. "We can be arrested here when we are grouping together. Let's wait to hear what will happen, but not from within." So we rushed and dispersed in a way that nobody saw what was happening—one at a time, one at a time— but within a short time, none of us was within Kiangua.

That evening very many people came to my home trying to see what would happen. It was me who knew where the Mau Mau were in the forest, and we were preparing if anything went wrong. I said, "Don't worry. We have people. If M'Nyiri reveals the secret, we will go to the forest. I have contacted people who will come and take us." Everybody had to take heed to see, "Where did *fulani* [so-and-so] go? Is he at home? Or has he gone to the forest? Or turned against us?" By this time we had a group of people looking around, seeing whether there was anybody [from the government] coming to our area.

Suddenly we heard the shot. We heard the sound of the gun, only one— *chuuu*—and we knew something was happening at Kiangua. People who were within the Homeguard camp rushed to my house to give us the report. They said, "Have you heard the shot?" We said yes. "The shot you have heard—it is M'Nyiri. M'Nyiri is killed. We don't know how many people he mentioned, and we don't know what will happen later on. So be careful."

We knew: *Ah-ha. Is this what is going to happen? We have also taken oath, and we will be shot as M'Nyiri was shot.* The man who shot M'Nyiri was Herodian. He was from this area, but he was on the side of the government and was a terrible Homeguard. Herodian was screening M'Nyiri with the DO. M'Nyiri would not confess to anything. Herodian was very serious [brutal]. I don't know [understand] the hatred he had for the Mau Mau. M'Nyiri was beaten, but before he mentioned anything, Herodian shot him. M'Nyiri died.

More people kept coming to my place. They said, "Let us see what people are doing at Japhlet's home." Around eight, it started raining. Seventy-eight people came to my home—old and young, men and even women came because they heard everyone who had taken Mau Mau will be shot. I had to sort people out. They wanted a decision.

To the women and old people, I said, "Now you—go home. M'Nyiri was shot because he has been a Homeguard, and he was planning to become *askari,* so that's their hatred. You haven't done anything. Go and confess that you have taken Mau Mau. They are concerned about younger people, and they are aiming at ourselves. Don't worry. They won't kill you."

We left twenty women and old people behind, and on that very night the fifty-eight *murani* who had an idea of the forest prepared to leave. We knew if we were caught being Mau Mau, people were beaten and thrown in detention or killed—terrible punishments, especially [for] myself, because I've been a spokesman.

It was very difficult. [Now] when people ask why I went to the forest, I don't have good words to tell them. I knew that I will suffer, but I had no alternative. I had quarreled with the *mzungu,* my employer, and we were not on good terms. I had broken the relationship with the missionaries. I could not confess to Dr. Irvine, because he would say, "Now, this is why that man has been so arrogant. He has been a Mau Mau, and Mau Mau are against the Europeans, so this is the time when I can get a hold of him." I knew he would hand me to the Homeguards for screening, and I would never come back.

I was a very good spokesman for my chief and the government, but I'd spoiled that side too. The chief loved me very much, but I was afraid for him to know that I am Mau Mau. That would be worse even than the European. I tried to think, *Where can I rush?* I found nowhere.

The *kaborio* [Homeguards] were shipped in to beat people. Would I dare to stay in the reserves, being beaten until I cried like a woman? Never. Better to die of a bullet, but not that way.

I decided that people are there [in the forest]. Do I look different from them? Let me join them. And I will work against the Europeans and the *kaborio.* I will fight against them. As they hate me, I will hate them—although I did not want anything to be done bad. Even the good chief was halfway like myself—in some meeting he gave the statement, "Now is the time that our people are dividing. We are dealing with Mau Mau, and Mau Mau are our people. So let us keep in the middle: Never go ahead, never remain behind. Let us move there in between."

The Europeans sacked him for that quote when the Mau Mau broke out. "This man has not been for us," they said. "He's been favoring *kina*

Japhlet and other people. He was trying to hide his people, telling them not to be in Mau Mau but also they should not be very loyal. They should be in the middle." I thought: *If that's what they did to the chief, then what about me?*

It was through the emotion [fear] of M'Nyiri that made us to rush without wasting time on that very day. It made us to be more in the forest. If they did not shoot M'Nyiri, I think very many of us could have been caught. By that time, we knew there was no sympathy. Even later on, the people responsible—the DO and the DC—knew they had made a mistake. They didn't know the number of people who had taken Mau Mau or any information. All of us went away before they had screened anyone.

I didn't want to leave anything behind, because I knew the Homeguards would take everything, and I never knew the steps that would be taken against Jesca. I had two big sheep, and I said to the people, "Why should we leave the sheep? Instead of [leaving them to] be eaten by Homeguards, why can't we eat them?" We killed them on that very day. I left all the fat for Jesca, because she could use it to make food. The fat is good for mothers and for babies, and [our one-year-old son] Kirimi was small by then. We had to eat as much as we could that day.

Also, I took all of my very nice clothes from my days of timber and teaching, and I spread them out before the people. Even the beautiful coat and one suit—I displayed them and gave the good clothes to good people. I remained with only one suit and another jacket. I thought it would be very cold in the forest, but when I reached there, I couldn't wear both, so I gave one to somebody who had no coat. I didn't leave any clothes to be taken by the Homeguards.

We had a nice party with my friends there. We had harvested a lot of maize that year, and I think we carried at least four or five big bags. By then, it was not so serious—people in the forest were all right with food because we were feeding them.

Luckily, before nine o'clock at night, a group of four came from the forest to see what is happening. "We cannot turn back now," I said. So I left that night. I left the mission and the chiefs and all that. My wife was very brave, and I told her not to worry. All the women by then had taken oath, and they were very brave. They couldn't mind whatever happened, and they were happy even that we have gone to the forest rather than being beaten. Jesca and I shook hands during the time of leaving on that Mau Mau day. After everybody said goodbye, we said, "If God wills it, we will meet again." And we kissed one another.

The General and Jesca (*front*) on their wedding day, August 16, 1947, in Chogoria
with the best man, Elias Nkonge, and the maid of honor, Alice Gatune. "That
was my greatest accomplishment," said the General. "I married the right lady."
(Photo used with permission from Thambu Family Collection)

The General (*left*) and his timber-dealing colleague, M'Arimi, in Nairobi, 1952, after selling their timber. In April, the two took the Mau Mau oath together. *(Photo used with permission from Thambu Family Collection)*

The General, 1952. *(Photo used with permission from Thambu Family Collection)*

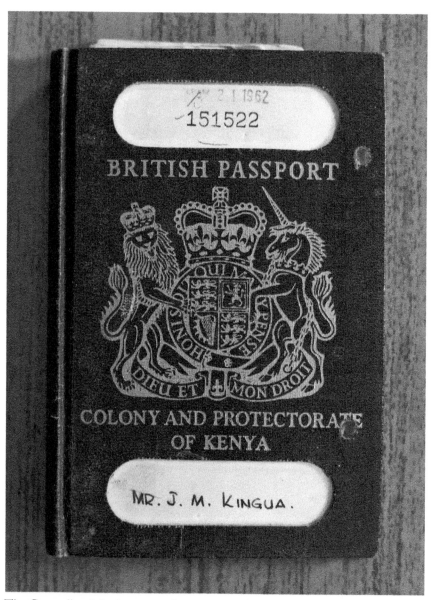

The General's original passport from 1962, used to travel to Ghana as a KADU delegate. There he met with President Kwame Nkrumah. *(Photo by Mary Beth Koeth)*

The General, chairman of the Kiangua Farmers Society, 1972. *(Photo used with permission from Thambu Family Collection)*

The General and Jesca at home in 1974. *(Photo used with permission from Thambu Family Collection)*

On the front porch at home in April 2009, plucking dried maize, which will be ground into flour for *ugali*. *(Photo by Laura Lee Huttenbach)*

Poster hanging on the wall of Naivasha, a Mau Mau soldier who fought under the General during the revolution. *(Photo by Laura Lee Huttenbach)*

The South Imenti Tea Growers SACCO (now the Yetu SACCO) Executive
Board meeting in May 2009. *Top row, left to right:* Josphat Gitobu, Zaverio
Muthamia, Gichuru Itawa, Gedion Gichunge, Japhlet Thambu, Festus
Kathendu, and Mark Gitonga. *Bottom row, left to right:* Gerald Njiru, John
Mwiti, and Isaiah Kiura. *(Photo by Laura Lee Huttenbach)*

The General, Juju Jesca, and the Thambu children, at a reunion in December
2011. *Left to right:* Jeremy Mutwiri (son of their late daughter Susan Muthoni),
Nkuene (their niece, whom they adopted), Rosemary Mugure, Jeremiah Nyaga,
Simon Kirimi, Betsy Kaari, Palmer Murithi, Florence Kaimuri, Dorothy Kangai,
and Frederick Kinyua. *(Photo by Laura Lee Huttenbach)*

The General and Juju Jesca with their great-grandchildren, December 2010.
(Photo by Laura Lee Huttenbach)

The General, December 2013. *(Photo by Mary Beth Koeth)*

Slopes of the General's tea farm, December 2013. *(Photo by Mary Beth Koeth)*

Jesca and Laura Lee "Nkirote" Huttenbach sorting tea at the tea collection center, October 2006. *(Photo from Laura Lee Huttenbach)*

For decades, the General's wife, Jesca, bore the weight of wicker baskets filled to the brim with over fifty pounds of freshly picked tea. The work left its mark. *(Photo by Mary Beth Koeth, December 2013)*

The Thambus' stone house, built in 1982 after a good tea harvest. *(Photo by Mary Beth Koeth, December 2013)*

PART III

THE FOREST

A VIOLENT RAINSTORM BLAMES THE WIND

The forest men told us that we were not allowed to go with our spears—only *pangas*—into the forest. They said that [the] Homeguards were using spears, and we could not tell who are the Mau Mau and who are Homeguards. I had mine on the very day we went to the forest, so I threw it somewhere under a certain tree. I remembered where I threw it, and it stayed there for the long time that we lived in the forest and when I was detained. [Six years later] I went and met my spear, next to the same tree. Nobody had touched that area, so I found it again.

I led fifty-eight men to the forest. From the other side, from Kiangua, we met another twenty-two. They took another way, and we found them there. So we became fifty-eight plus twenty-two. We were eighty. Entering the forest we followed in the path of elephants—by then there were very many elephants—and when they move, they clear each and every thing.

We met two generals: General Martin and General Simba.[1] They were the ones sent from the war council in Nairobi. Martin was from Nkubu, and Simba was from Chuka, but they worked with Mau Mau since the beginning. Martin knew all about the distribution of things from Nairobi and sharing of supplies through the war council. Simba was illiterate. He was one of the rogues and was taken for Mau Mau because he was an expert in stealing. They were very happy to know that they got a big number of people from Igoji joining the Mau Mau. East of Mount Kenya, we were around three hundred to begin with.

We were *itungati* of Kimathi, servants of Kimathi. All the Mau Mau belonged to him. The commanding chief is Kimathi. [Dedan] Kimathi was from Nyeri, and practically everybody in Nyeri took Mau Mau. Those people fought seriously. Kimathi had the education of primary school like myself, and he was in the Second World War. As I told you, those who came from the military—ah, they were not fearing Europeans anymore.

All of us have known [of] Kimathi, though he did not come to this side of Mount Kenya. He was in Nyandurua [the Aberdare Mountain Range],[2] where we had a lot of forest. I've only seen the picture of Kimathi, but his name was widely spread. He said, "Let us only use one name of General, General Kimathi." Put it to one man. No matter what you have to do, we could liberate ourselves, saying, "I have taken my commands." If somebody asks why—it is that cause, we were ordered by Kimathi. It went in that way, it was the spirit of the place.

All of our *kipande*s were taken. "Kimathi wants the ID cards," that's what they were telling us. "Kimathi must know we are in, and he'll do the records. If you see that you cannot tolerate this place and you want to leave Mau Mau, please just report to us, and you'll be given back your *kipande*." Later I came to know that was a lie. They burned the *kipande*s. If someone asked for the *kipande* back to leave the forest, he will be killed. Because he knows all the secrets of Mau Mau, and he will lead the Homeguards to us. And if he goes to the reserve without ID, it will be known he is Mau Mau.

When you are accepted in the forest, you had to take [another] oath. You had to say that you no longer belong to the reserve. By all means, you are a forest man now. They made something for you to go through [an arch], but we had already been Mau Mau, so it was not fearful like in the reserve, where they were using all these awkward things, rotten blood, to make people know if they went against it—ah.

I attended one ceremony of the second oath, where these women were taking it. I was hiding somewhere outside, but I could see what was going on. They gave the higher levels of oath to women in a very awkward way, especially the third oath. It was nasty.[3] You'd never like to see. Agh. They were fearing. The oath that they were taking was even, I think, worse than the men's oath. Women were naked—terrible, it was terrible. They [the oath administrators] were animals. Most of them died in the forest.

Jesca didn't take one of that kind. Jesca only took the first oath. Those who were given the second oath, if they got imprisoned, they did not mention it. The screening people would only ask, "Have you taken the second oath?" If the women said yes, the screener said, "*Pole. Pole*, mama." He did not want to go deeper than that. They knew how it was taken.

For us, in the forest, you only repeat, "As long as I live, if anybody turns from this movement, no matter whether my father or my mother, I will never be his friend. And if an enemy is killed in my presence, no matter whether it's my mother, father, or son, I will never reveal the killer. If I do, let this oath kill me."

This oath was for killing. If your wife or your brother turns [out] to be an enemy, and you are sent to kill them, you will do it. He will no longer be my brother, because he has gone against our will. We called the third oath *kugera ngero*, where people can do anything. *Ngero* means "anything," and *kugera* is "to do"—*kugera ngero* meant "to do bad things to your enemy."[4] Every forest fighter has taken that one.

After repeating, you were to get a new name. That was somehow a baptism. Our real names were completely hidden, to confuse people in the reserve and the government. When people surrendered later on, they [i.e., the Special Branch] analyzed it and knew who was who, but during Mau Mau, we never revealed our [real] names.

You could choose any name that you think will fit you. Some were taking Gikuyu names or Indian names, like Kassam. Some could take animal names like Simba [Lion] or Njogu [Elephant]. Martin was an English name. I chose Nkungi. *Nkungi* means a very strong wind, a whirlwind. In Kimeru we have a saying, "A violent rainstorm blames the wind." The wind is *nkungi*. If you want to do something, but something happens, then *nkungi* is your excuse. Whatever is happening in the forest, whether good or bad, people will be referring to *nkungi*. *Nkungi* is to blame. It's a widely known word.

So people may hear the name "Nkungi," but they didn't know "Nkungi" was "Thambu" until after I came out. Then they said, "Thambu is called Nkungi." But some people continued [to use] the name Nkungi, or General Nkungi, because they appreciated it.

We were new ones to the forest, and if we were not properly trained, very many could be killed, so we mixed with old members of Mau Mau from all over. One group went to Chuka with General Simba, and another group [went] to the other side with Martin in Nkubu. Until things cooled in our area, we were dispersed to other areas. We didn't want many people together—groups of thirty or twenty-five or twenty, that's all.

We had to move. We didn't build permanent camps. The other side [those west of Mount Kenya] tried to put up these temporary buildings, but we, east of Mount Kenya, were using *shuka* [a sheet] to put up our shelter, something like a tent. We pegged it tightly, and whether it rains or not, it doesn't leak. We were prohibited to use our *panga*s to cut anything around where we were staying. We never wanted to leave a mark in the forest, because that will be noticed by the Homeguards. They were coming all the time looking for Mau Mau. Only if we were trying to make an ambush, to have the Homeguards follow us a certain way, then we could cut a path. Otherwise, we could not make any marks.

One camp should be a kilometer or two away from others. When there is shooting or an ambush, the other camp can hear it and run away. If we killed somebody from one area, a *mzungu* or an *askari*, then we knew the government would follow us, so we would run to another side and stay for a month. When they looked for Mau Mau in that area, they don't find one. So we were nowhere. The forest was for us around Mount Kenya.

There was no smoking. We could smell it a kilometer away. Also, you could not use soap. We could wash clothes if necessary, but no soap. There are some plants in the forest that look like cabbages and grow around the river. If you crush them, it gives a powder something like soap but gave a different smell. People who passed here using soap, you felt a different smell. After a year, it was wonderful because even the elephants could not smell us. You could go near to them because we were smelling the same as animals. The elephant could smell the *kaborio*, but they could never feel any smell of the forest people.

Also, we were not allowed to wear shoes. The Homeguards and Europeans were wearing shoes. When we saw a mark, we looked to see whether it is foot or shoe. But we were not supposed to leave any footmarks, because those could be traced. When we saw [the mark of a] shoe, we knew the Homeguards were there. Whoever has shoes—we didn't want in the forest.

We woke up very early in the morning, and the first thing [we did] was to pray. We Mau Mau, and the people of Kenya, believed that our God lived in Mount Kenya, and we call him Mwene Nyaga. "Mwene Nyaga" means the owner of blessings, the owner of peace. Mwene Nyaga is our God, and there is only one. We were not praying as Christians seem to do. We were praying facing Mount Kenya.

We prayed thanking Him for the way He has helped us and praying that these people—our people [Homeguards]—should change their mind and know that we are not against them, but we are against the Europeans. We were praying that those who may not see that could see it. We prayed for those who went to look for food and thanked God for those who had come back.

After, we divided, and people went to do various jobs. Some were to go to look for yams, others were to look for honey. Honey was very important. There are certain trees here that give flowers and attract a lot of bees, so especially during April, you could get honey. We could use it for medicine if somebody was shot. When the bullet comes in, it makes a little hole, but the way it comes out, the hole gets bigger. We were to put honey at the entrance where the bullet passed through, and it will clear all the stuff that the bullet left in your body. Then tomorrow you add more, and in some time, you will be cleaned. There is a type of honey that is good for that—not sweet but not bitter—with a wonderful taste. Also, we had people with very good knowledge of trees who could make herbal medicine using honey. They could make a wonderful cough medicine, [because] in an ambush, we could not have somebody coughing in the forest. Even myself, now, I can make my own, better than you buy in the pharmacy.

For our meat, we were trapping these big animals called buffalo. They were very many here. They have their paths, their ways to go when they look for water in the forest. Those were the areas where we could take all the soil away and make a big hole. Then we cover it with grass [banana leaves]. When the buffalos are moving, they never know whether there is a hole, so they cross and—*whoosh*—they fall. We made it a size where it will be completely restricted, around eight feet deep, where it won't have space to move to any side. We had to look for them in the morning. Some were falling even during the daytime. We ate a lot [of] them. I think we ate all the big animals in our forest here—you can hardly find them now.

Although it looks very fat, it is all red meat with no fat, unless you kill one who is pregnant. That was fat, and we were trying to see whether we could get them because it was sweet and fat. You notice they are tasty. But we couldn't mind [pay attention to] the taste, [because] it was to keep us going. The meat was not specific for the people who killed it—no. We were to divide it according to the number of people within the camp. It was for the whole community. We could send a message to other camps that we have killed one, so they came for meat. Somebody even had to carry the big head. More than twenty people could not finish one buffalo.

In the beginning, food was an easy thing. We could get yams, maize— whatever was remaining in the *shamba*s of the reserves. But you could not go alone. There were some of that kind who went to look for food and then surrendered to help the Homeguards, so we did not allow anyone to go alone. We went in groups of five, or ten, or six—in those numbers.

When we left the forest, we were to walk backward across the *barabara* [road], so the Homeguards never knew which way we were walking. And we crossed one at a time because if we met an ambush, we could all be shot in a line, so we scattered ourselves. If someone gets shot, he will die one, not all of us.

The Homeguards knew we were to look for food in the *shamba*s, so the person in charge of the group had to go around the *shamba,* to survey and see whether anybody is there hiding in an ambush. After they scout the lot, they signal [*snapping fingers*] for the rest to come. If the rest hear a shot before, they run away.

If a group did not come back we had to follow immediately, to see what happened, whether they were caught or surrendered. If a person gets lost in the place you were looking for food, someone from the group must be sent back to the camp to say, "We were with so-and-so, and he got lost, so be careful." We move from that place because we fear that the one missing might bring the Homeguards back to our camp.

We were always taking care that all of us never left the camp, because people may come and hide and take over the position while we are out. We put guards all over the area where we were staying. We knew the paths where people could enter the camp, so we had at least four guards stay the whole day there, seeing those who are coming out and others that are back again.

People were not supposed to come at night because the forest becomes very dark after six o'clock. Ah, it's wonderful—terribly dark. You could never know your way and cannot walk. If you dare to use a torch, you will be aimed at and shot. If it becomes dark before you arrive in the forest, you spend the night somewhere and come to the camp during the daytime.

When we had only one month in the forest, we came and took food from Jesca. We were given *githere,* maize mixed with beans. We said that we should not go to the *barabara* during the night. By then these John-nies—we were calling them Johnnies, the Europeans who arrived from I don't know where—were ambushing. So we slept there [with Jesca in the reserve] until the dew came in the morning.

I went to collect something from somebody's home, and the other people left. I tried to follow them, but I missed the way that they went. I followed my own way. Just around six-something when I went to cross the *barabara,* I don't know what I felt. A few meters from the road, just before I was to reach it, I changed the route. I was diverted and took a different way.

After crossing the road, I heard "blablabla," these Johnnies, talking. They were covering all along our forest roads. I thought that they have seen me and would take aim, but they didn't. I ran back to the forest with all the things I was carrying. Ahead, I met six friends. "How did you pass?" they said. "We were trying to cross into the reserve, but they were there."

"I heard the Johnnies talking," I said. "They were calling their friend who was on the other side, saying nobody was coming, and they could move."

That was the first time I praised the Lord. I think God must have diverted me, to change the route. I said, "Eh, I could have died very early and been displayed by the Homeguards. It would be useless." We prayed. I knew God must have me.[5]

Around eight o'clock or eight thirty at night, when we knew nobody would come to us, we decided to cook. We did not eat the bananas, yams, and meat fresh [raw]. Most of what we ate we had to cook. We had *sifurias*—pots—and water was an easy thing to collect [because] there were many streams and rivers. We put guards around the camp to hear whether there were any planes coming, these planes going around Mount Kenya, especially in our area. If it comes, then we cover the fire with soil so the planes could never see the light.

In Nyambene, a bomb killed seven people. They heard the plane around them, and somebody gave the signal that the plane was coming, but they ignored it. They didn't know what the plane was looking for. The plane saw them and went back to Nairobi and then came back at night with great force and a new group of planes. We heard the bombs firing at Nyambene—*ooo-hoo-hoo-hoo*—we knew something was happening. There was one who hid himself and did not die, and he gave the report [of] what happened. Seven were killed. So we were very careful with the light at night. If we had a fire, we must have somebody outside, listening.

Before sleeping, we were to pray again. We prayed to our God of Kirinyaga, our God who was ever with us, believing seriously. That was the first and the last thing.

THE ONE WHO DUG THE HOLE IS THE ONE WHO FELL IN

Nobody could give good records in the forest, so, being a teacher and the only educated [literate] man, I took the position of secretary for General Simba and General Martin. I had to attend the meetings of the big people, to keep records of all the secrets. Within a very short time—three months—I was ranked a sergeant because I couldn't go to the committee that decides on forest affairs unless I am ranked. Although I was a newcomer, I had to take more secret oaths to qualify me to keep the minutes.

And in the meetings I was told to write the date and locality where *fulani* was killed but not who killed him. It was marked down that way.

I was in charge of the Mau Mau book of names. The books had all of the people who had taken oath, including people like Jesca from the reserves who were helping Mau Mau. I was *bwana mkubwa* when I took these books. I had two guards, two big people with guns, all the time. When we walked, we had to leave a distance [between one another] because if it happened for me to be shot with those books, they don't leave them. They should never run, because the whites would do anything to have our records. They wanted to know how many people belonged to the Mau Mau. If those books were captured, our people in the reserve would suffer. After nine months, I was promoted to RSM—regimental sergeant major—and then to the rank of lieutenant after one year in the forest.[6]

I stayed carrying those books in a big bag for two years. I slept in my own place, hidden where not even other members of Mau Mau knew where I was. We ate together, but after eating, I disappeared somewhere with my guards. It was a very serious, hard task.

When we went to the forest, we were expecting to have guns. But M'Nyiri was killed before our things matured, so we did not manage to get any guns. We had a general for Nyambene who was called Mwariama. *Mwariama* means a man who speaks the truth and gives full information. Before he went to the forest, Mwariama was a Homeguard in a European *shamba* near Nanyuki, but he took oath through General China in Mount Kenya West without the notice of the *shamba* owner.

When they planned to go into the forest, Mwariama arranged through General China a way to get the guns and take them to the forest. One evening, China came in with his group of more than six Mau Mau *askari*, and they were hidden in Mwariama's quarters. Mwariama went to patrol the *shamba* with the *mzungu*. That *bwana*, the *shamba* owner, had given them [his Homeguards] guns. After going around in the evening, they returned home with the *mzungu* to lock the guns inside. Mwariama followed the *mzungu* and helped collect the other guns to put them safely in the cabinet. Before Mwariama gave him his own gun, he grabbed hold of the *mzungu*. He called to China and his men to enter the home.

They took the European outside and killed him in the *shamba*. They burned the house and took the four guns. All of the quarters [African workers] went to the forest. In the morning, when people went to investigate, they found no *mzungu* and no Mwariama. It took no time to know that the *bwana* was killed by Mau Mau and Mwariama had left for the forest.

Mwariama stayed on that side [Mount Kenya West] for a bit with General China, but he decided to go back to his home in Nyambene. When Mwariama was leaving, China told him, "Because you are going alone, you cannot go with a gun; the gun might be taken. So, you go there with a *panga*."

After all that Mwariama had done for the Mau Mau, China took Mwariama's guns, and Mwariama went to his home territory without. When we met with Mwariama, he told us the story. We were very serious to China. We said, "Mwariama had four guns from his own source. Now when he tried to go home, to see his Meru people, you took his gun. Why?" He had nothing to tell us. "Did you care for Mwariama's life? Do you know who killed *mzungu*? Where did you get the four guns?"

China said, "Mwariama."

"Then why did you send him home with [only] a *panga*?"

He said, "We did not mean anything, we meant—"

"What did you mean? Mm-hm. You have to give that gun to us." We began to see these people, although we are [fighting] together, they are selfish. Our relationship with the Gikuyu, not because of politics or because of *wazungu*—we have got historical things from our fathers. We had a lot of quarrelling with the Gikuyu, but later on they agreed to give us one gun.

China was very active on the other side [Mount Kenya West]. Very unfortunately, he was caught early in 1954, I think February. I entered the forest in 1953, and by early 1954, he was caught. He didn't stay long. When he was shot, he could not run, so he threw his gun away and denied it was his. If you were caught with a gun or any cartridge or bullet, the sharia [punishment] was to hang. But the sharia [examiner] agreed that the gun was not his, so he was put into prison.[7]

Mount Kenya is surrounded by different tribes. The east[ern] lands are Ameru. Our Wameru generals were Simba in Chuka. Martin was Imenti South. Kaggia was Imenti North. Mwariama was in the lower area of Nyambene. Then we had General Kassam in Kirinyaga, around Mount Kenya, which was in Embu District. A man called Kubu Kubu was another general in Embu. Only General China in Mount Kenya West, near the settler *shambas*, was Gikuyu. Those were [the generals] around Mount Kenya. [On] the other side, in Nyandarua, we had Mathenge and Kimathi. Those are Gikuyu.

Mwariama and his people were taken as very good, brave people. But we were disappointed with China. Luckily there was a Gikuyu fellow who knew how to make homemade guns. It was an easy thing because we could get pipes.[8] We didn't take long before we had two homemade guns within our group. Every group leader was given a homemade gun, and I had mine. We did not play with guns. If you were a coward, don't take [it]. But if you mean that when you aim, you will kill one—we would give you [a gun]. We were very specific in that. Make sure that the bullet never goes out unless into somebody's body. If you fear, give [it to] me. I will do it. If you hear *TWAA*—somebody's dead.

Our homemade guns gave a very big noise. When the bullet comes out of the gun, it spins and makes a noise—*di-di-di-di-di-di*—then when it gets to the open place [the end of the barrel], *TWAA!* The Homeguards will get nervous hearing the sound, wondering what type of gun is that. They knew Mau Mau were not [equipped only] with *panga*s, they were [equipped] with guns.

The most difficult problem was to get bullets. Each group had a few bullets, two or three. If we knew that Chuka has bullets, they had to share. If they have ten, they can give us five. Each and every leader in the camp should have one or two. Sometimes we could get some bullets from the camps where the *kaborio* stayed. Some African people were in the *kaborio*,[9] and they could leave some bullets in the place where they camped, whether intentional or not. When you have ten or five or twenty—ah, that will remain [last] for a while.

When we saw Homeguards, we said, "Don't waste your bullet with an African. Leave him. Hide yourself. He's a fool, guided by the European. He doesn't know what he's doing. They are treated even worse than ourselves. They don't know why they're killing us. They were only told by that man. Aim—if you can get a *mzungu*—the whole field will feel that somebody has died. Even if he doesn't die, get a bullet in him. He knows he has to die. But this African—if you kill him, you kill ourselves."

Within each and every village our wives were there, and they were Mau Mau. Even the members of [the] Homeguards—some of them were loyal to Mau Mau. Before the Europeans detected it, the *askari* and the clerks that they had in the office were Mau Mau. So we had to get daily information [about] how things are changing, which side these patrols are seriously aimed at, and which side we should move [to]. We had a lot of communication with people outside the forest. They were allowed to look for firewood, so we saw them. It was a nice movement—difficult—but the cooperation was serious.

Women were coming to hide food where we can collect it in the forest. We could get some information from the younger children. We told them, "Go and take this tobacco to a certain place and meet someone," and then whoever meets him will give him something. You could never suspect these little children, naked, were related to Mau Mau, but they were our people. Even we used old people who could not walk.

Now, the matters of discipline were complicated. When Mau Mau started, the first people to take oath were the rogues, the great thieves of Nairobi, who had nothing of their own and could be used in any way. Some were very good *askari*, but, you know, rogues are disorderly. It was hard to get them in a system of integrity in the forest. If one of them misbehaved, and he had a rank from the war council in Nairobi, and you rushed to punish them—it could cause a lot of tension.

We had several meetings to see how to handle these people. We even had to refute some of the regulations being made in Nairobi. "Nairobi people are not in the forest," we said. "They don't know the problems that we have. To live with these bad rogues, we have to discipline them, or they will mislead and do any rough thing that they want."

But they had this terrible way of punishing people who break the Mau Mau rules in the forest. If you do something which Mau Mau does not want, they tied your hands together and hanged you from a tree by your hands, just inches off the ground, for a few seconds. You get paralyzed. Once you were cut down, you cannot walk. You have to take time for the circulation to go well again. That punishment was very common in the Mau Mau areas, but I didn't like it myself. I said that it won't be done in my camp. Some of the people said, "Nkungi has refused to use the punishment of hanging people." I was interviewed and had to explain why. I was fearing [to be outspoken] because I was new to the forest.

"It is wrong," I said. "If you punish someone in this way and if the Homeguards come while he is in that condition, who will take that man down from hanging? You will run away, and you cannot carry him. Supposing that man gets killed, who has killed him? Is it the Homeguards, or the Mau Mau? In our oath, we said we cannot reveal anything that will harm a fellow Mau Mau member. Now our friends have died." People listened and said, "It's true, Nkungi. That is, of course, logic. Let us change it to something else."

We also had beehives in the forest, but the people keeping those bee-hives—not all of them were Mau Mau. Some Mau Mau were killing the people of the beehives because [they thought] nobody should enter into the forest unless he's a Mau Mau. A group of us from Chuka had a meeting. "That is very wrong," we said. "These people of the beehives are helping us. They did not put them there because of Mau Mau, neither did they know Mau Mau could happen. So to kill them, because of good work that they did in the forest, and even you feed off that work—that is against the law, even of the Mount Kenya God."

We even sent some people to see them [the beekeepers]. We said, "The forest is dangerous. To us, it's okay. We won't kill you, but when these Europeans or whoever come to the forest and meet you, they will never know [if you are Mau Mau]. You could be killed. Can you please leave the forest, and if we get honey, we will bring [it to] you at home." They were happy.

Some Mau Mau were doing damaging things to those beehives. When they got honey, they dropped the beehive from the trees. "These beehives are serving us," we said. "Why should you break and destroy them? Where will you get honey from tomorrow?" We stopped that too.

Finally, I addressed in a meeting that I had a problem with some people [who] did not want to dig a big hole [to trap buffalo], and they were sug-gesting to make just a little hole and then sharpen a good, hard stick to put at the bottom. When the animal falls, it will be shot [pierced] with the spear and die. But I said, "Don't do it. This is bad because you don't know who will fall. All our people are within, and they don't know whether we have these holes. One of us might fall into it."

One afternoon, I spent the whole day making a nice hole for the buf-falo. We covered it very smooth—you could never know there is a hole. In the evening around six-something, I remembered I left my coat hanging on a tree. Turning to get my clothes, I didn't remember whether I was crossing the pit. At the very last minute, I stepped on one of the covering sticks, and it broke. I went—*shwoo*—into the hole.

My people had to come pick me out. Ah, we laughed very much. It was already the evening time, so we didn't repair it until the next day. That story went all over. "Nkungi was in the pit, which he made himself. The one who dug the hole is the one who fell in." People were to laugh at me. "You see?" I said. "If we had put that thing [spear] down there, you would have Nkungi being our meat." Although it was the shortcut way, I said, "Don't do it."

[Once, while we were] coming back from one big meeting next to Meru Town, it was very late in the afternoon. Walking back to our place, we saw elephants ahead of us. Those elephants were annoyed. When you see them trying to march in place where they stand—it's irritating itself and preparing to quarrel. If it makes noise, even the others could chase you, and the rest could become very wild. So when you hear them cry, making noise, it's telling others there is a fight now. Also, it was very foggy in the forest, and you could not see all the elephants around. "Let us not go that way," we said. "We may surprise them, and they may run toward us. Let's go another way."

Our friend Njuma was there. "Do you fear those elephants?" he said. "They are not animals [to be scared of]." So he took his own way, and we took another. These elephants were scared, so they rushed to stampede—*PADAPADAPADAPADA!* Then we heard the noise. When an elephant gets somebody, they trumpet.

We said, "Uh-huh. I think that fellow was met by the elephants." We turned. "Let us see why these elephants made a lot of noise."

I'm telling you—we didn't see any body, but we saw this bone, his backbone, and it was very long. Red and long, hanging from a tree branch. On their way running, the elephants had met Njuma. An elephant had got hold of him—I don't know, by the head or tusks—and threw him, pelted, kicked him, against the trunk of the tree. The skin—his body went away, and I did not see anything but his back. I never knew the back of a man was so long.

That was the end of Njuma. He was a very great friend of General Martin. "He said that elephants are not animals," I said, "and he has known now that they are animals." We didn't bother to look for the rest of his body, because he did not follow what we suggested.

We were telling our people, "Never rush with these animals. Especially the buffaloes—when you see an animal in the pit, wait. Don't rush." One time, one of our fellows went to check the pit, and he met two buffaloes in one pit. They were freshly down there, and the one on top had killed the other one trying to come out. The gentleman never knew that there were two. He only saw the buffalo [on top] playing, and he thought to come and kill it. So he rushed toward that buffalo with a *panga*.

Before the man reached the hole, the buffalo managed to come out because it could jump. *Whewwwww.* The big head of the buffalo went at him furiously. It took that man and threw him with his horns and flipped him behind. The man landed in the pit on top of where the other buffalo was dead. He had a wonderful fall and died.

When we came to the pit, we saw the man resting. We thought he was happy because the animal was in the pit. Oh-oh. To our surprise, that man was dead. What killed this man, we didn't know, but another gentleman told us the story. We had to take our man in and bury him before we could take up the dead buffalo. We were very sorry to eat the buffalo meat, because our fellow had died. Although we had to eat, we didn't enjoy it.

We were sharing the forest with animals. Even Mwariama was in the forest of [what is today] Meru National Park, living with the very furious animals—lions and leopards—but still those animals were far better to deal with than the British, because those animals could give us meat.

DIE WITHOUT NOISE

I met with Jesca only that one time to collect the food. The Homeguards took one month watching to see if we could come back to visit. Jesca was there waiting with the other women. They had to think and plan what to do now: *Should we join them in the forest? Do we know where they are?* Ah, it was serious. There was no alternative that they [the government] were to take my wife and other women for screening.[10]

They asked Jesca, "Tell us how these people went. What did Japhlet tell you? How many were they?" They were screened. They couldn't give proper information, [though,] because they didn't want to reveal the secrets.

"We don't know how many they were, but I know that they left. They went to the forest," she said. Then my wife went to prison. She went to Kisumu, very far from here, in western Kenya.[11]

In the forest I kept away from any thinking of my children and family. I was only thinking of the people whom we are fighting. We were claiming our land from Europeans. That was the agenda. If you are shot, before you die, you are to scoop some soil and put it in your mouth. That is to say that you are dying because of that soil. You are not dying because of any mistakes but because of that soil. You are innocent. And you can never cry. Never. When you are shot, you die without noise. You die without committing any wrong.

You did not go to the forest because you wanted to kill anybody, but you were against the people who took your land. That's the only belief we put in our head. If you can get soil in your mouth before you die, you have won. You are free now.

When I went to the forest, the *askari* and police were surprised. "Japhlet has gone to the forests, and he took practically every young person with him," they said. They knew people were under my command, so they would like to see me rather than anybody else. Even the Mau Mau people were telling me, "No, no—don't go to the reserves. Let us go ourselves. We don't want you to be seen."

A friend told me that when the *askari* were preparing to go hunt for Mau Mau, one was loading his gun. While he was putting in the bullets, he was saying, "This bullet will go to King'ua." My friend was listening to what this *askari* was saying. "That *askari* said when the bullet jumps from his gun, it will be King'ua's food. He said that he would never miss you, and he will feed you that bullet. God is good that you did not eat any of his food. The food went to his side. He died." My friend was proud to tell me that the man who wanted to give me a bullet—he died himself. Whether he ate the bullet, I don't know.

When my friend went to look for food, he saw my *shamba*. Coming back to the forest, he reported to me. "Japhlet," he said. "Japhlet, what I have seen there—I would not like you to see. These people have done wonderful [the unthinkable]. Instead of looking for you to kill you, they have taken your wife. We don't know where she is with the children. They have uprooted all your coffee—not cutting, but uprooting and burning. I understand that they killed the two cattle you had.

"Let me tell you, Japhlet. These people, instead of trying to kill you, they have killed each and every thing that you had. So make sure that you never die. These things have paid your burden. They have done horrible things, so feel free. You will not die."

I said, "Yes, you are very right."

Before I left for the forest, I was in a very nice permanent house. I built it with this tin, *mabati* [corrugated iron sheets], and timber. Also, my coffee was completely red [ripe], giving lots of wonderful beans. In November, we could have had a very nice harvest. But, oh—when Jesca was taken and I was in the forest, the Homeguards demolished the house and took all of the timber and *mabati*.[12] Only some stones were left. But it was lucky they left the stones, because I used them when I came back again to the house.

All the things that I had were taken. I had very nice tables, a round one and an oval one with six good chairs. These were taken by our local Homeguards. Even the pictures—they were all taken by the *kaborio*, for the *wazungu* to see who is Japhlet. I lost all of my pictures. I got only one back from the wedding, because my sister-in-law gave it to me.

When I came back home, I met nothing. Nothing. Even I lost my brother during that time of Mau Mau. He was cut by Homeguards, and they messed him up mentally. He was captured and cut [on] one leg, and he went off his head. He died later on. My other brother was imprisoned. People didn't term Mau Mau like people. We were counted as animals. Brothers were going after other brothers. And if there was an enmity that came from before, then this was the time that someone could kill you and know that he would not be charged for it. So we were killing one another. In fighting with the Europeans, we killed ourselves.

If somebody got a man like myself, he could be paid ten thousand shillings. That was the money offered by the government. If you could kill Kimathi, I don't know how much you could be given. The government had the list of the people whom they can pay for. The ordinary people [Mau Mau] also could get you a little money. To prove that you have killed someone, you had to cut [off] the hands and bring them to the Europeans. Then they check the fingerprint, to know whether it is the person you have cut, because people were saying, "I've got the hand of a very big man," but they had to check. The record had to be official. If it is proven by the fingerprint that is the one, you get rewarded. People were selling parts.

We were trying to hide bodies from the Europeans. If a Mau Mau died accidentally, we buried you. But once Homeguards cut [off] your hands, there was no need to bury them, because, from the fingerprint, the government already knows you have died. We never buried the bodies of Homeguards.

Those years in Mau Mau—they took me wholly. I was not of my own mind. A human being is wonderful [strange]. He can do anything he likes, but if one is poisoned by [the] oath—ah. The oath kills human thinking, and it plants something new. From what you were—you are taken away completely. Fully. Oathing does that. Nothing else but oathing does it. I never knew why people killed each other. It is during the Emergency that I knew—bitterness. If it goes beyond their control, people kill one another. A person kills himself even.

We were talking of *mzee* Johnson, the one who started the Independent schools. This old man went to the forest during Mau Mau, with two of his sons even. His sons came out first, but Johnson was caught later because he could not run. In the group that caught him was a European and some police. They began to screen him while he was in the reserve. They said,

"*Mzee,* do you still like the Mau Mau? You were in the forest fighting for independence. Now—did you come here on your own, or was it because we caught you?"

"It is because you have caught me," he said.

"Supposing we allow you to go back, would you prefer to go back to the forest?"

"I will never waste time—yes!"

"Then go," they said.

Johnson turned and started for the forest. They shot him. He was an old man, and they shot him. They killed *mzee,* for nothing, because he didn't like to be captive.

Our Homeguards were mad [crazy]. If you put something in people's head, if you poison someone by giving oath—especially when you mix poor and rich, educated and illiterate—then you can never recollect it. If you make the mistake to teach them together, you get only a few with reason. The rest will never turn around. They will go against you even. Some will make it their duty [to continue fighting] because they have got free things to eat. They like taking things. That is the problem we have with this oathing business.

In Chuka, Mau Mau did a mistake and killed a very good Christian woman. She was called Mama Miriam in Kimeru—that is, "Mary." I was educated with her sons. Mama Miriam was a very wonderful, good Christian fellow. Mau Mau came to give her [the] oath, and she refused. She said she has taken the Christian oath, the Mau Mau of Jesus. Mau Mau asked her, "Are you going to say that you've seen Mau Mau?"

"Me, I've never seen Mau Mau," she said. "I've seen people. Do you differ from me?"

Mau Mau killed her. Very many people gave evidence, and the news spread that Miriam died because she has taken the Mau Mau oath of Christ. Those people did [a] mistake. It was not within my presence. I think they were young, not with a grown-up fellow, and it was a bad lot. Most of them died in the forest.

Everybody felt bad. "Why could you kill a woman?" asked [General] Mwariama. "If anybody has taken the Christian oath, and he says that he does not want to take the Mau Mau oath—okay. If he says he won't mention anything concerning the Mau Mau, leave him."

I don't know the date, but Mama Miriam was killed in '54. She was buried in Chogoria. Even today there is a good grave for Miriam. She has very good sons, Christians, who are still alive. Other Christians who were caught and repeated the very same words were not killed. We even had a man in the forest called Apollo who had a Bible and led us in prayer. He was shot in the forest but was a very good Christian.

In Chogoria, everybody was fearing me. "Japhlet knows Chogoria all over, and he's going to be serious with a gun," they said. But when Gikuyu wanted to burn some houses in Chogoria, I said no. I said, "This is our hospital, this is our mission. Take whatever you want to take for eating, for clothes, *nini* [whatever], but don't touch people. We are not here to fight [them]. If you attack the hospital, you won't get any medicine, or if you happen to get it, what are you going to do? Do we have any doctors here? No."

I told the men in the forest, "Let's go to my place [in Igoji] where we have the proper Mau Mau system, and you can have whatever animals. But leave Chogoria alone." So we made arrangements with the people [in Igoji]. They would give their cattle voluntarily to the Mau Mau. And after taking their goat or cattle to eat in the forest, we told them, "Now you wait an hour, then make noise. Cry that Mau Mau has taken whatever. Awaken everybody. Cry—*ooooooo*—that's what will free you. Nobody will beat you, because even themselves will fear to come out during that noisy time. They will know Mau Mau has ambushed, and you are against the Mau Mau because you did the alarm. When they were doing that, we had left an hour before.

One time, a Gikuyu team said they wanted cattle from Chogoria, and they had eight good rifles, G3s. "We will allow you to take as much cattle as you can," I said. "But never shoot anybody there. We will arrange with our people that you take the cattle peacefully, but after an hour, or a half hour, they will say the cattle have been taken. So the *kaborio*, the Homeguards, will follow. That is where you can make an ambush and shoot them all." They agreed.

They went there and took cattle. But before they moved with them, they talked amongst themselves. They said, "Now, we have left some. Can we go back and collect the others?" Then they decided yes, and foolishly they went back. Before they took the second lot now, women thought that those people had already gone, so they made the cry.

The Homeguards began shooting. Those cattle which they [the Gikuyu Mau Mau] had taken before were not moved to the forest. When the people heard the shots, they had to run away. They didn't take the second lot, neither the first. Foolishly they came without any animals. They wasted a lot of bullets, and they did not shoot any Homeguards.

The other side of Mount Kenya is where Europeans had big *shamba*s, and we had no connection with them. Gikuyu did some terrible destruction there. There's a place called Lari, a camp where women were detained, mixed with men. When Mau Mau got into that camp—that was 1954, I think[13]—they killed all the people who were there. They didn't spare anyone. To make it worse, there were two women who were pregnant. It was—ah. We were shown these pictures—they were spread all over the forest by airplane. Mau Mau took a knife and cut a woman that way [across her stomach]. This woman had twins, and they were dead, falling down from the stomach. We were—oh, so terribly ashamed. Not ashamed even—it reached beyond. We could hardly believe whether this was the action of Mau Mau.

That demoralized us seriously. The Europeans took that chance. The *wazungu* displayed those papers all over, to reveal the work that is being done by the Mau Mau, to see the fight that Mau Mau are fighting. They said, "These are the people who are fighting for *uhuru* [freedom]? Mau Mau are against the Europeans, but are these [victims] European? These [Mau Mau] are killers—it's not a matter of *uhuru*." They converted many people to hate the Mau Mau.

Children are innocent. They never commit any mistake against anybody. What were children to do with the Mau Mau? That was bad—beyond the Mau Mau activities. It was painful even to us. We denounced it. That action made a lot of Gikuyu turn against the Mau Mau. Gikuyu were calling it "Muito wa Lari [Lari Forest]." No one, none of us were happy. This was not Mau Mau but other people. But I was telling you that most of the Mau Mau were rogues in Nairobi, mad rogues without any morals.

In our area, we had only two European farms—even today, very little here are owned by Europeans. The *mzungu* who had a *shamba* next to our forest during Mau Mau was called Bwana Mali. One night, Mau Mau went and took five big bulls from his *shamba*. We killed the bulls and ate them. The following day, it was reported that Mau Mau took all of Bwana Mali's cows. The Europeans wanted to put Homeguards on his property and chase the Mau Mau. But Bwana Mali said, "No. Leave them alone. They do not have any food to eat. They are hungry. I don't want them to be followed. I don't mind."

Because of this, the *wazungu* thought that Bwana Mali is a member of Mau Mau. They accused him like that. They wondered, *Why wouldn't he like to have Homeguard posts to save his animals?*

Bwana Mali said, "Whatever you want to call me, I won't mind. You don't know the trouble that these people have. They have never taken my dairy cow—they have taken bulls. They have not killed anybody. They have never burnt my garden. Let them eat." The other *wazungu* wanted to detain him, but they could never prove anything. Bwana Mali knew [that] Mau Mau are people, and they are annoyed, and he knew the reason that they are annoyed.

Bwana Mali's response converted each and every Mau Mau. We thought that he's a good man. "That *mzungu* is on our side," we said. "That is our friend. Anybody who touches Bwana Mali's animals will be punished. They will meet Mau Mau."

His *shamba* was next to the forest, but people were to pass there and go to the other side to get cows or goats from another *bwana*, not Mali. He was widely honored—Bwana Mali, the good *mzungu*. He said that we were good people. He had no Homeguards, but nothing was touched.

His *shamba* remains, and he has been a friend ever since. I don't know if he is still alive. Mali became a Mau Mau, the first [*mzungu*] Mau Mau. That's why I say not all the [European] people were bad. We came to realize that Bwana Mali was even better than General China. China was not thankful. He did not honor Mwariama.

TAKE HIM TO KIMATHI

We did not forget Herodian. I don't know how Herodian hated the Mau Mau so. That man was serious. When he shot M'Nyiri, Herodian was very honored by the police and the DO. They thought he was the one that could fight against the Mau Mau. In March 1954, some forest people visited Kiangua, and women told them, "You should know that Herodian will be a chief tomorrow. He is very proud. There's been much preparation. Now, when he becomes the chief, all of us who are Mau Mau will die."[14]

That information touched Mau Mau. Mau Mau said, "Can we learn the way that he will take to go to the ceremony?"

They organized that night. They found a good place in Kinoro, near the *duka*s [shops], where they could hide in some good depressions [ditches]. The *barabara* was narrow and surrounded by bushes. I think there were nine Mau Mau properly hiding themselves. They took their heavy clothes and went in the middle of the night and waited. There was somebody called

Nkari—Nkari, that name means leopard. He said, "I know Herodian. I will be on the lookout. When you hear me blow the whistle, arm yourselves. That will be Herodian."

At eight o'clock, people started passing, going down the hill, but the gentleman didn't blow any whistles. Nkari said, "Not yet." People were tired of waiting. They thought Herodian might have gone another way around. At nine-something, they saw somebody cycling. They waited, and then—TWEET—Nkari blew the whistle. Herodian had come, and he was carrying another agricultural assistant on his bicycle. Whew! Mau Mau came out very quickly, and before Herodian turned the bicycle, he was cut [with a *panga*]. *Paw!* Trying to take his gun—his hand fell down on the ground. [They cut off his hand.]

The other fellow tried to cry because he knew one of the people. "Don't cut me!" he said. Ah, this friend cut him first, and he fell [to] the other side. No sympathy. Some people were born to kill. We had one here, called Kairo. Killing to him was like a cat with a rat. He was quick—once you mention you are against the Mau Mau—no sympathy.

They stripped Herodian and his friend of their uniforms and took everything—the whole attire, the shotgun, the watch. They left both men dead and naked in the road. By eleven o'clock, our men came to the forest with all their possessions. They were wearing Herodian's uniform. I saw them approaching and said, "Who are these people coming with agricultural uniforms?" One had a shotgun. Then we recognized them. They were very happy.

We said, "How did you—"

They said, "Herodian is not with us."

"Say it again!" we said.

"See his uniform. And this, the shotgun is here with his bullets. We have done it. We have killed him. Herodian is dead."

Ah, we prayed and thanked God. "We have avenged the death of M'Nyiri," we said. "The person who killed M'Nyiri, we have killed him." I wonder whether there is anybody who cried for Herodian. No, he was a beast.

As we celebrated in the forest, the government received the news. The DC was waiting [for] Herodian to crown him chief. The message came that Herodian and the person whom he was carrying on his bicycle had been killed four kilometers from the camp. There was a terrible commotion. When the DC heard the story, he could not believe. They went back to Meru being very annoyed.

Our people in the reserves were happy. Women? Ah, they were happy. Herodian was very serious. He abused them. Mau Mau were fed after that—anybody could give Mau Mau food or whatever you wanted. People were annoyed the way that he shot M'Nyiri. We said, "The Bible said an eye for an eye."

We were caring for our wives and children who were left behind in the reserves, but also people who were not in the forest, especially ladies, played a wonderful role. Women were ever good. They could kill because they were friends of both sides—the Mau Mau and the Homeguards. Here [in Igoji] we had no time to train the women *askari*, because when M'Nyiri was shot, things were broken up in the very beginning. Our women were known as Mau Mau in the early stage, so most were imprisoned. But in Embu and Chuka, they had wonderful, wonderful women.

In Nyeri, there was an inspector who had this machine gun, a billygun— the one that goes *Ku-ku-ku-ku-ku*. That side of Kirinyaga was very strong with Mau Mau, so the police had guns. We had a lady there who had taken Mau Mau, and she arranged to be friends with the inspector who had the gun. She became a very good friend of that *askari*.

One day, Mau Mau gave her money to buy a chicken and make nice food. The lady arranged with the inspector to meet for dinner. "Make sure you get this man in the house," Mau Mau told her. "If we get that gun through you, don't worry—we will save you." The inspector wanted to be alone with that lady, so he didn't go with any other *askari*. Inside the house, in the corner somewhere, there were two brave people [Mau Mau] hiding. There were another two outside. They were told, "If this man comes in, and you let him leave with that gun—you, yourself, will never come out. You will be killed then and there. Also make sure—don't leave the lady."

Ah—the inspector came in the house very proudly with that girl. When he started playing with her, his gun was there [on the floor]. That lady had a knife. When they were about to—*HUAK!* Before [she was] sleeping with that man, the knife of that lady cut him across the belly. That was all. Everyone left. They took the gun. The gentleman was left inside the house, and it was locked from the outside.

The Homeguards were to search for the man. "He left us," said his *askari*. "He did not tell us where he was going. He has been a friend of a certain lady. Has anybody seen that lady?"

Nobody had seen the lady.

"Let's go there." The room was locked and flies were in the house. "We have to break [into] this and see inside," they said. When the house was broken [into], the gentleman was there, with all his intestines hanging out. There was no gun, no bullets, no lady. And it was known that the Mau Mau killed him.

I tell you that billygun saved us. The Mau Mau leader of that area was called General Kassam, Njogu. He is still alive.[15] The gun was given to a man called Munyi—that's his Mau Mau name. *Munyi* is a name for a rhino, which can pass anywhere because he can clear his own path. He was in the Second World War, so he knew how to use the gun. With that gun, nobody could ever reach his camp. He killed very many people. Munyi was honored. That man was fed. Anybody could suffer hunger in Mau Mau, but not that man. Any area that was very serious with Europeans and Homeguards, Munyi was to come along with the billygun. Those Europeans wanted to die. If they were in a line, they fell all in a line. It would make the noise—*Ku-ku-ku-ku-ku*—people thought there were Europeans in the forest.

All of that was managed by a lady. The inspector with the machine gun was killed by the friend whom he was sleeping with. The girl was taken into the forest, and she was lucky to come out alive later on. She was honored—very, very honored.

When Europeans appointed a young chief who was a terrible Homeguard, we convinced another lady to become a friend [mistress] of that chief. One night, she made arrangements with him. Around eight thirty or nine o'clock, the lady came with the chief to her house, and two Mau Mau were hiding there behind the bed. The lady and the chief had their tea, and when they were ready to go to bed, the men jumped out. The chief was startled. He said, "Who are you? What are you doing here?"

They tied him up and took him to the forest. I had given them instructions: "When you have the chief, don't beat him. Don't do anything. Come with him and make sure he does not say a word."

In the morning, there was no chief. People heard no quarrel, no sign of anything, no cry of Mau Mau. Ah, they were surprised. People feared very much. They asked the lady in the morning, "Where did our chief go?"

"I don't know," she said.

"But did you go with him?"

"No, I didn't go with him," she said.

"Did you follow him?"

"No. I said no." The girl refused completely, [saying] that she hasn't seen him.

They brought him to my camp. He was called Kiruja. Nobody could sympathize with him. He had been punishing people, and now he was in the hands of these people. Watch out—now he will suffer consequences. I said, "Kiruja, what are you doing with the Mau Mau?"

"Ah, I've decided to join you," he said.

"Oh—have you decided to become a Mau Mau?" I said. "You will be a good *askari*. This one should be trained at Kimathi's camp. You tell him exactly what you have told us, and you work in that camp before you come this way. Take him to Kimathi."

He was going to take oath in Kimathi's camp. I knew the oath that he was going to take. When they got to a point in the forest, they said, "Kimathi is not seen by anybody who has not taken oath. If it is revealed that you have been Homeguard—well, things will be serious. So let us first give you oath, and you can give report that you are Mau Mau." He agreed. When he was going around in the circle, repeating the oath, somebody was waiting with a *panga*—*hooo-shwoo*—they cut his head off. That was all.

Some very senior people were appointed to do the job of killing. My junior people never knew where they were going. It was a *siri kali. Siri* means "secret" in Kiswahili. *Kali* means "very hot, very serious." So *siri kali* means "a very serious secret." A very strong one—hard for anyone to break. There's no good word in English like Kiswahili, *siri kali*. The headquarters were for Kimathi, not for everybody. These things were only known by the big, very official, people. We could say that the man will go and learn everything about the training at Kimathi's camp and then he will come back. That is the story we told our junior people. Someone made me to laugh because he said, "Also you'll be given uniforms."

I was with my friend when I sent a man to Kimathi, and he wanted to follow them. "Don't go," I told him. "You don't want to follow. Let them take him." I didn't want him to see people being killed. It is later on that I revealed why I stopped him. He said, "Nkungi, you saved me." Even myself, I'd taken the oath of killing, and people were killing us, but I never liked to see a man being killed. If I did it, it was better with a bullet, but not with a *panga*—never, never cut anybody with a *panga*. That's improper killing. I didn't like that action to be associated with me.

Especially in the reserve, we said, "No matter how someone might have wronged, if you think that you cannot take him to the forest—leave him. Don't kill him. Because this will link you to the witnesses. You will be known by all the people. Let them say he was taken by Mau Mau, and that's all. If somebody wants to follow, he follows to Kimathi."

We never knew who might come out of the forest and surrender first. If a man in the reserve who has never gone to the forest gives evidence that somebody has killed another person and then someone in the forest gives the same evidence—that [accused] person will be hanged. No more is required—only two witnesses [from two different contexts] to give the same report.

Killing means with a *panga*. If it's the case of a bullet, then that was no case. Bullet was fighting. You can never witness that the bullet shot by one person killed anybody—no. With a *panga,* if the forest evidence supports the reserve—hanging, direct.

Only if someone has been very horrible, and we want people to know that a big man has been killed by the Mau Mau—then we were doing these very strange, wonderful things. In 1954, when I was at Embu, one of our *askari* guarding the books was shot. Around three o'clock [in the afternoon], the books were taken to the big camp next to Chuka Town. The chief there was a terrible man called Wasto. The ladies and gentlemen in the camp cried. They knew now that they would be revealed because all their names were in the books.

In the village, we had four *askari* of the Mau Mau mixed with the other three *askari,* who were not Mau Mau. Our *askari* sent a message through the network to the forest: "Please, make sure you come for those books today in the evening. We will fight to make sure that these books are not with us."

"We should come at what time? Nine o'clock p.m.?"

"No—ten. Ten o'clock p.m.," the *askari* said. "The books are in the chief's camp at his house. His second wife is a Mau Mau and lives there." She was a young lady and had only one child with that chief. "We will be guarding. When you come to the gate, fire your guns. While we are taking cover, we will get rid of these three Homeguards. If you hear shooting, don't worry. We will be taking care of the other three. After we kill them, we will fire in the air. That means to come in."

To the lady, the chief's second wife, they said, "Now you, once you hear the first shot, the chief should be cut. Make sure that you cut [off] the head."

The lady said, "No. Don't tell me what to do. You fire. I will know what to do."

The lady prepared the chief. She had gone to town earlier, and she bought local beer from a good Indian. After eating their supper, the wife purposely fed the chief a very strong drink so that he would sleep. She was thinking, *Once he takes this, I will do whatever I like with him.*

The chief was very happy. He took the wine, became very tired, then went to sleep. That woman took the chief's good knife, and when she heard the shot, she was quite prepared. She started here, up to this [*dragging his finger in a line across his stomach*]. She sliced the chief, making certain she would never miss him. After the first shot was fired—*PAH!* Wasto did not move. He died as he was sleeping.

By then the books were out. It was surprising that the Homeguards had taken the books the day before, and now the books went back again to the forest. The other side was relieved. I was at Murang'a there in the morning. I saw the books coming. "Our *askari* are safe now," we said. If the Europeans had got those books, they would have known each and every registered Mau Mau.

The lady pretended that she ran away and hid down in a trench with her children. "Because everything—the house was broken, I don't know what happened to the chief, but I ran away, because there was a strong bang," she said. But of course it was done by her.

For Wasto, we wanted it known [that] Mau Mau had killed a big man. We wanted the Europeans to see. So this chief's head was taken and put in the gate there, on a post, looking the way that Mau Mau had come. The three *askari* died too, but nobody bothered about them. That was done to Wasto, as an example in the camp. When the first European came and met the head of [the] chief, he said, "Ah! Those bastards. God damn." He didn't even pass there. People wanted to see that we are animals, so we did it.

When things were hot, women were the only ones with good information. They fought. They were *askari*, not wives. You meet a lot who were loyal. Very few went to the side of the Homeguard. Many were killed through them. The *wazungu* warned the *askari*, "Now, if you go with these women, be careful. They are the Mau Mau, and they have husbands in the forests. Know that they are double-dealers. She loves you because of her husband. When you go with her, you never come back."

"THE YEAR OF MAU MAU"

Feeding was very complicated. I think that's the thing the Europeans used to conquer the Mau Mau: hunger. You could send people for food, and they stayed two or three days without getting any. 1954 and 1955 were horrible times to people in the Central Province. Europeans took our wives and brothers who were not detained or imprisoned to little camps. They were not allowed to go back to their *shamba*s, because the area where they were living was [defined as a] "Special Area." Those were Mau Mau areas, close to the forest. You could never be found in this area. You will be shot.

People left the *shamba*s full of bananas and yams. We were to feed from them, but when the Europeans knew that we were not coming out because we have food, they uprooted each and every thing. They took all our years of work and uprooted everything that we had. And once the elephants noticed there were no people in the Special Areas, they came through the area and cleared all the bananas, so it was a bush.

There was nothing left for us, neither [for] the people who were in the camps. Our people were helpless. They had to work in the *shamba*s of their subchiefs and chiefs. They were doing free, useless work, making roads for these people to go search for Mau Mau. They were terribly punished, men together with women. It was most serious for women with children. One day, when we hunting for food, we saw a group of women. They were too dusty, all brown, covered with soil, and very weak. They had poor dressing. I don't know what they were eating. They were cooking with nothing.

Even we were giving our people warning not to go and be with their wives. I said, "Supposing you give your wife a child, where will she go? Who will look after her? You are creating another problem within."

Some women went to the forest together with us and gave birth. They struggled. On the side of General Martin, two women were in the forest. One happened to have a baby. She survived because her brother was also in the forest, and he guarded the area of his sister and her baby, but a bomb exploded in the place where they were living, and a piece of the bomb hit the brother. He died. Her other brother took over the situation. They survived and came up with the boy, but we did not encourage that.

Even [in] Muthambi, a lady from our area got a child, and her man was shot dead in the forest. That lady suffered until she offered herself to surrender with the baby.

We said, "Once a woman has taken all the oaths similar to those you have taken, she becomes your sister. When you go to the reserve, never commit anything [have sexual relations] with a woman who has taken oath." [But] somebody from my camp abused a woman when he went to look for food in the reserve. That man raped her.

The woman reported what the man had committed to another person who went to collect food. The woman's husband was in prison because he was a Mau Mau, and the woman was a Mau Mau also.

When the people she reported to were near the camp, they handcuffed the man. They said, "It has been reported that you have messed up with a woman. Is that true?" He was trying to argue, but the *askari* said, "I was told by the lady that you have committed [this act] with her. So now you are going to wait here. We will go and give the message to Nkungi to see whether he will allow you to come to the camp or whether you will be taken for a cleansing."

So two men were left there. When they reported it to me, I instructed the *askari* to bring him to the camp. Those who reported to me are still alive, even the woman is alive. The man had done it before, but nobody had caught him. This time, he was caught. He admitted that he had done the action. "The punishment for that thing is not done here," I said. "You have to explain this to the further authority that is Kimathi's camp. They will escort you to Kimathi's. Go." Two people, sergeants from that senior group, took him to Kimathi's camp. In the evening, the men came and said, "Ah, that man has gone there." That was the end.

I called a meeting and had a long, good speech to tell the people. "This act is prohibited," I said. "It is a nasty thing. If anybody is caught doing something against these women, you know we will be more serious than [we are with] Homeguards. By all means, you will be punished. Kimathi will judge for you. And you know he doesn't like that. Now, we are cleansed. We are not repeating. If anybody messes, please report it. He is dangerous to you. A curse will come and stay with us, and it is more likely that we could be killed or ambushed by Homeguards because of the sin committed by that stupid fellow.

"Those women are our friends, and they are serving us. They are fighting, seriously, as we fight, and our women are suffering. Their fight is even worse than ours. They are being raped by Homeguards, and they cannot turn from them. Why should we join the Homeguards and punish our wives?"

I tell you, my mother was left with our three children when Jesca went to prison. They were detained locally, in the chief's camp. My little kids, my mother, and also my father were in that camp. They were suffering. My mother was an old woman, and they were eating only bananas. Europeans didn't bother about these old people. It is God's will that we met them.

One time, we went to look for food in the Special Area. I was to guard, but I did not know the place, so a man in our group [who] came from there told me which way to watch. Very unfortunately, the Homeguards did not come the way that he showed me.

I don't know what I felt. I was looking one way, but I heard something and turned the other way around. I saw somebody aiming at me, and he dropped down. He was kneeling, with a gun. Then *TWA!* I fell down. The bullet passed me. Then *TWA TWA TWA TWA.* I was already down by then. All my people rushed away. They thought that I was shot.

We had the good training to take cover and hide yourself flat *kabisa* [completely]. After waiting, I moved. I went down to the valley, but I knew these people might follow if they thought I was without a gun. So I turned and shot once—*TWA.* Then I ran away and followed the others. When my people heard my shot, they knew I was not dead. We left what we had from the *shamba,* so we had to try and get food from the other side of the forest.

We collected some bananas, the remains that an elephant left behind, and we waited until the morning. At six, we were to cross back to the forest. Just after leaving the Special Area, we heard *oooo-hooo-hooo-hooo.* An airplane was coming. They knew that this was the time Mau Mau usually crossed back to the forest from the Special Area. Somebody had seen us.

These airplanes had a billygun, that sort that gives bullets *babababa-bababa.* No bomb, but they have bullets in a chain that goes across, very fast—not in the magazine, but in a chain. I was fearing. I jumped next to a very small tree to take cover, and the baboons were in this tree. They were jumping from one branch to another, but even the baboons were quiet when they heard the planes. Bullets were popping and jumping next to me. I laid on the ground, rolling from one side to another.

The airplanes passed once, and turned again, firing all along where we were. I couldn't see what was happening—only *babababababababa.* Leaves were falling. Then—*PLOP.* One of the baboons was hit and fell on the ground next to me. I looked at it and closed my eyes. I knelt there and waited. The planes turned again, sprayed all over, and then they left.

I tell you, God is good; none of us were shot. We were six in the group, and we were in the direct line where these people were shooting. And we didn't lose anything we carried. I had two sugarcanes and a bag of *githere* that a woman gave to us. We went back to the forest and met our people being very worried. They knew we had been seen and [thought] we were dead. "How did you come out?" they asked.

"God is good," we said. By noon, some *askari* followed the path on foot, to see whether they have killed anybody, but they didn't find anyone dead. None of us was shot. I tell you—when I was sitting and the baboon fell down next to me—it was serious. We had not reached the forest yet, so there were only little trees and bushes, and the planes had a lot of bullets. If you rubbed the face, it was all black because of that soot, from the gunpowder. That was 1954. We call it "the Year of Mau Mau." The bombing was very serious.

Another time, we were in an ambush waiting for Homeguards, the police. We knew we were going to be followed, so we walked forming a path so that it would lead those following to us. Then we waited for the Homeguards to come. I was second in the line. Very unfortunately, when we were almost to shoot, somebody stood up, trying to see where the people were. It was General Martin. He made [a] mistake and was impatient to see why these people had not come. He was seen before these people [Homeguards] had lined up the way we wanted them to line up. When they saw Martin, they shot at him first.

They didn't get him, but we had to shoot. One was very close to me. He turned with the bullet, he aimed to shoot me, and it hit the butt of my homemade rifle. My gun slapped my hand.

I did not take notice because I had to shoot. I was moving backwards, pushing to get out of the ambush line. Bullets were passing over the hair of my head. I shot two bullets and then ran away. Each person on my side shot twice. Racing to the valley, I met my people close to the river Maara. We gathered there. It was then when I noticed that I couldn't find one of my fingers. I realized very late, after running several meters. I thought, *Am I shot?* But then I turned my hand over and found my finger lying on the other side [against the back of my hand]. I took it and folded it back. I didn't know how my finger jumped, but then I saw the butt of my rifle was shot at a very close range, and a piece of its wood was the thing that bent my finger.

When we came together in the valley, we counted ourselves. "Everybody is alive," we said. "And luckily, we shot three."

We knew the police would be very serious in this area, so we ran away to Embu. On the day we were going, very unfortunately, planes were bombing. We could hear them. These people knew we were crossing, and they bombed the place where we were. It was around three o'clock in a hilly area.

The fellows I was with ran down to the valley, and I was left alone on the hill. I wanted to see how these planes were going, whether they were going to bomb the valley or the mountain. I was standing on this sloping place between. Although they were bombing in the valley, one of the planes turned and bombed where I was. I was covering [myself] with a small tree that was there.

When the bomb fell near to me, it threw [up] all the stones that were nearby, and all the smoke turned to me. I took time to stay there, because I never knew whether I am alive or not or whether the other plane was coming to bomb the same thing. But after a while, I opened my eyes to see all the stones which were there; even the tree was leaning to one side. There a big *shimu,* a hole, next to me. I coughed for an entire month because of the *moshi,* the smoke, from that bomb.

In 1954 Kenya shook—a lot of killings, burning *shambas.* We knew now it is a matter of punishing one another. We were to burn whatever *shamba* we could reach, set fire to them, because Europeans had started [the] destruction. A lot of wheat was burned and animals were killed. If a group found something—take what you need and then kill the rest, as many as you can. It was a culture for destruction.

I think this touched the Europeans very much. Remember when Kenyatta got imprisoned, Mbiyu [Koinange] was doing communications with the colonial government [in London]. He was representing the grievances about the Kenya *wazungu.* Mbiyu was going there daily, telling them why there was a mess in Kenya—that the Europeans were there, doing messy work. He impressed the people in London. Finally, people came from Britain, and they met Mau Mau.

That's during the time when a man called Erskine came. He came from the Colonial Office to see and find out why there was war in Kenya, why people dared to die. He had a meeting with the Mau Mau and some European leaders and the minister of home affairs. China was there; I think also Kassam attended the meeting. It was around the Mount Kenya lodge, the other side of Nyeri, and I remember in 1952 when King George died, Queen Elizabeth was there, in Kenya.[16] Kimathi did not attend the meeting of Erskine; also I think Mwariama wasn't there. Erskine said, "There should be no fighting when I'm calling these people [together]." So there was no bombing.

Mau Mau explained exactly why we were fighting. Erskine went back [to London] with full, good information. He knew that the Europeans in Kenya were the people who engineered things to fight with the Africans. General Erskine said, "These white people are misusing Africans the wrong way. They are the ones who made this war because they have seriously suppressed these people. These Europeans are not living with Africans. They are *bwana mkubwa*, all of them. Africans have no right in their country, and they have realized that this is their country now."[17] He gave the report to the colonial secretary: "Unless you harmonize, which I believe you cannot, there must be changes."

Erskine pushed forward a scheme that would give the Gikuyu incentive to be loyal. He said that negotiation was going on in the colonial secretary's office and that our representatives were there, so we should not fight anymore. Erskine made a cooling time, and very many people came out of the forest.

There was a promise that if you come out, there will be no case. You will not be punished. Very many people heard it, and even Martin, our big general, came out and surrendered himself early in 1955. Me and Simba remained inside the forest. Martin was our leader and knew each and every way of the forest. He talked to the Special Branch. He said, "If you want me to call my people [to come out], I can go alone or with your *askari*. But since they know that I've surrendered, I fear that I could be taken captive. Let me go with *askari*, but please make sure that you never fire to them."

Martin wanted us to see that he is with Europeans, and he is not killed. "I want them to hear my shout and see that it's me who is calling them," he said. "But please, whether they run or not, don't shoot." They agreed, and they visited very many of our camps.

When we saw Martin the first time, we ran! We did not wait for him. "That is Martin," we said, "but who is behind him?" He was with a *mzungu* and *askari*. We disappeared completely from that area. He said they wouldn't shoot, but people could not believe it. We thought, *Now if these people have seen us and we have not surrendered, the police will follow the way that Martin has shown them. We will all be killed.*

When Martin left our forest, I was promoted to general and took responsibility of the people that he had. I was given a group of a hundred and three men in my area. I was in charge, and I divided them into groups along Mount Kenya.

Martin sent me a message through one of the local people, a man called Giatû. Martin was afraid because we had these homemade guns and the sharia [law] was that if somebody was caught with a firearm, he will be sentenced to death. So Martin sent Giatû and said, "Go and tell Japhlet that when he decides to come out, get rid of that [fire]arm. Also he should never let anybody know whether he had that book." People were coming out speedily, and he didn't want anybody to report that it is me who carries all these things, because it could delay my screening, and I could be sent back to the forest to collect them. There were a lot of names and very certain things in the book that could even affect some of the government people who had taken oath. "Let him burn that book." That's the instruction Martin sent to me. "The book will kill us. Our case will be done against us. Burn it." So at night I started tearing the papers where everything was written, and I burned them. I couldn't burn the hard covers of the book, so I took it to a muddy place by the river called Irarû, to the main place where the elephants cross. And I buried the book by that river. It was kept in the forest, and my people never knew where I put it. I told them it was taken by a Gikuyu fellow.

People were not at ease. It is the time when many people turned from Mau Mau into Homeguards. When people left, the Special Branch thought they could use all these surrendered people as kaborio. Europeans told them, "Help us to get other friends of yours in the forest. We will never reveal you—you are our people." The Special Branch took them to their own special camps so they were not seen by their friends in the reserves, and they remained as they were in the forest with the same clothes, same beards, same bags. A man called Kingani [Crocodile] was of that kind.

Kingani was shot in the forest, and the brother of Njiru cared for him.[18] Njiru's brother treated the bullet wound with honey, and it healed within a month's time. When Kingani was healed, he had to go back to where he was from in Tigania, near Mwariama. Very unfortunately, he was caught by Homeguards. [While] being screened, he said, "Don't kill me. I will show you where the General of Imenti stays, General Nkungi. It is from his camp where I got nursed. I will show you where he lives."

Kingani explained [to the Homeguards and the European], "This man has his own place to sleep, and if you try to go during the daytime, they have wonderful guards. Whatever done in the reserve is known, so if you try by the day, you will be seen. Now if you want to get him, let's wait until eight o'clock, you sleep in the forest, and you attack them very early in the morning."

When this was being planned, somebody came and told me that there was quarrelling in another camp. He called me to investigate. As general, I was in charge of keeping order in the camps. I had to visit and listen to every group, to see if there were any messes. I was always moving. "Okay, yes," I said, "I will go there to see what is happening." Some of my friends were asking me, "Why are you leaving at night? Why can you not go tomorrow?"

I said, "It is night to you, but it is not night to me. Why wait for tomorrow? Why not now?" So I went with that gentleman around six o'clock. Before we reached that camp, we met another group who had something to tell me, so I was delayed. I told the gentleman, "Let's sleep here. We will go to the other camp in the morning."

Around this time, Kingani was prepared with the police. They slept in the forest, and very early that morning, around five, Kingani led them to the place where he left me. First they aimed at me, to the place where I was [supposed to be] sleeping, but they saw there was nobody, so they moved to the camp. The brother of Njiru, the very boy who was nursing Kingani, saw him first. "Has Kingani come back again?" he said. But before they finished speaking those words, they saw people behind Kingani with a gun pointing at them. "Hands up!"

They did not surrender. Homeguards started firing, and they shot four people dead. It was through that [incident] that Njiru lost his brother. After all, Kingani killed the nursing man who helped him survive.

Two of the people escaped from the camp and met me. They explained what happened. "Nkungi, the people in our camp were killed." Those two survivors reported the story that Kingani had betrayed us. That man was coming directly to where I was sleeping. That first bullet would have fallen to me. They could have shot me dead before I even woke up. But it is [because of] God's message that I left camp that very evening—a wonderful miracle. Njiru's brother was a good man. We lost very many in that way.

Kingani was very honored when he went back to the *askari*. He was taken back home with a vehicle because he had done the best, but unfortunately he didn't get the General. The General wasn't at his house.

In my group, I was caring for a man called Mberia and his brother, who was shot. One day, without my knowledge, the gentlemen left us. I was thinking that Mberia has gone for food. I waited for him for a day, and he didn't come, so we changed the place where we were.

When Mberia came out with his brother, the brother was taken to the hospital, and Mberia was taken to that private camp of Europeans. Mberia knew all that area very well [because] his father had been a beehive hunter even before he entered the forest. The Special Branch talked to Mberia, and he became one of that group being used by the *wazungu*.

After two days, he came back with a *mzungu* and Homeguards in the forest. The European and the others went somewhere to hide, and Mberia went to the area he left me, but we were in another place. He met two people looking for honey and said, "Do you know where Nkungi is? He is looking after my brother who was shot. I left them to go look for food. I got stuck somewhere, and I need to find them."

The people looking for honey brought Mberia back to their camp because they wanted to help him and he had some food to eat. In the evening time, Mberia sneaked out of camp. He came back and brought the other people, the *mzungu* and *askari*, with their *pangas*. Early in the dew, before everybody in the camp woke up, they were killed. It is very unfortunate [that] one family had two brothers there, and none of them came out. That group of Mberia killed eleven people in the camp, but it was a good miracle that one of them didn't die. He was terrible with cuts all over, but he survived until the morning time. As the rest were dying, this man tried to move, and by good luck, he met someone from another camp who was looking for honey. The man helped him to walk and took him back to his camp, and he gave us the story.

"If you go there, you [will] find that all the people are dead," he said. "They killed all of us—even myself, I don't know how I managed to come up. Mberia was there." That fellow was treated with honey, and he survived, so the story was known.

Mberia would have been one of the ones hanged by the British because of his actions. He was an *askari* in the Second World War, and he could shoot. But what he did in the forest was forgotten, never to be reported. According to the Europeans, Mberia did a good job when those eleven were killed.

People said, "Now, don't trust anybody, because Mau Mau are being used by the *wazungu*, and they are killing us." Those were the worst that killed our people. The *wazungu* did not kill many people, but those were the methods they used. They were hated.

Someone from our place killed one of his cousins in that way. He couldn't hide his cousin from the rest of the group, so the cousin was killed. The reserve and his family knew that he killed his cousin, and [he] was hated all around. I don't know what he felt, but that man didn't take long—he hanged himself.

After all, those people were not even detained. They were freed by the Europeans. Even today they fear people because they did wonderful [unimaginable] action. They never like to talk about it. But we know that it wasn't their will. They were terribly badly used by the Europeans. They had a bad job.

Ah, if there's this confusion—when people turn against themselves—it is a terrible, everlasting war. Nobody knew whether it will end. One day, I was hiding in the forest, and people were running that way and that way. I looked and saw someone. I thought, *I know him! That man is like myself. But if I am seen, I differ from him because I am Mau Mau. He will run, saying that he has seen the Mau Mau. But we know one another. Ah—I said, 'Mzee, there will be a day when we are together.'*

But nobody knew whether we could get together—no, no, no. The Homeguards were thinking that when the Mau Mau ends, they will kill us. Nobody will ever live.

Toward the end of 1955, practically everybody, even the big people, left the forest. By then, even myself got tired. All the clothes we had were torn up. We had funny dressings. We had run away from Martin, but we had nowhere to hide from him. I called a meeting around August. I wanted us to come out together. "Now, Martin has been our leader," I said. "He knows all the places where we used to stay. Can we stand him? Instead of us going out one by one, would you like me to write to the police and tell them to wait for us, at a certain place, on one day?"

The group was big—I think there were seventy-eight people in that meeting. Some people agreed, but a few said, "No! Everybody came to the forest because of his own will, with everybody having different reasons. Whoever wants to leave, let him leave. Even Martin came out."

One of the people was very serious, and I listened to him because we were relatives and went to the forest on the very same day. I had given him my nice coat. His wife was imprisoned together with Jesca, so we were very friendly. He was the one to argue. I didn't have words to tell him.

Most of the group knew that I wanted to come out, so the following day, a good number of them left the forest without my knowledge. Very fortunately, they gave a good report to the police, even the *wazungu:* "We had a big meeting. [The] General gathered us, and he wanted to take us out. But somebody argued, and Nkungi got annoyed. We have decided ourselves that if Nkungi wanted us to come out, we have come out."

Those who went out also reported that I was protecting Chogoria. "Japhlet is saving us," they said. "If it were not him, Gikuyu wanted to beat us." That, too, went back to the European.

"Is it true? Is that true?" Dr. Irvine said. "Let us pray for Japhlet, he's a good man. Let's pray for him that he decides to come out." Some of the people who were praying were the Mau Mau. They reported to me, "Dr. Irvine still loves you. He wants you to come out. He's praying that you should not be killed."

"Ah, let him continue," I said. "He's a hypocrite." But I had a wonderful record because of that meeting, and the government stopped coming to the forest for a month, saying, "Never interfere with Nkungi. He is gathering people to come out." During that time, most of the people in my area came out.

Within two days' time an airplane was in the forest. Out of the speakers it said, "Nkungi, we know that you are doing a good job. We will give you time, and there will be no interference with Homeguards or whatever. Could you please repeat your meeting and bring all these people out?" The plane went all around, from Chuka to the other side.[19] Even my sister was taken by Europeans in a small plane, calling me: "Japhlet, come out! Whether people have refused to come out—you yourself better come out!"

The military and the *kaborio* were told not to fight Mau Mau, because Nkungi was busy. We were given three good weeks with no military, no *kaborio*, no bombing, no police coming to the forest. It was a quiet time. It was at the end of September that we decided to come out. I called another meeting and said to them, "Now, gentlemen, most all of our people have decided to come out. Would you like to come out?"

They said yes, so I said, "Follow me."

Yetu Savings and Credit Cooperative Organization (SACCO) headquarters, located in Nkubu. The General, at ninety-two years old, continued to be elected chairman of the board of directors. *(Photo by Mary Beth Koeth, December 2013)*

The General admiring his tea *shamba*. *(Photo by Mary Beth Koeth, December 2013)*

The General shaking hands with President Kibaki of Kenya, April 16, 2010.
(Photo used with permission from Thambu Family Collection)

Tea plucking on the *shamba*. *(Photo by Mary Beth Koeth, December 2013)*

A resident washing clothes and collecting rainwater at apartments in Kinoro.
(Photo by Mary Beth Koeth, December 2013)

The interior of the Presbyterian church in Mutunguru, where the General serves
as elder. He also donated the land for the church.

The tea *shamba. (Photo by Mary Beth Koeth, December 2013)*

A full basket of tea leaves. *(Photo by Mary Beth Koeth, December 2013)*

Children gather in front of the tea collection center. *(Photo by Mary Beth Koeth, December 2013)*

A little girl posing in front of the tea collection center. *(Photo by Mary Beth Koeth, December 2013)*

A tea plucker waiting under cover for the rain to pass. *(Photo by Mary Beth Koeth, December 2013)*

Makena, who had just graduated high school and was helping the Thambus with household tasks, straining tea in the kitchen. *(Photo by Mary Beth Koeth, December 2013)*

Stocked shelves of the Thambus' kitchen. *(Photo by Mary Beth Koeth, December 2013)*

Portraits hanging in the Thambu living room. *(Photo by Mary Beth Koeth, December 2013)*

The General *(right)* and a building manager, standing in front of the South Imenti SACCO Complex in Nkubu. *(Photo by Laura Lee Huttenbach)*

A *matatu*, on the road from Meru to Nairobi. *(Photo by Laura Lee Huttenbach, December 2013)*

Murithi Thambu and his family in Nairobi, 2009. *Top row, left to right:* Timothy, Kawira, Zipporah, Murithi. *Bottom*: Phoebe. *(Photo by Laura Lee Huttenbach)*

The General and Laura Lee "Nkirote" Huttenbach. *(Photo by Mary Beth Koeth, December 2013)*

PART IV

UHURU

SURRENDER

We spent three days in the Special Area, preparing ourselves to come out. There was a camp at Kinoro here with the *kaborio* and the chief. On the other side was a police post with the *mzungu*. I said, "We are going to come out in the place where the *mzungu* is." I decided not to go to the place of the Homeguards and the chief because the locals might gather and say, "These are the Mau Mau!" We didn't want that.

We wanted to see somebody who could give one final decision, so I told my men, "Let's go to the *mzungu*. The *kaborio* cannot decide anything unless they escort us to the police station." We wanted to go to a quiet place where things will be done properly.

It was the seventeenth [of] September 1955. We were to carry these things [twigs] to say that we have surrendered, but I said, "I will never carry anything. I am enough. I will tell them that I am Nkungi. If they want to shoot me, they will do it. I know they will not."

It was very early in the morning. An *askari* at the police station saw me coming. He reported to the *mzungu*, "There are Mau Mau coming. One must be Nkungi." I had a big beard, and they knew that I'm a tall man. One *askari* knew me. He said he was married to a fellow in my family, but I never knew him. He said, "Is it you, Nkungi?"

"Yes."

"Ah, come on, brother."

When the *mzungu* came, he said, "Nkungi, are you the leader of Mau Mau?"

"I hope. I am, yes."

He said to give us *chai* [tea] and porridge, but I did not take [it]. We had already fed ourselves before we came out. We had eaten yams where we stayed in the Special Area. Most were uprooted, but we managed to get a few.

They were taking pictures of surrenderees. When the Mau Mau came with their beards and were given food, they were photo[graph]ed looking spoiled [defeated]. Those pictures were copied, and papers were being sent all over the forest. We had seen them, and we didn't want to be in any of those pictures. They would advertise that Nkungi and his men surrendered and ate all the food. We said, "No. We are not hungry, we have already had our food."

The *askari* tried to persuade us. They thought we were fearing to be poisoned. They said, "See, there's nothing wrong."

"No, we have taken enough," we said. "We don't want it."

"Nkungi, I'm related to your family. I won't poison you." But we didn't take [it].

The European police inspector prepared things, and then we left. We went in his Land Rover with his two *askari* to the Meru police station, the headquarters. They told the others who came with me to go home. They said, "The General has come. Go on. They wanted Japhlet. You go." So my people were released and joined the other people in the camps.

They had this radio and said to the Meru DCs, "Nkungi came on board. Nkungi is with us. Over!" They replied, "Roger!" When we arrived at Meru, many people were awaiting us. It was known that a big man of Mau Mau came out.

I was taken to General Martin. Ah, Martin was very happy to see me. "Thank you, Nkungi. You have come," he said. "I've seen you several times in the forest."

"Yes. I saw you twice. I tried to organize people to come out, but they refused," I said.

Everybody was happy. We had an African DO, I think the first in Meru, and he was my friend. Before we went to the forest, he was a teacher, and I was a teacher. "Brother, don't worry about these people," he told me. "Once you have come out—you are out. We are together. Follow me."

We went to Kinoro. On that day, it was a show day, where people display their animals, their wood, their agricultural products—all sorts of things. It happens once a year. The African DO gave me a microphone and told me to say this speech:

"You are with General Nkungi. Whoever has anybody in the forest, go and tell your fellows that the General has come. I am Nkungi, and I am speaking to you." Everybody in the show left all [of] what they were doing and came to see me, and I was not frightened. I could speak freely, knowing I'm with Martin. I thought, *Ah, let them give [a] decision whether they want to hang us or not. We are not the first.*

The DO said, "Nkungi, my brother, has come. Everybody now—go and tell your friends or sons who are in the forest that the General is out.

We are with General Martin, and Simba will come out, so there's no more Mau Mau in Meru anymore. The three generals are out." We went back to the police station, and very many people from our area who had known me followed us.

I was told now, "General, Mr. Nkungi, there is nothing wrong with you. Here is your friend, General Martin. We are not going to do anything with you." And Martin had intelligence, an *askari,* going with him everywhere, but [dressed] in plainclothes. We left the police station being escorted by only Martin's police friend, who was not wearing [a] uniform.

Then I went with old teacher friends and people from the [coffee growers'] union who had known me. People bought me new clothes, and my beard was shaved. In the afternoon, you would never know whether it was me, [the] General, because I looked exactly like who I was before.

The following day the DC came and wanted to see me. He was on *safari* [traveling] outside the district when I came out. He went to the police station and called us, and we went to meet him. I never knew him before, and I didn't want to talk much.

"Is it you, Nkungi?" he asked.

"Yes," I said.

"When did you come?"

"Yesterday."

"How is the forest?"

"I cannot tell you how the forest is. It is forest."

And he said, "Did you leave some people there?"

"Yes, of course there are."

"Why didn't they come out?"

"I tried to gather them for the first time, and they refused, so I decided myself to come out."

"Good! Leave them! I think they'll come out," he said, "And who shaved you?"

"Me, ah—I've got friends."

"And these are the ones who bought you clothes, is it?"

"Yes," I said.

He was shaking his head. "Ah. I wanted to see the General, the Mau Mau, with a beard—not you. I heard you had a big, full beard. Now you are not the General. Anyways, that's okay. I will see you later."

He walked away laughing. He didn't talk much. He only said he's happy to see us. I thought he would be the fierce one, but he was very friendly. He knew my full story, the bad and good—the whole story. He would become a very great friend of me. He was a good man, Bwana Cumber.

The *mzungu* who was staying with Martin said, "Now, can you make the same effort that Martin made? Can you go and call Simba, the general of Chuka?"

"Yes, I can," I said. "Let's go together with you and me and Martin. And we will call with a loudspeaker because we don't know where he is. But once he hears my sound, and Martin's sound—if we ask, he will come out."

We went to Chuka in the evening, calling Simba with the loudspeaker, "Go, Simba. When you come out, never go to the *kaborio*. Please, go to the police station in the morning."

The following morning we understood from Chuka that Simba was out. We were congratulated, and it was declared that there was no Mau Mau in Meru now.

We three generals stayed in Meru Town from the end of September through December. We stayed in a local house—not detention, but people would pass through, be screened, and then be sent home. We were very comfortable. We were given food by the chief. We were told we could go anywhere. Whenever we met people, they wanted to give [us] some money. We were honored as generals, so our local people fully equipped us. We looked very well in those three months we stayed in Meru.

One of the screeners on the screening team was a very good European. He made friends with us instead of harassing anybody, so we could tell him more. He was called Tom, Bwana Tom. He asked me, "Do you want to say hello to your wife?"

"I don't know where she is," I said.

"I will show you," he said. Then he told Martin, "I will leave you today. I want to take Nkungi home to see his wife." He brought me to Igoji, where Jesca was staying at the Catholic mission, next to St. Mary's [Catholic school]. Jesca and the women who left prison were gathered with their children in these small villages, and they were getting food and aid from the government because they couldn't do otherwise; everything was uprooted or burned. Instead of being taken to the chief's camp, they went to the Catholic mission camp.

Bwana Tom left me there in Igoji, and he continued to Chuka, where he had business to attend to. "I will collect you when I come back from Chuka," he said.

I met Jesca, with our three children. I was not sure we would meet again. I was very happy to see that we came together. We prayed. Jesca explained to me all of her time and experiences, the difficulties that she had. When she was taken to Kisumu [prison], we were lucky that the children were left with my mother. When she came back, she met the children very weak, but they were okay. The firstborn had measles. Our other little girl was very weak but okay. Even the boy was very young and anemic.[1]

The Father at the mission was very good. He helped Jesca with the feeding of that child, and he recovered. Although they were sick and weak, we were lucky to meet our children. Those people who went to prison with children—not all of them came back with children.

The Padre gave us a house to stay in, and we talked a lot. We stayed together for the afternoon. Jesca and I were given a room, and we stayed—[I was] alone with Jesca—for a good time. She said hello to me. We loved one another for the long time that we ha[d] never met. During the time of leaving [on] the Mau Mau day we said, "If God wills it, we will meet again." And when that *mzungu* brought me to see her, we said, "God is good, we are back [together] again. I think all our children are here, and they will be all right. So we begin again."

That afternoon I waited for Bwana Tom on the road because I expected him to come back. When it was around four, I worried because the chief had known that I was there. Nathan—the man from the timber, my former student—had become chief. He was serious [against me]. When he passed, I greeted him. "*Salama. Jambo.*" [Peace and greetings.]

The chief went to the European DO and reported me. He said, "I have seen Japhlet. He is there plundering the village and abusing everybody." He talked a lot of useless words, nonsense. Around five, I saw two *askari* coming. I was there at the road. The *askari* said, "The DO wants to see you." We walked to the chief's camp.

"What are you doing here?" the DO asked me. "How did you come to this place?"

In Kiswahili, I said, "I was with Bwana Tom, who went to Chuka but hasn't been back."

"If he didn't come back, what were you going to do here?" Somebody else was there to interpret. I didn't want to speak English to him.

"I don't know where he is," I said. "*Pole.*" Bwana Tom didn't come back. They put me in a cell, and I stayed there. At night, one of the *askari* came from this area. He was my age-mate, so we knew each other. "Japhlet, let's go and sleep together," he said. So I spent the night with that *askari,* not in the cell. In the morning, I came back.

"Has Bwana Tom come?" I said.

They said, "No, he hasn't." The *askari* and the DO at the camp were going to Meru, so I was transferred to the Nkubu police station. *Whey!* Messages were sent to Meru, and Bwana Tom got the information over the radio. He met me at Nkubu when I was still in the cell. He came back worried. "Bring that man out," Bwana Tom told another *mzungu.* "It was me who was with him."

I was taken from the cell. "I went to Chuka and did my things, and by mistake I stayed the night," he said. "This morning I heard the story. The DC called me; he had information from the Igoji chief, and I understood that you were taken to the cell. The chief was saying that you were abusing each and everybody on the road."

"Bwana Tom," I said, "do you even think that I could do that? Could I dare to talk to anybody? Am I released? Even supposing I was released, could I do that?"

"No, I believe you couldn't. You better forget it, please. I'm very sorry."

He took me to the DC straight away from Nkubu. We went to DC Cumber's office. Bwana Tom explained to the DC how everything happened. I didn't say a word. Even the DC didn't ask me anything. He only said, "Did you see your wife?"

"Yes," I said.

"Are the children okay?"

"Yes."

"Okay. Don't worry. Never go there anymore." The meeting ended, and we left the DC's office. Bwana Tom didn't take me straight back to the place where I was staying. We stayed together and talked for a while. He told me [that] when he heard how the story had been cooked in that way, he had gone straight to the DC's office. "I had already talked to the DC at his office before I came to get you," he said. "I knew there was a former history from your place between you and the chief. I'm very sorry. I didn't want you to have problems."

That chief was a terrible bad man. I did nothing to him—why did he treat me like that? I don't know. I was telling Bwana Tom, "Remember that I helped him to get that job? Nobody else would take him in class because he was an old married man, but I agreed to teach him and let him mix with the younger children. I sympathized. Ah—but he became an animal. Not even after the Emergency—our history was from before."

The chief was very serious during the Emergency. Whoever was detained at his camp worked in his *shamba*. He had a big farm where people were working free of charge. He took great advantage [in] abusing them. Funny—if the Mau Mau continued, Nathan was to die next. That man was to die like Chief Wasto.

I think the story that he formed that day helped me very much. The DC turned to my side, and he understood that the chief was [out] to get me. Bwana Tom took me back to the place where I was staying with *kina* Simba and Martin. The story ended that way, and I didn't come back to see Jesca anymore.

Martin was certain that we won't be detained. When I came out of the forest, he told me so. I said, "You are saying this, but you don't know them. I doubt."

"Believe me. You won't be punished," he said.

"But why don't you go home?" That's the question I asked him. "You have been with them for more than six months. Why are they keeping you here? You say that you are freed—you are not. You don't know."

He said, "King'ua, you don't believe."

"Why does this *askari* stay with us? Hmm? He leaves in the evening and then comes in the morning to take us around wherever we want to go. Who pays him? Martin, you don't know these people."

One morning, very early, Europeans saw some [Mau Mau] people who were still in the forest. There were not many by then, but Europeans surveyed and knew where these people were. Mr. Malcolm, a *mzungu* from the screening team, went there with *askari*. We heard the bullets—*kakakakakaka!*—when we were at Kaaga. After an hour or two, around eight [o'clock], Mr. Malcolm came to us with a Land Rover, and in the back, he had the people [corpses] piled on top of one another. Mr. Malcolm and the *askari* had killed ten people, a mix of Gikuyu and Wameru, but luckily one girl was shot but not dead. There were ten bodies with blood running down all over, and the girl who was shot but not dead was sitting on top of all of them, with blood all over her and falling [dripping] from the Land Rover.

Mr. Malcolm brought the people to us. "Now, General—can you see?" said Mr. Malcolm. "These are the leaders of Mau Mau. I think they have got *uhuru*."

We were not happy at all. "Okay," we said. "You have done it. What do you want?" We did not talk to him. We were very, very annoyed. Malcolm could have gotten a hold of these people instead of killing, but he killed them, and he was showing them to us—I don't know whether he meant, one day, to kill us as he had killed those people. Ah, we were almost to go back again to the forest,

One of the *askari* noticed that we were upset. When they went down to the mortuary at Meru General Hospital, that *askari* told a good chief, "General Nkungi and Martin might go back again to the forest," he said. "They were very annoyed by Bwana Malcolm when he showed them these people." The good chief, named Herman, came to us with that *askari*. He wanted to see our mood. We spoke to them openly. We said, "Kiungo is a rubbish fellow." We were calling Malcolm "Kiungo" because he had a big head. [*Kiungo* means "big head."] Even we meant to kill him during Mau Mau. "Why did they show us these people?" we said. "And why did they not get hold of them instead of killing? Also, they didn't help anything to put a girl sitting on top. Why didn't they kill her?"

"You know, these people are mixed up," said Chief Herman. "They are not our friends—no matter whether they look [like] our friends, they are not. You forget them. Let them do whatever they are doing—they are going. Forget them." The thing [news] spread all over. Even DC Cumber was not happy about that *mzungu*. I think he told Malcolm that he did wrong. He knew we felt it.

We told Martin, "You see? We were brought here by your friend, Malcolm." That was sometime in November. Still, Martin was telling us that we won't be punished. And we waited. In December, things changed. It was on the twenty-second of December that he knew, and it was very hard.

EATING SAND

A *mzungu* prison clerk came with a file. He called out our names. "General Nkungi."

"Present," I said.

"General Simba, General Martin."

"Present," they said. We were handcuffed. We went to the Land Rover and drove to prison in Meru. Simba and I turned to Martin and said, "Martin, are we going home now? Is that where we are going, Martin? What were you telling us? That we'd never be imprisoned? That we'd never be tried?" There were two ways for Mau Mau—either we would be taken to the detention camp, or we would be taken to court for trial.

To be tried, there must be some accusation, some truth or evidence given against you. Detained was the better thing because it meant that you had no case to answer. It meant only that you had taken Mau Mau, and that was not serious. I was not worried about a trial, because I knew I had never committed any crime that would make me go to trial. I was very careful in the forest. All through Mau Mau, I knew I could never be charged.

We spent that night locked in Meru Prison. The following day they put us in handcuffs. We were four—General Martin, General Simba, myself, and somebody called M'Inoti. We met that fellow in prison. He was accused of killing some *askari,* but there was no proof so he was to be detained.

We were tied together two-and-two. I was chained with Simba, and Martin with M'Inoti. We got into a lorry, the prison vehicle, and we were very sorry. Simba and I sat on one side with an *askari,* Martin and M'Inoti with their *askari* on the other side. We didn't know where we were going.

We made our journey to Nairobi and went to an old prison that is still there today. We had never taken anything in Meru—no food, no water. We arrived in Nairobi around two p.m. That was the second day. The *askari* led us each to our own cell. Each had his own small, dark cubicle room. When I entered, I saw one iron ring on the floor in the middle of the room. It was like the ones you see in the slaughterhouses where animals are killed. The rope is there, the animal is tied to that ring, and then it falls down. It can't move, because that strong iron bar is cemented in the floor.

[The] *askari* removed Simba from my chain, and they tied me to the floor. They put the chain through that iron ring and then fastened the handcuff on the other side. I was locked and couldn't stand—on one side, my hand was cuffed, and then it went through the ring, and the other hand was cuffed.

Nobody said hello to us. For the whole remainder of the day, we had to sit there alone in that room. They brought a blanket, an old blanket with dirty things. You could cover yourself at night, but it was very dirty. I spent the night moving from side to side because I was chained to the ring. It was very hard, horrible, to sleep.

In the morning time around eight, I heard somebody open the door. They said, "How are you, General?" I said, "Okay." He came and opened the part that was nailed [fastened] there, so I could stand up and walk out.

I met Simba and Martin coming from the other rooms. M'Inoti by then was already sitting somewhere. We saw the *askari* who had taken us from Meru, so we thought that we are moving again.

I was chained with Simba, Martin with M'Inoti, and the doors were open. We were given the luggage that we had. We went to the lorry, the same one we came with the day before, and got in with nothing—no food, no water—and that was the third day.

We started to drive, and we took the way to Mombasa Road. It was then we realized we were going to Manyani [Detention Camp]. We were talking to Martin very severely. "Martin, didn't you tell us that after all we shall go home? Is this the way home? They were telling you that there will be nothing [to punish us]. Do you see it now? We are being taken to Manyani, where bad people are taken." He was very sorry.

We drove farther and farther until we reached a place called Mutito. That's halfway to Manyani. It's a long way from Nairobi to Mombasa, although I had never been to the coast. We asked the *askari*, "Why don't these people give us anything to drink, neither to eat?"

"We don't know," they said. "We are under command." There was somebody with files sitting in the front with the driver. They left the lorry to go and get something to eat at Mutito. We begged them to give us something, but none of them dared to. We were annoyed. Even I thought it would have been better if we were prosecuted.

When we arrived at Manyani, our vehicle was not allowed to enter the gate. We met some other soldiers, and we were handed over to them with our records. We didn't know we were going to be detained, so we brought our clothes that people had bought us—shirts, pants, even coats. They took our things and put them in another stall, labeled with our name and number.

Everybody got a number when entering Manyani. It stayed with us during the whole time. You wore a wristband with a clasp that covered your number, and nobody but yourself will know it. We hid our numbers, because somebody may use your number in a very terrible way. My number was thirty-two-oh-nine [30209].

The *askari* guided us to the dip. There was a big, deep dip there, like the ones we have for cattle, to get rid of ticks and things. Nowadays, we spray, but we used to have the dip. This was a detainee dip, for people. You had to go before you can join the others. The clerk didn't go to the dip. He entered his own gate and was to wait for us on the other side.

We were told how to dip with only our trousers. You have to make sure that every part of your body is touched with that water. It had some *dawa* [medicine] in it, some white stuff, to make sure you don't have skin diseases or lice or whatever. It kills any insect or germ. A whole man my size could go under water. You walk down these stairs, you go under water—*bloop-bloop*—then push off the bottom and walk out the other side. They said if you stayed too long, you could swallow that *dawa,* and you could die. You have to hold your breath and shut your mouth, being careful. We could hardly come up, because we were very hungry.

We were calling it *munanda.* You had to follow that channel to get into Manyani. The people enjoyed seeing us dipped like cattle. We ourselves even laughed, reaching the other side, water dripping off the face. You know people take things easily when it becomes serious.

We entered Manyani. We walked a distance inside the barbed wires. We passed another gate and followed in a line. There was a place called "Main Cell," a cubicle made of *mabati.* We stayed there and complained that we had never taken [eaten] anything from [since] the days before. "Unless we have something to eat, we are going to die."

"Very unfortunately, everything is gone," they told us. "You have come late, and everything here is taken during the afternoon at lunchtime." We had stayed three days without food or water.

Somebody went somewhere and got us a loaf of bread. We divided it. He gave us two loaves, and we shared it between us four. We ate it with water. Again we went each one of us into our own cubicle. It was one building but divided with four doors. We entered one after the other. That was [the] twenty-fourth [of] December 1955. We spent our Christmas in Manyani sleeping on the sand.

Manyani was called a "Special Detention Camp." It was called "Special" because it was hell. That was where "dangerous" people were taken to be screened. Anybody who has passed through Manyani knows that it was a horrible camp. The seriousness of detention was that you were not supplied with anything. You were not working for or imprisoned by anybody. The law that detains you was proclaimed by the governor. There was no proof whether you have taken Mau Mau, but—according to the declaration of the governor—you were detained. It was a time of Emergency. So whether you had clothes or not, it's upon you. You only have food to live. And shelter.

I remember my good friend Stanley who came into Manyani properly naked. All of the clothes he had got finished [fell apart] at Mackinnon

Road [his previous prison]. He came in with just strips of material, pulling across his body in tatters. After months of staying at Manyani, he was called to go home. He told the *askari*, "Gentlemen, I don't have anything to wear. I am exactly as you see me. Can you give me something?" They couldn't.

Stanley said to me, "I have been called, *bwana,* to go home."

"But how will you go, Stanley?" I said. "Without shorts?" We laughed.

"What can I do?" he said.

I sympathized with him. "Can you arrange to meet me, and I will find you something to wear?"

"Very much," he said. "I can."

"Let's meet tomorrow. Report that you are sick, and we will meet at the clinic."

In the morning, he reported that he was sick. I also went, wearing two shorts. I had trousers, longer trousers, covering the shorts inside. I gave him the shorts. He was very, very thankful. "Man, you have saved me," he said. "I don't know how I could be put out without clothes."

"Ah, Stanley, how could you face the people? You would have gone naked." We have been friends ever since. Even when we meet today, I say, "Where are my clothes, Stanley?" and we laugh.

At Manyani there was no time limit. You stay as long as your record made you stay. It depended on the time it takes for you to confess, so you imprison yourself. Or that's what they were telling us.

Manyani is [means] "monkeys" in Swahili. There were very many monkeys there. Even today they are the most common animal. The Europeans wanted to put us in a place where no one could escape. Or if one manages to escape, they make sure he never survives. It was in the middle of nothing, inside a large game park called Tsavo near the coast. I think if you left that place you had to walk more than sixty kilometers to reach where people are. If you try to run and catch the train, you'll be eaten because it has very many lions and wild animals.

When you read of Manyani, you know [learn] the story of the old Tsavo lions. When the British were building the railroad from the coast to Nairobi, these two man-eaters killed very many Indians—more than a hundred and fifty, I think—who were building the railroad. The railway could not pass there, because of those lions. You could have your gun, and the lion lies down entirely. It would come closer and closer, and you could see it coming nearer, so you get worried and shoot all your bullets. Once you finish your bullets, then it comes and kills you. It was called the *simba* of Tsavo, a furious one. The story is in our Kenyan archives, in our history. An expert was brought from London who killed that lion.

There were some who tried to escape from Manyani. I remember a good group of five people who tried when I was there. Two got completely lost. I don't know what happened to them. They disappeared. The other three made it all the way by train to a river near Nairobi. It's only when they jumped from the train that they were caught. People saw them running naked, and they thought that those people were thieves. But when they were caught, it was known that they escaped from Manyani. Police asked where the other two went, but they could never give [find a] trace, whether they jumped from the train at night or whether they were eaten by lions.

Manyani is a very plain, flat place. It has stone hills around it, so you could never see past those hills. It is a semiarid area. We were to sleep naked on red sand without covering. They had these rugs, old pieces of blankets, which were meaningless. But it was a hot place, so we didn't need blankets.

We woke up at seven in the morning. We had only to carry the buckets [of human waste] to the end of the camp. We poured them in the big pit, washed them, and then came back. Once the pit filled, we covered it with sand. *Askari* were at the gate watching you; [others were] at the *githuu*, the tall watchtower. We were not handcuffed—there was no need, because you could hardly get out. We were completely inside the very tight barbed wire fences within strong gates guarded by *askari*.

If a guard gives a signal blowing the whistle, someone is causing trouble or something is wrong, so you are to lie down. Wherever you are, you lie down because you don't know what is happening. You listen to whether there will be any shot. If the *askari* shoots in the air, you can get up.

The *askari* were very many covering Manyani. There were half as many *askari* as detainees. The British employed people from Tanzania, people who were very primitive and illiterate, foolish even—so that if one is ordered to shoot, he won't take time [to think about it]. Most were taken from very remote areas, and they were told that Mau Mau were animals, that we could take their guns and run away and disappear.

I was escorted by four *askari*, two on this side and two on the other side, with their guns cocked and pointed at me. I was almost naked, wearing only shorts, but they were told, "Don't play with this man. These people can kill you and then eat you with nothing." They were very fierce with us because they believed we were not people.

At nine o'clock, we took our breakfast, a cup of porridge. Then at one o'clock. in the afternoon, we had lunch, a cup of *ugali* with some mashed beans. That was all—just one mugful for twenty-four hours. Feeding was terrible. We looked like skeletons. The thing that they punished us with at Manyani was feeding—we were given very small portions. Why? Because they wanted us to surrender and know that we are nobody. Before the end of the [month of] December, I think everybody had lost very many kilos. Within three months, we were all like one another.

In 1956, I met somebody called Elias Makundi who was wearing a shirt that was very big. Makundi was very skinny. The shirt he was wearing looked like a lasso and could go around him twice. I asked, "Elias, why do you wear that big thing?"

"It was me, General, this was my shirt," he said. "I was as big as that." Makundi used to be a trader and very fat. These big, rich people of Gikuyu were punished. All of their things were taken, and they were detained without reason, because nobody knew who had taken oath. But he said, "Don't worry, General, things will be okay. We won't stay long here."

I didn't bother much about the food at Manyani. Because, you know, whether you bothered or not, you have to take that food. People were looking hungry at the kitchen throughout the day. I didn't bother myself. People were making the *ugali* in the kitchen, and the wind would come and carry the red sand into the kitchen and into the *ugali*. You could hardly see it, but when you get your cup, you taste the sand. We were eating sand, but nobody died because of that.

There was only this disease that people got with hard skin. We were calling it *ferangera*. I think it's because of the diet. You find people scratching. I don't know what language is *ferangera*, maybe Indian, because I used to see some Indians with hard skin, especially the neck. You could put oil on it to soften. We had a clinic there where it was treated.[2]

The clinic was run by detained people. Some had worked in hospitals and were very learned, with good experience. The government did not lose money to employ people, so the detainees treated the other detainees free of charge.

For four good [long] weeks we stayed in the very place where they brought us on the first day, called the Main Cell. Every morning we had to do PE, with the *askari* abusing us. It was punishment with any horrible exercise. We had to jump. They were not supposed to beat you, but if you fall down, you could be kicked by people wearing shoes. The Main Cell was terrible.

I met one of our Wameru, a learned man called Kabere. He used to be a Mau Mau fellow but surrendered before and now was on the screening team at Manyani. He knew all of us because he came from the same place of General Martin. We had contributed for him to study in East Africa, where he went for a degree in agriculture. General Martin had led the *harambee* [fundraising] for him to complete his higher education. We were very happy to see him.

We were near the gate when we talked to him. He'd heard that some big people had come, the Meru generals of Mau Mau. He said to me, "I understand, General, that all the things you had, all of your possessions, were taken by the Homeguards."

"Yes," I said.

"And did you get *uhuru?*" he said. "After all of your things being taken, did you get *uhuru?*" He taunted me. He was very proud. "No? Is it what you wanted? Did you get *uhuru* then?"

I stopped the conversation. All of us were annoyed, and we didn't talk to him anymore. We refused to be screened by that man. Mr. Kabere was there to screen the Meru people. He said he was the leader of Mau Mau and that he knew Meru people, but we said he didn't. The words that he spoke to us showed us that he was a horrible man. He thought that by being *kali* [mean and fierce] to his people he could be released sooner. If you say that you didn't take oath to Kabere, he directed people to beat you. Ah, he was naughty. Kabere was brutal. Hoo-hoo. Wameru people were beaten seriously.

Kabere came to my home many years later. He was running for parliament. He came to ask me to campaign for him. I tricked him. He got only one vote from the whole area. Even I tried my best to get that one man not to vote for him, but they were relatives. I bought a lot of beer for that man, but he didn't get convinced. When the votes were counted, I revealed to Kabere what I did. The woman, his wife, was very furious to me, but they couldn't do anything.

"Kabere, what did you tell me in Manyani?" I said. "I got *uhuru* now. Did you get *uhuru?* Have you gone yourself, to parliament?" He was very annoyed.

"To hell with you," he said. Even today, he's a good farmer for himself but isn't a good man.

So we stayed for one month in the Main Cell. From there, we were transferred to Compound 21 in Black Zed One.[3] It was hard to make friends at Manyani. When you try, you are fearing that the other person was sent to gather information about you and then tell the Special Branch. You never knew who were the informers. "Among the lot, there are some government people, so be careful," they told us. "Never talk freely with anyone whom you don't know. We are mixed with the government people, who later on will take people from our camps and kill them." Of course we feared one another very much because of the propaganda.

In Compound 21, I met a very learned fellow called J. M. Kariuki. He was in form six during the Emergency and was caught. JM, Josiah Mwangi, wrote to the colonial secretary from Manyani. Communication was an easy thing. You could bribe the guards and mail letters. He complained to the colonial secretary about the conditions at Manyani and how we were being treated. He wrote our concerns, that people are dying of hunger and that we live like animals close together. "People are eating the sand," he wrote.

His letter went through the *askari*, through the officers—all the way to London. When it was received, it was known that it came from Manyani Special Detention Center and was written by somebody called Mwangi. One day, all of us were told to go inside a house in the Compound 21. We were told to lie down with our face covered on the ground. We didn't know what was happening. We stayed there all day. Then an *askari* leaked it. He said, "Kariuki was taken." And we noticed that JM wasn't with us.

We said, "Why?"

"Because he had written a letter to the colonial secretary." Kariuki was detained by himself on his own island, Saiyusi Island, in Lake Victoria.

Ah, Kariuki was a good man. He was very bright and handsome—merry all the time and loved by everybody. When he said hello to somebody, they stayed smiling. Before he was transferred to Saiyusi, he was teaching us a nice history of form four. He told us not to fear and that things like this have happened all over the world. "Independence never comes freely," he said. Kariuki had nice things to tell.

He was telling us that if the Gikuyu were like the Maasai, the Europeans could never have possessed all of the country because the Maasai fought with [against] the Europeans. But the Gikuyu didn't. Even the Gikuyu helped the Europeans to fight against the Maasai. That was the history.

He told us about the coming of the Arabs. The Arabs were cheated by the whites, too. They were given just a little land, some ten kilometers, along the coast. The sultan, the leader of the Arabs, was honored to be given the land to rule along the coast. He never counted the Europeans who passed through Mombasa to the Upper Country, and this was the force that chased him from the leadership.

Kariuki left us teaching one another at Manyani. We had been idle because there was no work or hard labor in detention. Mau Mau who were imprisoned did hard labor. Whenever there was something to be done, the Mau Mau could do it. They built the airport. A gang of a thousand people were to go every day to work there. My brother was imprisoned at Kajiado and he told me they were working there. The government enjoyed [having the labor] to make a new airport and took great advantage [of the prisoners].

But in detention, we had nothing to do during the day, so we said, "Do you want to learn?" People said yes, and we taught classes. We honored ourselves and loved one another. Very many people came to Manyani illiterate, and they learned how to read and write with sticks in the sand. Fingers and sticks in the sand make good pens. People came out signing their names and writing. I had a group myself. I made very many friends teaching illiterate people how to read and write.

There was a missionary Bible society. They gave a lot of books to the detainees, to read and rehabilitate them. They had a team of missionaries going around the detention camps, preaching and telling people that we should cooperate. Even Kimathi was converted by a Catholic priest when he was in Kamiti Maximum Prison. But of course, Kimathi did not leave there. He may have been converted in prison, but that didn't help [keep] him from hanging.[4] No matter how far the Father could go, the rope was still at the end for Kimathi, whether converted or not. The law said that.

We were even with some Luos who had taken Mau Mau. It was not only Gikuyu, Embu, and Meru, but we had some Luos. I remember we were with this one very educated man called John Washike. He was a court interpreter in Nairobi. He helped with a lot of cases. He defended very many Mau Mau on trial, and through his work many Mau Mau were released. When it was known that he was a Mau Mau, he was almost to be shot, but luckily he was detained together with us at Manyani. So even with other tribes, they were not wholly trusted [by the government]. Washike was very honored during the Independence.

Another Luo who helped us to come up from the detention was Tom Mboya. Mboya was a politician, not a Mau Mau. He was very powerful. He was the one who helped even Gikuyu to go to America and study abroad during the Emergency time.[5] He had an organization called the Kenyan

Federation Trade Union, or something of that sort. He led the trade unions as secretary general, and that body worked very much for us. They had good say in Nairobi because they were not Mau Mau. When we first got African representatives [in 1957] in parliament, he was one of the six. He was an MP [member of parliament] in Nairobi. They negotiated for us—especially Mboya.

In Mau Mau we took oath saying that if you see somebody killing another person that you should never mention them. But people turned. They were bribed or threatened, and they got emotional. They said who had killed people. They were told, "That person now is at Manyani. Supposing we took you to that person, and we covered you so that nobody knows who you are, then we lined up people—do you think you could identify that person?"

And they said, "Yes."

Then the Special Branch would come to Manyani. We knew when the truck came, and we could see the covered window. "*Nkunia* is coming," we said. "He is trying to get somebody from us." We called those people *nkunia*. They had a sheet, a *shuka*, over their heads with only two holes cut out for the eyes.

The Special Branch checked the records to find out which compound the accused was in. Then a clerk comes out. We all gather together. The clerk says, "I want these people—number 30209, number 5202, number . . ." They call out the numbers and get three from one compound and three from another compound and so on. They order you in lines. You are naked. Then you see the guard coming around with the *nkunia*. They pass, *pole-pole, polepole*. You never know what is happening.

When the *nkunia* points to somebody and says "stop," then that is the one. Then they change the order of the detainees. Two or three are transferred from one line to another line. Then the process is repeated.

They move again. "Is that the one?"

"No."

They go to another row. "Is that the one?"

"No."

Then he says, "He's number three there." If he gets you twice in two different lines—ah, you cannot get rid of him. He knows you thoroughly. They say that if the *nkunia* can recognize you when you are naked, it's not the clothes that he remembers.

The rest of the detainees are returned to their compounds with their records. The *nkunia* leaves without notice. Then, you go to prison. You get very terrible screening. You will be taken back to where the action occurred, together with that man being covered. And if somebody else again gives the same information, you will be hanged. Very many were taken in that way from Manyani.

You never know who is the person covered in a sack. Later we came to know. You can never defend yourself. That's the worst—being caught by somebody whom you do not know.

KENYATTA WON'T COME TO MANYANI

We Meru generals were very surprised at our treatment. They told us that if we confessed we would not be punished, so what were they doing now? We were seeing [that] these people had lied to us. We were harmless, and they liked us—but they meant for us to test their Pipeline. That's what they were calling it, the Pipeline.

We were asking why we were in Compound 21, for Black Zed One. That's where they kept the hardcores. We said, "Didn't we confess? Why are we, the generals, being treated as badly as the hardcores?" The hardcores were these people who would never confess to having taken oath. They refused. Most of them were in *machege* [chains], with their legs cuffed. They moved shuffling their feet. If an *askari* pushed them—*BOOM*—they fell down. Hardcores said they didn't know the Mau Mau. All through the screening, they refused to confess.

They were the dangerous people, always trying to escape, so they were feared. Hardcores were not allowed to move from that compound. If anybody's sick, the doctor could come and treat him there. They could not even carry the buckets to the pit. Hardcores were angry with us, the Meru generals. They said that we were cheating the people in the forest. They accused us of doing intelligence for the Europeans. They told others, "They say that they were in the forest, but they were not." They were funny.

They were not happy with us, revealing the Mau Mau oath, but how can we say that we have not taken oath, and we have been in the forest? That's what we were asking these detained people. "You tell us what to say," we told them. "You say you have never taken oath, and you were detained from the reserve. But what about ourselves? We are from the forest, and we have fought with [against] these people. Why did we go to the forest if we had not taken oath? You can talk anything you like, but we are telling the truth."

"You fight!" we told them. "Continue to fight, gentlemen. But you are inside barbed wires. You are beaten any time that the *askari* want to beat you. Is that fighting?"

They looked at us.

"You are beaten by *askari*, and you cry like women. Who are you fighting? Do you find any Europeans here inside the barbed wires?" In detention, you are being fed by the people you were fighting. You can never retreat. We were telling the hardcores, "We have fought with these people, but here, you can only say, *'Jambo*—hello!' to *bwana mkubwa* because we are within barbs. He can do whatever he likes to do with you. Oooo-hoooo. You are empty-handed. Don't play."

Even some compounds rioted. The whole compound was thoroughly beaten. If somebody fought with an *askari*—uh-huh, you will be beaten. You see some people like the GSU [General Service Unit] with big batons. They enter into that compound, and all the doors will be shut. Then, no matter whether you were the one, you were beaten. People run this way, run that way—until they heap themselves lying on top of one another. They were given time to wake up.

We were calling it a "trip." You think you are going somewhere, but you are not going anywhere. You are beaten, until you are tired and make no effort. It was a very difficult trip. "Have you taken enough trips?" Many people had to attend [the medical] clinic the following day. These people were telling us that we surrendered, so we said, "Now, look—do you hear what is happening in Compound A? They are crying like women. Are they fighting Europeans? The whites have really tricked us."

"Kenyatta did not confess," they said. "Why should we confess? Has he said that he took Mau Mau? So, we have not taken Mau Mau." They were talking a lot of propaganda. They were very hopeful. "Kenyatta will come, and he will be very big. People who fought against the Europeans will be put in big posts." They were believing that they'll get rewarded because they fought. You could be very tired listening to them.

Some were pretending they were mad [crazy]. You find them putting the buckets on their heads, full buckets that people had used for the toilet. They turned them over and poured them on their heads. They don't want to talk, they don't want to do work, they made themselves mad—for nothing!

We were not even laughing. We were running away from them. We complained to the *askari*. We complained of one in particular—ah, he was with a terrible smell. We said, "Better to take that man to prison." And he was taken, chased from the compound. People were doing ridiculous things. There were some who made their legs not to bend. They used sticks [as canes] for the entire time they stayed in the Manyani. Why? Because they didn't want to cooperate or do any movement, so they complained that his legs could not move.

One of the Europeans told me, "Do you know these people are pretending to be crippled?"

I said, "I doubt it."

"Why do you doubt?"

"Because they have always been like that, in all the prisons and detentions. I don't know whether they can be faking it."

"General, let me tell you. If something is wrong with the leg, with the hip or thigh, he will lose muscles because he can't use it. The leg will be smaller than the other. That's one thing. Secondly, you have to note that these people are complaining of the right-hand leg. Do you know why? This is the thing that they can control. They can do whatever with the stick, because it is in their right hand. Nobody is complaining of the left leg."

I saw he was right. They were pretenders. "They are cheating," I said. But there was one man who could not walk, because he had polio. I asked, "Why is this man detained?"

"Do you think Mau Mau is about walking? It is not. If he cannot walk, he can talk. He can pass information. Mau Mau is not legs; neither [is it] hands. These are the Mau Mau who are even more dangerous than you." And I realized he was right. Mau Mau used people you could never suspect. They were the ones to pass information.

We Meru generals were not happy to be with these hardcores. The son of Kenyatta, Peter Kenyatta, was the one who cooled us down. He came for screening in Compound 21. He spoke to us, "Forget these hardcores. They are bitter. We don't want to keep you here. Tell us all the stories that you have done, and we will take you off from this compound. This is the compound for bad people who say that they have not taken Mau Mau. Why should you be mixed with them?"

Peter was a very good man. We told him the story of Kabere and said that we only wanted to be screened by Peter. He was very happy to hear that the three generals from Meru wanted to be screened by him. The screening team wondered why.

"You yourself have been in the forest," he said. "Let us go and confess, then we go home. Let these people wait for Kenyatta here, with cuffs on their hands and legs. Follow me. Remember that Kenyatta is my father. I will remember you, General, when Mzee [Kenyatta] comes. No matter whether I have taken Mau Mau, I will become the son of a president, and I won't leave you here.

"Don't try to impress anybody but speak the truth. We want to become leaders of our country and have these Europeans go. That's why we have taken oath, that's why my father was detained. We don't want our people to continue killing one another, and these people have understood that we don't want them. Let's tell them that we are not going to fight anymore. We want peace. And don't worry, whether you have killed or what—tell them! It was a fight, during the fighting time. Even those who are asking you—some have killed people. That was a matter of Emergency, and we are no longer in that state. Let's say the truth, and we leave the camp. Leave the hardcores to stay here and wait for Kenyatta. Kenyatta won't come to Manyani. If he comes, he will go direct to the State House."

Mr. Peter made sense. He was very courageous, and he was speaking the truth. We thought, *He is right. Kenyatta will not come to Manyani. He'll go to the State House if he comes. We cannot wait for Kenyatta here; let us go. Thank you.*

As generals, we had taken the top oath. Hardcores said we revealed what we said we shall never reveal. But we believed that we fulfilled what we had promised to do with the Mau Mau—what else remained? Now why should we remain in this condition? The hardcores were furious with us— ah, they were naughty. But we didn't fear them, because we were beyond their oath. They were drugged—cursed—in a horrible way.

The hardcores stayed for a long time. They suffered greatly but never surrendered. They could die before revealing that they'd taken oath—to date, even! I'm telling you there are some who have never shaved their beards. "Not yet *uhuru*," they say. Some of them could move from detention to rehabilitation, then back again to detention. When they got released, they agitated. They tried to recruit others to be like them. You saw them coming back and wondered what happened. But you could not believe those people. We met them there, we left them there.

We talked very freely and followed Peter. We did not stay long in Black Zed One. After one month, we were transferred to Compound 10 and stayed until the end of the year. We were very cooperative. There were people in Compound 10 who were still not very cooperative, but nobody bothered about us because we had already said what was needed.

On [the] eighteen[th of] November 1956, we left Manyani. We left from Compound 10 and were transferred to Mbeu Rehabilitation Camp. We were very happy to leave Manyani, very happy indeed. We suffered there—ah, we were skeletons, very weak. We found a new land when we came to Mbeu.

FOLLOWING THE PIPELINE

Mbeu was a rehabilitation camp. It was for people coming from different detentions and prisons on their way home. They weren't imprisoned anymore, just following the Pipeline, to go back to the people whom they left. These screening teams were the ones who can say who goes home and who needs to stay. "How do you behave when you are nearer to the people? Are you cooperative, or do you still keep the enmity? And what happens when you are near your brother who was a Homeguard? How do you feel about him?" These were such things and questions [they asked] to see whether you have evolved to a certain standard where you can go back home. We were detained, not imprisoned. We had no date to leave—only the time that these people feel you have stayed enough.

We were calling Mbeu a working camp, where people had to do jobs and work for their food. Mbeu was a very fertile place, and we had a big piece of land fenced for the detainees who were there. We were digging, weeding, planting, and harvesting maize and beans for our consumption. All the food there was ours, but we harvested more than we could consume. Especially beans were doing very well. We even took some and sold it to Meru Prison. We were working freely—[for] no payment—but we were eating.

The portions were done by the cooks. People recovered quickly when they came from Manyani. We told new people, "Don't worry. We have food here. Eat *polepole, polepole*. Don't take too much. You get each and everything that you want, so eat *polepole*."

Life at Mbeu was okay. I met my brother [Zacharia] at Mbeu, and we were very happy to be together. He came from Kajiado Prison. People felt free. You only knew that you were in camp because of the barbed wire. There was no seriousness even with the *askari*. They knew nobody will escape. And we could talk freely with one another. We were not worried about spies, no. We were all surrenderees in one category and had nothing to hide.

People could come from various places to visit us. And *askari* would allow us to go to the gate and talk to them. Tobacco was not prohibited, as it was in other camps. Every month people were coming from detainment and others were going home, every month.

We were still using buckets for the toilet but with good holes within the *shamba* not very far [away]. We were staying in the same types of temporary houses made of *mabati* and had only three compounds. We slept on the ground but had blankets. And we were given uniforms, not prison uniforms, but they were marked, to say that we are of the camp.

At Mbeu I was communicating with Jesca. She was writing to me, and I would reply. She wrote saying that she was released from Kinoro chief's camp. She said, "We are allowed to put up our houses in our former places, in our *shamba*s. Everything we had is bushy. Where shall I build?"

I told her never [to] go back to the exact place where we were but put a house next to it. "How are you going to manage to put [up] a house?" I asked.

"I've talked to my father, and he has said that he will give me his laborer, Kanike, who will help to put up a little house for us." Her father helped us very much. He let us work with Kanike, who built the house and helped us to clear the bushes from the *shamba*. When I was released, I met the man, [who was] doing a wonderful job.

[My daughter] Mugure was born in 1956.[6] I didn't feel good when I knew that Jesca had a child, because it was during the time that she was helpless. I was at Manyani, then Mbeu. I wrote to her, and she told me she was all right and that our child was okay. She said the problems were being helped by my father and some local people who supported her.

I was prefect of my compound at Mbeu. I was counting the number of people in the camp for the sergeant or the *mzungu* every day in the morning and the evening. I gave reports to the person in charge. Before you reach the camp, the screening team already knows who you are because your records follow you. I had the same number from Manyani.

I had just arrived when a European who[m] I didn't know called me "lance corporal," the very first rank in the military. I didn't know why he was mentioning my name in that way. He said, "I'm calling you lance corporal because if we keep calling you 'General,' then you won't leave this camp. So now you are lance corporal." He was kidding me. He said, "Mm-hmm. When I demote you from that lance corporal, then you will go home."

So I was demoted—*polepole, polepole.* He was a friend of me, called Mr. Ingram, a good European from Britain. He had a very good lady for his wife, and I was teaching her Swahili. Mr. Ingram could even give me a little beer. "Don't tell anybody that I'm giving you beer," he said. We were thinking he was Christian because he never beat anyone. No, no, no—he sympathized with them. There was another one who was very brutal, but Mr. Ingram was a good gentleman. He knew anybody could be imprisoned.

When I first came, I went to work with a group of men in the quarry. I did this for two weeks. I was out working, taking stones from the quarry. Then I heard somebody calling me, "General!" It was the clerk with a file. "You are being called in[to] the office." I wondered why. "You will be helping Mungane," he said. Mungane was the clerk there. They had gone through the records and had seen I was a good, educated man and could help in the office. "Aren't you happy? I don't want you to work in the quarries."

"Okay, thank you. I am," I said. And I reported there to the office. They gave me a clean shirt, an extra one that I could keep clean and wash. The good European, Mr. Ingram, said, "General, you cannot wear a dirty uniform. You are not imprisoned. The rest can have that, but you are not in prison." So I had a white shirt.

They asked me about the hardcores, the ones chained and sent back to Manyani. They said, "Do you believe these people?"

I said, "Ah, they are foolish. We have confessed. Each and every Mau Mau has claimed it. Why are they saying they don't know? I don't know. Leave them alone."

One day a European from another camp dropped off a pig and asked Mr. Ingram to look after it. His camp, Ririaba, was closing, and he could not take the pig with him. It could get food at Mbeu. Now when that pig came, it was served [pregnant]. It gave six piglets. After three months, the man from Ririaba wanted to come and see his pig. He was at another camp by then. Mr. Ingram knew that this man was coming, and he called me out from the office, "General! Come out."

"Sir?"

"Come with me." We went and selected two of the piglets. He told me to carry them, and we hid them somewhere. When the white man came, he found his pig with four piglets, and he was happy.

When the man finally came to pick up his pig, we hid those two again. The man was so grateful that he gave us two piglets. He went with the mother and two piglets. And we were left with four. I did not say anything, because I was fearing. Then Mr. Ingram came to the office. "Hello, General," he said.

"Morning, Sir."

"Let me tell you a story of one European called Williamson. He was from Britain, and he had a very big farm in South Africa. When he planted wheat, the locusts came at the harvest time and ate all of the wheat. He tried again a second time, but there was a terrible drought. The wheat didn't come up. The money that he had was all gone. He couldn't survive. He decided to move to Zimbabwe [Rhodesia]. He knew the soil was good there.

"The European was given another loan and a very good big farm because he was known to be a good farmer. On the first day, he took his tractor to survey the area and see where he will put his fence. Just a few meters before his property ended, he saw something very bright. It was gold. Ah-hah. The group from South Africa came and found that it was real gold, the highest quality. There was wonderful gold all around that farm Mr. Williamson was given. And Williamson, poor Williamson, became Lord Williamson." Mr. Ingram looked at me. "Do you know why I'm telling you that story?" he asked. "Because not everyone will be as lucky as Williamson."

Everybody has his own living, his own way to survive. You have to take what you are able. Because we can't wait until we become like Williamson.

The owner took his two piglets, and he was very happy! He didn't know that we had more than what he had taken. I liked it and laughed with Mr. Ingram. We laughed so hard that the clerk came to see what is happening in the office that made us to laugh so seriously, and we did not tell him.

Mr. Ingram said that he would go to Meru Town to sell the pigs. I knew the place and told him where to go. He took the pigs—they were good enough porkers by then—and showed them to the man at Meru Town. I don't know how much he sold them for, but when he came back to Meru, Mr. Ingram said, "Now, I have money, and you are detained. I do not want to give you money. What do you want me to give you?"

"Oh, you know—anything. Anything that you think," I said.

"Supposing I give you three new blankets; where will you keep them? Will you manage to send them home?" I told him I thought so.

I went and consulted my friend Francis. He had a house separate from the compounds because he was a screener. They were given houses outside the barbed wires. He said he could help. Mr. Ingram gave me three very nice big blankets. I took them to Francis, and I gave Francis one. Then I told him to keep the other two at his home until I could get them to Jesca.

So we sold the *mzungu's* pigs because "not all the people will be as lucky as Williamson, the poorest man becoming lord." I kept that story in my head.

Now the same Bwana Malcolm, Kiungo, from the Land Rover story, was the European in charge of the screening team at Mbeu. Malcolm told me that the *wazee* of Njuri Ncheke wanted to meet with me and asked me if I would like to meet with the *wazee*, and I said yes.

Bwana Malcolm took me to the meeting, but he was not allowed [in]. I went to meet with them alone. The *wazee* said, "Ah, welcome, Thambu! Welcome. You are a good man. We know who you are. Would you like to join us?"

"Why not?!" I said. "Yes!"

And I was oathed there—not seriously, but it was only to show that I agreed and to say that I'm very loyal to my people. My friend Francis was within the *wazee*. He was already a member of Njuri Ncheke. The *mzungu* waited for me at the chief's camp. "Are you finished with the *wazee?*" he said. I said yes. "What have they said?" I did not reveal to him that I was accepted. Then we went back to Mbeu.

Later, the chief, the very Nathan who did not like me, told the *mzungu*, "The people do not want him. The *wazee* do not want the General. They told me." And Kiungo was surprised. But then Francis gave a report which was contrary to what the chief told him. Francis said, "The General is now an *mzee* of Njuri Ncheke. He has taken the oath, and the *wazee* were happy to receive him."

Malcolm was confused and asked, "Was the chief there?"

"No, we couldn't allow the chief to come, because the chief has not taken Njuri Ncheke." Then Malcolm said, "That's okay." He went to see DC Cumber and reported the story. The DC said, "I know of Japhlet and the chief."

At the very beginning at Mbeu I had told the DC that I would never go to work in the *shamba* of Nathan. "You can send me to any other camp but not his," I said. "All of my people would see me working in Nathan's *shamba*, and he doesn't like me. The chief at Nkubu is my friend—I can go there. It is where all of us from the division want to go. He knows the returning detainees are harmless. But if I cannot go there, I will stay at Mbeu." The DC said he knew where to send me.

Finally Malcolm told me, "Your chief said the *wazee* do not want you."

"Ah—That's lies," I said.

He was laughing. "Now, where should I take you: to the chief's camp or to the *wazee* of Njuri Ncheke?"

I told him that if the *wazee* did not want me, then he should send me to Mageta Island, an island where they sent all the hardcores who had been refused by their homes. I told him, "Save me a place at Mageta Island. I will go there and make my *shamba* before all the land is taken."

"Ah, leave the chief—he doesn't like you," he said.

There were always people going home from Mbeu. But I think we generals stayed longer than most of the other detainees. Even some people were telling the screeners, "None of the Meru generals have been released. What's wrong with them? They do confess and have agreed to everything in the screening—why don't they leave?"

By then, Martin had become a screener and was spending nights out of the compound. He had more knowledge than ourselves, because he was involved from the start of Mau Mau in the Nairobi War Council. He could get more information from screening, and he had fame. It was him who called us out of the forest. Simba never was a screener. He was a good man and a great friend of me.

On one Tuesday in March 1958, the DC came to visit. He was visiting the camp all the time to get reports. He gave us a good speech and told us how the people who had been released were doing well. He said that everyone was cooperating. "When you get released from here, I want you to go and follow the same example," he said.

We all said, "Okay. Yes." After addressing the meeting, the DC said, "I want to see [the] General." I stepped outside to talk to him. He laughed. "I've heard the story of you and your friend the chief," he said. "Now don't tell anybody, but I will recommend that you be released on Thursday of this week. I want you to see me before you go home. If you come to my office at Meru on that very Thursday and do not meet me, I want you to wait for me at the chief's camp in Nkubu. Do not pass Nkubu before I see you."

I was happy to know that. So on Thursday I saw the clerk coming with a file, the list of numbers to be released. I knew that I would be one. We gathered, and I heard him call my brother's name, which I did not expect. I was very happy. There were a good number of people—I think twenty-eight. The last name he called, he said, "And General Nkungi."

I was the first general to be released. I left Simba there. [The] *askari* said, "Go and take your things from the camp and line up." The truck was already there. I said [to the other detainees], "Okay. Bye! Do well!"

"Don't forget us!" they said.

"You are coming next—you will follow us!" We got in the lorry and went to Meru. The DC was not in his office. So they gave us food, and we spent the night at the chief's camp in Nkubu. Around eight thirty the next morning, the DC and the chief came. He repeated what he said at Mbeu. "Those who have gone to the reserve are performing good work, and they are farming well. I want you to do the same. I don't want clashes. You must get along with your chief. If you find that someone has taken your wife, do not look for her, because maybe a Homeguard is waiting for you. Get another. If there is a complication with regard to land, do not quarrel with anyone. Come to my office. You know my office is open to you, and I will resolve it. Yes?"

We all said, "Yes. Thank you."

"Good, but I'm sure that you won't come. We've had very few cases. I hope you do like the friends that you meet." Then he said, "I want to see the General." People scattered to go to their home places.

The DC was with another *mzungu* whom I didn't know. I moved to talk to them. The DC told me, "Now, these people are going to their chief's camp, but your friend the chief doesn't like you. So, I think this man will want you." He was talking about the other *mzungu*, and he was smiling. "This is Mr. Bachman. He's in charge of the Kaguru farm, a general agri-culture institute. I want to give you to him, where you'll learn the way of farming instead of going to the chief's camp." In every province, in every district, there were these agricultural farms headed by Europeans to teach people the method of farming.

He told Mr. Bachman, "This is General Nkungi. His chief doesn't want him. They have been enemies from the beginning, even before Mau Mau. The chief would be telling me that he's revolting all the time. I want him to go to Kaguru, to do the general agriculture course. How long is the program?"

"One year." And Mr. Bachman said that class had already started. The students had already been there for two months. The DC said, "Don't worry. He has been a teacher, so he will catch up. Don't you think so?"

"Yes, I will do it," I said.

He told Mr. Bachman, "I'll be receiving his progress reports. Please give them to me. And you, General, if you perform very well, it is me who will employ you."

"Thank you, sir," I said. "Do you want me to start today?" It was a Friday.

"No, no. Go home. Say hello to your wife. Do you know where she is?"

"Yes."

"Go home, say hello, and join the school on Monday."

People never knew what we were talking about. He told me, "When you come to Igoji, tell the chief that I have released you but don't talk to him anymore."

I said okay, and I left with my brother. We had no means of transport, but we saw the brother of Mr. Mate, who was secretary of the coffee union. He gave us a lift to Igoji. The chief was not there, so I reported to an *askari*. Then we started to climb up the hill. After a couple kilometers, we heard a vehicle coming. It was the DC's vehicle. The chief was riding with him. He stopped when he saw us. He said, "General, where are you going?"

"I'm going home."

"And who is the other one?"

"This is my brother."

"Ah-hah. I did not mean to release you. I meant to release [the] General. But anyway I will never take you back. Why didn't you tell me you were coming here so that I could have carried you? I never knew we were coming to the same place. Come on, let me help you."

We got in his car, and he carried us up the hill until I said, "I have to drop here, Bwana DC." My home was in the direction of the forest. The DC said, "Is that your home? Are you going back again to the forest?"

"Yes, I am going back again to the forest, but not going to the forest. That is my home." We were laughing.

"Okay. Go on—but don't go to the forest anymore. Do you remember what we have said?"

"Yes. I remember."

The DC said, "Okay. Bye—see you!" The chief was very surprised. He never knew what we were talking about. I dared not to say anything to him in the car. It was later on that he knew I was not to come to his camp. The chief was not happy, but everyone who loved me was happy.

I reported to Kaguru on that Monday in March 1958. I started my course in general agriculture, and I did very well. Kaguru was a camp to demonstrate how to farm. We stayed in good sturdy houses. We had two good dormitories, one for male and the other for female. It was a nice institution.

General agriculture included husbandry, learning how to keep animals, and how to do mixed farming using a little land, five or six acres. We call it "small-scale farming." We learned different fertilizers for different crops, sprays that you use for animals and sprays that you need for pests. You can put [on] a lot of manure, thinking that the more you put [on] the better it will be, but no, no, no—it's the opposite. They knew the measure of how much fertilizer and manure.

The training at Kaguru helped us very much, and I'm still using it. That's why we have spinach and *hohos* [peppers], cabbage, and *sukuma wiki* [a kind of kale]. Instead of buying everything, you have a farm and depend on yourself. You keep one or two cattle, [and] they give calves alternately, so you always have milk. When one becomes dry, you serve [impregnate] the other one. You never have time without milk. I live that way.

All the teachers whom I met at Kaguru used to be my pupils. I knew how to write on the board even better than themselves. They told me, "Now, *mwalimu*, take the chalk and give notes to your people." So I learned as I gave notes. The instructors were happy. They were to teach, and I wrote on the board.

The rest [of my classmates] were earning money to take the course.[7] I was the only detainee. They knew my situation, and at the end of the month when they were paid, they bought me beer. You could hardly know that I was different from them. Even I studied with Jesca's sister there.

Bachman was a good fellow. He was slender, small—good people but not married. He was very social. We could even dance with Mr. Bachman. He was employed by the ministry, so he had nothing to do with Mau Mau. He ran Kaguru to train agricultural people. He had a diploma of veterinary [science] and agriculture. He knew anything concerning farming.

We were allowed to go home every other weekend. I had an agreement with Mr. Bachman. I ate the food on Friday night because it was rationed for everyone. You couldn't break that system. Then I left after dinner to come home at night. I wanted to be already there by Saturday so I could work all day. We worked terribly hard during that time to clear the bushes. After we had taken food and the children were sleeping and the moon was full as if it were daytime, I would say to Jesca, "What are we doing in the house? The children are asleep. We want to plant coffee. Why can't we go and work?"

Jesca said, "Why not?" So we would go out and dig wonderful holes during the night.

The next day, one of my workers said, "*Mwalimu*, some people are working in the *shamba* at night. Who are they?"

I laughed. I did not tell him it was us. I said, "We are going to find out." In the morning, they found us working, from the night [before]. And on Sunday, we joined them in the fields. We said, "This is the time now to help ourselves, to go back again to the place where we were. We were good farmers, and we have to repeat it."

The man that my father-in-law had given to Jesca to help build the house didn't go back to her father. When I came, I said, "You stay." I made another house, a little one, and I was to sleep there with Kanike, that man. He helped us very, very much. We worked with him very nicely for at least five years and made wonderful progress.

Before Jesca was taken to prison during Mau Mau, she had some coffee beans that we picked, and she gave a sack to one of our neighbors who was not involved with Mau Mau. Jesca said, "I know ours will be burnt, and you are not involved with Mau Mau, so please take this bag and sell it for me when the people sell coffee."

In 1958, when Jesca knew that I was back, she went to that woman. "Jesca, I sold that coffee, and I have money," she said. Jesca got ninety shillings from that lady. With that, she made me a sack bed, a cot made of sacks, where you could fold it up like what you see in a hospital. With the money she had left over from the bed, Jesca bought me trousers.

All of us left Kaguru in October 1958. People were to return all the *panga*s that they had, but I said, "I will go with mine. I worked with this *panga* unpaid at Kaguru, but it [this *panga*] was very nice. So I'm going to work with it in my *shamba*." I hid it and bought another *panga* to replace it.

In November, I tried to see whether I could get employed, and I could not do it. But Mr. Cumber got me an interview to be the marketing assistant at the cereal board in Meru. Bwana Cumber gave me a hundred shillings to get a pair of trousers for my interview at Nyeri Provincial Headquarters. One hundred shillings! The ones that I had from Jesca were short, so I went to the tailor who was making suits for the DCs and government officials. He was called Mr. Rovel, and he made me the best trousers with wonderful material. Nobody could wear such nice clothes as I had from him.

Mr. Cumber bought me these nice, wonderful trousers. They were the best. It reminded me of the clothes that I had before the Emergency that I shared with my friends.[8] Mr. Cumber is the good one—he helped me to come back into the government. That's what he was telling me. He said, "I will help you 'til you come back again to the government." I tell you, there are some good people in the world, born by women, with wonderful minds. I cannot tell you why, but that man loved me. We had no connection of any sort. I remember the first day that he met me without seeing a beard. He said, "No, I don't want you. I want to see the General." And I was foolish. I was a prisoner, and I did not like to see or hear from him.

He was a very good man, a gentle man. He talked slowly, in a very humble manner. J. C. Cumber—a wonderful, lovely DC. He understood me in a good way, very quickly—rather than Dr. Irvine, who had stayed with me from youth up to maturity. Mr. Cumber understood me twenty times better than Dr. Irvine, who had been a friend forever.

Mr. Cumber hated when people messed with the detainees trying to go home. Some people were released, and then people were not friendly to them, and they quarreled. Some chiefs mistreated people. Especially in my area, people who came to Igoji were laboring in the chief's camp, and they were punished when they should not be punished. The chief can say, "This man is only pretending. He's not fully rehabilitated. He is dangerous to the people. He can continue on and make another Mau Mau." He could put anything on you and accuse you without your notice [knowing], and you will be taken back to prison.

But DC Cumber told them, "Remember that those people have been away for a long time, and they have come through the proper channel. Luckily, you were not detained, but they were detained. Now if you don't think that these are good people, and also you have been Mau Mau, then you can be exchanged with them. You have to give reason why this man is not good. You cannot say only because he has been in detention."

There was [a] jealousy of some sort in families, maybe related to land or wealth. There was a hatred. Some people didn't want their brother to come out or people like me to come out, because when we meant to work, we worked. They were jealous to see us surviving. One of the subchiefs within the area worked very hard that I may lose my *shamba*. He was saying that my *shamba* doesn't belong to me, but it belongs to his friend. But when I came, I beat [refuted] him thoroughly.

Ah—we were termed as animals, bad people. Later on they came to see that some of us who were detained from the forest were living better than themselves because we followed the instruction we were given. They told us to work. But people were not happy to see Mr. Cumber helping me.

I WAS FEARING POLITICS

In November [1958] I went to Kiambu for training to see how marketing was done there. The Gikuyu, Meru, and Embu people still had to carry a pass for employment to move from district to district. The man who is now our secretary of Njuri Ncheke, *mzee* Moses, was the passbook inspector and the DC's clerk. He wrote me my pass. You couldn't move without this permit.

Before I left, the DC gave me a salary advance. They were paying a good amount of money—four hundred eighty shillings per month. I left Jesca with money when I went to Kiambu. Somebody at the cereal board had tried to prevent me from getting employment. I don't remember his name, but he was an old horrible European. He had a very colonial mentality of the Mau Mau. He was not like Mr. Cumber, who had no discrimination. This European didn't want me to enter into that position, but the DC was his boss, so he couldn't do anything.

In January I started my work in Meru at the cereal board as assistant to the European marketing officer, Mr. Cross. We had cereal boards to control our produce—maize, beans, peas, chai, grains, millet. All produce was controlled. We had to sell it to the cereal board, and then the cereal board sold it to the brokers to distribute it. The market was for the Europeans, because they pay you for the produce, but they never let you know the price that they are selling.

So the farmer brings the produce to the cereal board, and there are a lot of charges. You have to pay the inspection fee, whatever fees, then you get [a] very little [low] price. Big trucks of [owned by] Indians will come and collect the produce and drive it to Mombasa, where Arabs buy them. You find a European in every situation. They are manning the produce in the stores. A farmer can never sell it direct to a buyer, no. You could never pass through a barrier even with a tin of that produce unless you have a letter from the boss at the cereal board, because they didn't want anybody to interfere with the market where they are selling those things. That was very direct corruption.

Mr. Cross was very secretive. He used to hide the selling price from me. He locked the price in the cabinet, fearing that I'm going to tell people how things are. I was his assistant, but he could not share the information with me, because the difference in the price that the board was buying and selling [for] was very great. Mr. Cross was too proud. But I could ring to my friend in Nyeri, because he worked at the cereal board there and was the same rank, and the marketing officer was an African. He gave me a copy, although I did not show it to Mr. Cross. They were buying [at a price] not even one-quarter [that] of what they were selling [for].

Corruption. And exactly what they were doing—it turned to our coffee. Nowadays, you never know the price that they are selling [for]. They are still doing it. They saw how the controlled produce was, and it turned to the other side. They are terrible. Stealing, sucking other people's blood—I labor hard but get nothing because my labor turns to be your profit. And somebody ahead of you gets more than you.

The cereal board was in Meru, and we were given a house to live nearby. I could come home to visit Jesca at the end of the month. Even the DC helped me to borrow a *piki-piki* [motorcycle] from a garage in Meru Town.

Very luckily, around this time, I saw Elias Makundi, the very man I left in Manyani. I met him in a market in Thika. Makundi was as big as can be. He was wearing suspenders to hold up his pants. "Makundi!" I said. "Is it you?"

He said, "Now, come now, General, come. I'm Elias Makundi. General, where are you going?" I told him where I was going. He said, "Are you okay?"

"Yes. I am well. This is my lorry." I said I was working as a produce inspector.

I was looking at his shirt, and he was filling it out. He told me, "You see? This is the very one I showed you. Look at it. Anything can come back to normal. Don't worry, you'll be back to normal. We will all go back to normal."

Makundi gave me five hundred shillings, and that was too much by that time. I was very, very thankful. I didn't know whether we could manage, but later I remembered the words of Makundi, "We will all go back to normal," and saw that he was very right.

While I was working, the DC became secretary of the cabinet and went to the State House in Nairobi. He left his position in Meru. Sometime in September 1959, I went to inspect the Chuka Barrier and collect data. When we were crossing the river, the driver lost control of the vehicle, and it fell down off the road. It was about six thirty in the evening, and the driver had had a little beer. In the morning, we went to see if we could get help from the office. The car was pulled up, but it didn't move.

The following day the *mzungu*, this European that didn't like me, got the information that the Land Rover had an accident. He could never speak to me; if he phoned to the office and Mr. Cross was not in, he would not talk to me. The driver and I were both sacked, and I did not complete the year.

Now the same Mr. Cross who would not show me the reports decided to help me. Although we were not so friendly, he advised, "Now, this man has dismissed you together with the driver. You had worked for eleven months and had almost to complete a year. If you finished the next month, you could qualify as an officer, and you were due for one-month leave, and that month is payable. We are going to work it in a way that gets you some paid days."

Mr. Cross taught me good arithmetic, and I got my salary for September plus the payment of the thirty-three days of paid leave, which included some holiday. I received nine hundred and fifty-three shillings in cash, instead of receiving four hundred eighty. With that money I did not come home. I had information that people were splitting timber, so I went straight away to the place where I used to deal in Tigania.

I bought timber for seven hundred shillings. I had only a hundred and something, one hundred and forty shillings, to keep in my pocket. I spent very little from that amount. I squeezed myself. I sold the timber for one thousand eighty [shillings], which was not bad. I made sure that the timber I bought next would be more than a thousand.

I met many old friends still doing the old business. Even some were left there during the Emergency, while we were in the forest. I met my friend called Mutwiri who settled there. He got a wonderful, big *shamba* when we were in the forest. Mutwiri helped me very much. I was staying at his *duka* in Mikinduri, so I had no problem of sleeping, neither of food. People were properly settled, and they sympathized very much with me, the General.

The timber business was still seriously black market. Remember it was not yet Uhuru. Africans were not to get such money as they could get from timber. Our people were fighting to abolish this policy in parliament of one man having three votes. We were not voting one man, one vote. No. One man could have three votes—one for the man, one for his education, and one for his wealth. If a man could get four thousand shillings, he could have another vote in parliament and got more power. Only Europeans and some Indians could have that much money. From timber if you managed to sell two lorries, that could give you four thousand—another vote, so we were not allowed [to sell]. The European voted three times. They were less [in number] than ourselves, but this was the technology they used to multiply themselves. We said no. These persons vote three times only for themselves and not for the country. We said, "One man, one vote."

When I came back I made the same arrangements with my Indian friends, and I employed local people to split the timber for me. I only bought one or two trees at a time, had my people split them, then stored them at night in the shop of Mr. Kassam.

I stayed two months without seeing Jesca. When I came back from Nairobi, I spent one night with her and left her with three hundred shillings. I went with my one thousand shillings, and it took me three weeks to get another [load of] timber to Nairobi. I was also selling the Meru oak; an Italian in Nairobi was making coffins. The Indian shop owners, the Singh[s], bought the timber. Africans did not own shops by then.

I worked in my timber [business during] September, October, and November—by December, I had money. I had over three thousand shillings. That was a lot of money to a man who had been in the forest. I earned [regained] my confidence without people's knowledge. I didn't want any of the chiefs to know that I was buying timber.

One day, on my way from the Indian's *duka*, I spent the night at my friend Isaac's house in Kanyekine. In the middle of the night somebody tried to call me out of that house. They were people pretending to be the Mau Mau. Mwariama was still in the forest by then, and he belonged to that area. They were against the surrenderees like me. They said that we were inviting the Europeans to stay in our country. I told Isaac, "I cannot leave this house. If somebody tries to take me out—just try. You will see that I'm the General."

Isaac said, "Somebody ought to greet them."

"Ah, let them come in the morning; then they will greet me. I know better than yourself," I said. Those were people of the forest. I never knew whether Isaac had [a] connection with them. I never thought they could dare come to that home. But without my knowledge, they had consulted with Isaac.

"Isaac, go if you want, but don't come back into this house," I said. "I have a *panga* here, and we are with your wife. If somebody tries to come inside—ah, I will never let your wife come out. So you try."

He feared. He went back to the people and said, "Leave the General alone."

I did not sleep that night. I was very, very aware. I understood that I was in a dangerous situation. They meant to kill me. But I said, "If they don't get me today, they won't get me tomorrow." I ended my friendship with Isaac and didn't sleep there any longer.

I reported it to the chief: "There's a lot of Mau Mau going on down at Kanyekine. A group of people were trying to call me out of the house from Isaac's home, but I refused. If you contact Isaac, he will tell you whom those people were." The chief didn't take any action. Later on these people were known, and some were arrested.

I was fearing politics because I knew the consequences that I suffered. I was in detention for [a] long [time], and I was tired. I was busy doing my timber [dealing] and had no connection to politics. It is Mr. Mate who forced me back. I used to teach with Mr. Mate at Chogoria, before the Emergency. During the Emergency, Mr. Mate was awarded a bursary to study in Ireland. In 1957, Mate was elected as one of the few Africans in parliament.[9] He became a member of parliament very early.

What happened was that, in 1960, Kenyatta was still in detention. KAU, the party for us all, was fighting for him to be released. But before Kenyatta was released, KAU members said, "We have to elect the officials of KAU." They met at Kiambu, and [Ronald] Ngala and [Daniel Arap] Moi aimed [intended] that they would get big positions.[10] But KAU appointed [James] Gichuru as president.[11] Ngala was treasurer.

Ngala refused. He said, "No, it is we who fought for Kenyatta, not *kina* Gichuru. Gikuyu had no say because Gikuyu were not around [they were detained or in the forest]. It is we who were fighting for the release of Kenyatta. But why did you appoint another Gikuyu to lead the party?"

Ayeeee—Ngala said he will never take the position of treasurer. Moi too. So another group formed. That split into two parties—KANU, the Kenya African National Union, and KADU, the Kenya African Democratic Union. KANU remained with Gichuru, and Ngala became the president of KADU. He was a good leader from the Giriama [people] of the coast. Mr. Mate was very friendly with Ngala. They went to Alliance High School together, so Mr. Mate joined KADU. KADU wanted Majimbo-ism. They wanted a federal government system, like you have in America, where you have states and a national government. We wanted provinces to become like states, and each handles its own affairs, and then you have a federal government.

But KANU did not want to work with Majimbo. With the one-government system in Nairobi, everything goes to Nairobi. The government only feeds where the president is [from] or whatever tribe the president belongs to. All the other areas are forgotten. With Majimbo, states are treated equally because we are all taxpayers. KADU was saying [that] the government should represent everyone and all the areas and provinces should benefit because we are all taxpayers.

KANU was mostly Gikuyu people. It had the support of the Central Province, the people of Mau Mau—that is, Gikuyu, Embu, and Meru.

Although Mate was Meru, he joined KADU because of his friendship with Ngala. And because Mr. Mate was my friend, I also liked KADU.

KANU people were taking oath against KADU. Instead of campaigning, they were oathing that you can never vote for KADU. It was widely known. KANU members were calling it "tea." A big man, [a friend] of Kenyatta, tried to give me "tea." He told me, "Let us go take tea." I didn't fear him.

"No—you are taking Mau Mau!" I said. "You are calling oath 'tea.' Even Kenyatta himself—I can give him oath because the oath I've taken, as a general in the forest, Kenyatta himself has never taken. So who is going to give me tea?" It was true—even Kenyatta did not take the oaths that I took.

The people looked at me and feared. They said, "The General has said no."

With KANU, everything was oathing. I said, "No, I won't go back again to detention because of oath." I had surrendered and confessed everything [and promised] that I will never repeat. If I did the same mistakes again, I would be in prison forever. I would be silly if I were associated with oathing.

In 1962, Mr. Mate appointed me to go to Ghana. By then, Ghana was independent.[12] We were invited by Mr. Nkrumah to attend a meeting there. I wanted to go and could not refuse. We were four KADU people and four KANU people, and I was a delegate for KADU.

I tell you I was happy. That's the first time I got my passport, and Mr. Mate helped me to get it. I was very proud. I still am keeping it. That was March 1962. It said I was a British subject, a farmer from Meru, Kenya. And we had to get the certificate to say that you had the yellow fever vaccine.

We went by the airplane. That was my first time sitting on the plane, but I was not scared. It was wonderful. I was very, very happy. Very, very happy. There was an MP of my age who helped me to pay for the flight. It cost four thousand shillings. We boarded the plane in Nairobi. We had a stop and spent the night in Addis Ababa, and then to Khartoum in Sudan, and then to Kano and Lagos, that's Nigeria, and then to Accra, in Ghana. There was war in the Congo, so we could not go that way. It was a long journey—two days—crossing the continent.

We stayed for a fortnight in Ghana. Mr. Nkrumah called the meeting to reconcile KANU and KADU. He told us [that] we do not have only two parties [in Kenya], because the Europeans make another party. If we [KANU and KADU] started quarreling, we would defeat each other.

"Don't play with these Europeans," he said. "Europeans are strong because they have people and money to back them. If you play, you will struggle longer." He wanted KANU and KADU to become one party, to unite and defeat the Europeans. "Leave your differences and unite together. If you work together, I think it will be an easy thing. All your [partisan] things will be solved after you are independent..

"Say that you have no bitterness, no desire to fight anybody. We are not rich here in Ghana, but we are settling our things, and we are not enemies of the Europeans. We are still with them. Never show any enmity."

Nkrumah was a very good adviser. He was a big man, dictating, somehow like Kenyatta. He was tall, strong, and black, with big lips. He looked like a Luo fellow. You feared to look at him, Nkrumah. He ran a very strict government. We noticed that we were shielded from something, because he did not want us to mix with the local people. The people who were looking after ourselves were ladies and men of the General Service Unit.

Ghana is a state land. Nkrumah didn't introduce the system of individual lands. I think that government works very well in Ghana. They have these big *shamba*s with these big yams which are not like our yams. I don't know where they got that variety of seed.

There was somebody from Tanzania [Tanganyika] who attended the meeting but had to leave right after. There was no flight direct from Ghana to Tanzania, so the shortest route had to go through Britain. I tried to see if I could manage to go with him, because I wanted to see London, but I couldn't. From that a curiosity remained. I said that I must go out and see now not only Africa but other places.

Coming [back] from Ghana and having represented KADU, I said, "Well, I have touched it; now let me become a full member." I became general secretary in Meru region. KADU was a strong party supported by Europeans, but you could never tell in the Central Province. Central Province was for Gikuyu, Embu, and Meru—they were taking the oath of KANU. I was to educate people and campaign for the party—the party which was not violent, not the Mau Mau.

Kanike, the laborer from Jesca's father, was still working for us. People from his Tigania area were harassing him. They said, "You are working for KADU. They are friends of the European."

"Don't worry," I told him. "It is me who will give you money. Let them go. Remain here [and] nobody will touch you." I knew the way that people were looking at me. I had no friends. But I had Jesca, and I had my *panga*.

There was a time when I was taking Jesca home, and [KANU] people were harassing us, and Jesca didn't know why.[13] "You should not worry that people are threatening us," I said. "They don't know what they are doing. Follow me. We [members of KADU] are very big—come and see." I took her to Nairobi for a good week. She enjoyed drinking and staying in the big hotels of Nairobi. I introduced her to many honorable members. When I ran out of money, I went to tell the chairman, who was a friend of mine. I said, "You know, I am here with my wife, and I don't have money."

He gave me a check and said, "Go to the bank and borrow five hundred shillings."

I even saw one of my European friends, Mr. Hilliard. I had told Mr. Hilliard that I wanted to have knowledge of social development. Mr. Mate was sending people to Israel, but he did not select me. I told him I would like to go somewhere else to learn. "I would be very happy to study social services abroad," I said.

Mr. Hilliard said, "Now, if you don't fear politics, my brother, I have got a friend who is one of the big fellows of social service. He will get you a direct connection and recommend you to go to Zambia. The *siasa* [politics] are very *kali* there. You go there for two years and study in a big nice college where you'll learn social services and get a diploma."

"I'll go there," I said, and we arranged to meet again. So during the time that I was in Nairobi with Jesca, Mr. Hilliard saw me. He was a floor above us. He whistled down and said, "How are you, brother?"

Jesca got surprised to see a white man calling me brother. Then we climbed up and walked to him. We greeted one another, hugging. Jesca was very surprised to see us hugging. "Who is he?" she asked. Then I explained to Jesca how we had known one another.

Mr. Hilliard's friend was supposed to come to Nairobi the following day, but, very unfortunately, that man died in a car accident on the way, so the connectivity of going to Zambia ended. But I wanted Jesca to see that she should not get worried when people shout at us. "We are very big—I am a big man," I said. I bought Jesca some nice clothes, and we turned back up in Meru.

People thought it was a joke; they wondered how a Mau Mau general could favor the party of the Europeans, the people we had been fighting against. We said that it was not a competition. We said that Europeans are no longer our enemies. We created friendship with the people whom we fought against. They said that I was bribed to surrender, to turn to the side of the European.

There was even a song about KADU being crucified. They were singing it to me and Jesca. They were singing that Jesca and I will be chased together with the *wazungu* when KANU won. "Okay," I said. "We will follow them." But what I say is that you should never suffer carrying your own cross. Whoever wants to take it will take it. But do not bear the burden. Put it down. If you carry it or don't carry it, they will try to crucify you. So let the people who want to crucify carry the cross.

I saw things early. I saw that all the talk of Mau Mau being compensated—ah, it was propaganda. I'd suffered in detention, and nobody helped me. Why should I go to that side again? No. I did an about-turn. I said, "I'll join the other side now. I'm now with the *wazungu.*"

In Meru there was no KADU, so I had very little to do as secretary. I was fortunate not to work in Nairobi, because there was much to do there. But in Meru, I took great advantage. It was a good time—I was selling my timber, and I had that additional salary of five hundred shillings per month. That was big money, and I used it to make my farm.

After the Emergency, I wanted to come back again and to plant all [of] what I had before. My mind [plan] was to clear the bush. This was all forest. In Meru we were lucky because we had communal lands. The land doesn't belong to the individual; it is community land. No one could sell land, because it is of the family. So they uprooted my coffee—burned my coffee—and took all my things, but they couldn't touch the land. The Njuri Ncheke Constitution protected that. It cares for our Meru Land Unit.

And I knew [that] unless I got back again to the position where I was, when I had nice coffee and vegetables, I could not survive. And I didn't want to cry about it, no. I meant to work. I knew [that] the only thing that can help me is the *shamba.* My business was to farm.

I was trained in agriculture at Kaguru, and that helped me a lot. I knew all the cash crops. In 1961 I had my surplus money from the timber, so I bought a lot of coffee. I planted more than a thousand trees. In 1962, a friend of mine, a very good Gikuyu, was an agricultural officer. He said, "If you plant this Napier grass for the cattle, then I will give you a loan. Plant two acres, I will give you three thousand shillings."

I did it very quickly. Within one rain, I had two acres. He gave me three thousand shillings. Then I bought three grade cattle. They were not pure grade, but there was this *mzungu* who wanted to breed the Friesian that he had with a more resistant one. [The Friesian] had a pedigree, and it could not resist most of the diseases, so he wanted it to become a bit more native.

He hired this Indian bull called Siwo, the one with the big hump, and bred it with his grade cattle to lower the grade so that it could survive. The price was low for mixed breeds—with five hundred shillings I could buy one cattle.

There was a European here called Bowman who was from the Netherlands and worked in Meru. He was a good man, and he came to teach us how to keep animals with zero grazing—not ranching but keeping them together in a house and feeding them there. You plant Napier grass for them. They never look for feeding [in pasture], but you give [it to] them—zero grazing.

So I used my three thousand shillings to buy four cattle, and I was left with a thousand. I used that to fence the area. All this area of mine was fenced. That was 1962. I had already planted at least a thousand coffee trees, and I added some more to make two thousand. That's how I started again earning from my *shamba*. Those three cattle gave calves, and I had to sell milk. The MP [member of parliament] was buying, and the sister of him was buying, at least four gallons per day. I was even selling milk to Njiru, to his wife. Later on, when I returned to teaching, I told his wife, "Do you know how much money you have paid us for milk for your two children?"

She could not recall. I said, "Madame, I'm a teacher. Njiru is a teacher, and you are a teacher. My wife works in the *shamba*. But can't you manage one cattle and see that you feed your children without buying milk? You have given us a lot of money. Don't be silly. I will give you one of mine with a very cheap price." The lady agreed.

I gave her a cattle which was to calve within one and a half months. From there, that cow gave them nine calves. Njiru and his wife were very thankful. All the children that he had grew without buying milk from anybody. Even today, she has cattle.

So within three years' time I was earning from my *shamba*. The work that I did surprised everybody. They wondered where I got that money. They thought that through *kina* Cumber and the *wazungu*, we were getting helped by the government. I said, "You keep saying that, but unless you work hard, you cannot [survive]." Ah, we worked. We helped ourselves, and people know that.

WHO WAS FIRST BECOMES LAST

That meeting with Nkrumah worked in some ways, because when we came back we had a coalition of KANU and KADU. KANU was praising KADU because KADU had pressed very much for Kenyatta to be released. KADU built the house of Kenyatta. Oginga Odinga, the father of Raila Odinga,[14] organized the party to build Kenyatta's home. In 1961 Kenyatta was released from prison, and he took over from Gichuru as leader of KANU.

They said, "Now, we cannot form a government unless there's a new constitution. Where should it be done?" They said it should be done in London, in the presence of the Queen. "We are going to have a government where we harmonize everybody in the country." That's when they went to Lancaster House, where they made the constitution. I remember Mr. Mate was telling me, "When we went to Lancaster House, *mzungu* was number one, followed by an Indian, then an Arab third, and an African was fourth. When we came back from Lancaster House, African was first, followed by an Indian and an Arab, and the *mzungu* was number four." We said it was an about-turn—who was first becomes last.

When they came back, there was [an] election. They had [an] election to see who had to form the government—KADU or KANU? That was the question. We said, "Now let us vote. The majority will form the government." I voted in Kinoro at our local polling place [in May 1963]. I was very happy—*sana, sana* [very much]. We were counting down the days. We felt free to vote and know that our vote will be counted. You mark the name on the paper ballot. First you vote for the presidential candidates, then you move to the next area, you get the paper with all the members of parliament. Then, you get another form for the candidates for the civic positions. If you are illiterate, someone will help you, and an agent will stand there to see whether the person put the tick next to where the illiterate fellow said to do it.

I voted for KADU. Even myself—I was competing for a seat of the Regional Assembly as a KADU member. There was only one KANU man whom I voted for. He was called Simon Kamundi. He was manager of the Meru Coffee Union and a close relative of mine. My mother had come from his family. I voted for him as MP. I saw him later that night, and we had a lot of drinks. He was very sorry because he did not vote for me, and he knew that I voted for him. "Mto, I did, silly," he said. "I have understood from the family that you voted for me, and I didn't vote for you. Now you hate me, don't you?"

I was telling him, "Why don't you differentiate the party and the person? Me, I didn't vote for KANU, but I did vote for you."

We all knew that KADU would be defeated because Central Province was too strong for KANU. Even all the Luo people were for KANU because Mboya was in KANU. All the KADU people in this area were defeated. Mate lost.

We had a coalition government called "Internal Government" and had two flags from June up to December—Kenyan halfway and British halfway—a time to see whether we are able to do the arrangements. There were two big people, Governor MacDonald and Kenyatta, who were equal and checking to see whether we can govern ourselves. Then on [the] twelfth [of] December 1963, the governor said, "Okay, you can do it by yourself," and the British flag was taken off. We got Uhuru. We were no more [a] colony of the British.

On Uhuru Day, we were all friends. There was no KANU, no KADU anymore—we were the government. KADU agreed to join the ministry, and we were given posts. Most of the *askari* were KADU. It was only we [who] were holding up fingers to show that KANU was the party of one government, one man's government, and KADU was the party for us all. But everyone celebrated. We were Kenya, and we had Uhuru.

Even we elected some Europeans. Bruce Mackenzie became the minister of agriculture. Europeans never expected for us to elect Mackenzie. They wondered why Mackenzie was being elected when others were being chased away. Many Europeans left Kenya because of Mackenzie. They thought he colluded with Mau Mau and Kenyatta and was going to take over *shamba*s. There was a lot of misunderstanding between Europeans.

Another European, Humphrey Slade, also remained. He was elected as Speaker of the National Assembly. Mr. Slade never took sides. He said, "If you are *mzungu*, and you have messed [up], say you are sorry. Apologize and say that you have messed [up]. If you continue [old ways]—get out. Leave." So we said let us continue with Mr. Slade and Mr. Mackenzie. They were the Europeans who knew how to farm, and agricultural things should be taught by someone who is a good farmer. They were good *wazungu*.

Each and every party joined the government and had members in the cabinet. The day was wonderful at Uhuru Park. It was colorful with Europeans mixed in—wonderful. You could never see who was *mzungu* and who was African. There were a lot of bands. People were shouting. You could not even listen to the whole speech because of the noise. People wanted the ceremony to end [so they could go and celebrate]. They were only interested in seeing the KANU *bendera* [flag] go up. The other business was for the government, but people wanted to see that the British Union Jack was not flying over Kenya anymore.

We saw a great change when Kenyatta moved. All the people were being cleared away because the president was passing. The one who was greeting and shaking hands now became somebody whom we could never come close to. We had never seen that before. Now the [colonial] governor had no escort. He had to go by himself with the flag. We enjoyed seeing the comforts that Kenyatta had. We could stand on the road watching his motorcade and never know which vehicle was his. We were happy to see how our president was guarded, to see how he is an important man.

Also our cabinet ministers—when Mr. Mate became a minister of health we could hardly see him. Once the cabinet meets nobody was allowed to go near. We came across a lot of differences. We understood more about Independence.

That night in Nairobi there were all sorts of celebrations. Every bar had music, and people danced throughout the night. For us [politicians], we had a party in the State House. It was a farewell party to the British officials. Mate had a lot of beer, and he didn't attend that function. A car was hired, and I entered Parliament with my own car. I was sitting behind the driver like a minister, and the driver saluted the guard at the gate, and we joined the queue.

I tell you, that State House is big. You can get lost there. I was walking around, and you know who I saw? I saw my old DC Cumber. He was surprised. By then I had a suit, and he was very happy. We had a glass of wine, and he said, "Now, I want you to say hello to my wife." So I followed him to another room in the State House. I met Mrs. Cumber. She was talking to another group.

He asked his wife, "Can you remember this man?"

She looked at me and said "No."

"Do you know somebody called the General, from Meru, who is our friend?"

"Oh, yes. I can recall him," she said. We were laughing and greeted one another.

Cumber said, "Look at him! Look how he is. He is exactly like what I wanted him to be." Ah, we shared another beer, and he gave me a tour of the whole Parliament. He was very happy to see that I'm in the government and to hear that I'd even gone to Ghana.

That night, somebody, called Munyao,[15] went with a plane and put the Kenyan flag on top of Mount Kenya. After that long day, he put our flag on the tallest peak, called Batian. It was raining, but he dared to put it on top.

Our tradition was that our God lived on top of Mount Kenya, so [for] any good that came to us, we had to remember him. Our flag was put where our Lord stays. It was Him who helped us to get the *bendera*. People clapped that night on [the] twelfth [of] December 1963.

When I came back from walking with Cumber, it was night, and I was drunk. I left there and did not want any more drink. I didn't see Mr. Cumber any longer after that night. That was my last time. I think he left the country, because someone else took his position. I will never forget him. In all ways, he tried to help me. Although other people tried to stop me, the lovely idea [impression] that Cumber had [of me] helped me to overcome. I wonder if he is still alive. I would take him a very big goat.

That whole week of Uhuru was a good quiet time. There were no rogues. We took [had] a week without any bad incident or quarrels. People were well behaved. And we could go into any hotels in Nairobi, where we could never step in during the colonial time. We were anxious to visit the New Stanley Hotel, the Norfolk Hotel. We could enter into parliament, where we had never entered before. There was a lot of change after Independence. There was no *bwana mkubwa*. Everything Africanized, seriously, and we liked to be Africanized. We had a feeling that this is our country.

Mau Mau changed our living. We said, "We have to fight the Europeans to leave our country. Let the Colonial Office feel it, because we have talked to these people [through peaceful means], and they never felt it." Mau Mau changed our country. That's why General Erskine and the colonial secretary were sent to find out what was happening, to investigate why there were such problems. They found out there were mistakes on both sides. The Europeans were taking our things harshly. They criticized the Europeans: "It is you who imprisoned Kenyatta before consultation."

Any people, whether white or black, can fight because of suppression. If some ruthless people governed you for a long time and prohibit you to keep the standards of the rulers, you can never cope. People will say, "Ah, these people are suppressing us. They don't want us to come to that status they are."

When we struggled with the Europeans, the Catholic Fathers told the PCEA [Presbyterian Church of East Africa] missionaries, "It is you who sharpened the *panga* on both sides—religiously and educationally—and now they are cutting you with the same *panga* that you sharpened." It was true. Catholics were for the religious only. It is only after the Emergency that they gave people education. People of the Catholic areas are still far behind.

The Gikuyu were ahead of us [in education] by twenty years because the missionaries came here very late. Europeans came this way [to Meru] in 1908, but those were [colonial] administrators. Only missionaries came later with education. We had very few primary schools. All the teachers who were here during my primary education were Gikuyu. We had people from class three teaching class two. Not many of us were educated even in Kiswahili.

We have the saying in Kimeru that [if] I'm very weak and you save me in my weakness—after all I will never thank you. I can even abuse you because I'm healed now. Europeans were the ones who educated the people who turned against them, and that is natural. Even the Americans fought. Europeans fought when America got independence not because some of the people were better than the others but because of the ruling, the feeling that "this is our country." Here in Kenya—the colony we became, through the hard rules and the hard labor—we fought. After all you must fight for independence. It's not given.

Now we have to ask, "Why did we fight?" This is the time that we are to heal. After Independence we came to know very many countries and very many tribes, and it is the time now that we can compare. Were these people bad, or is it something that went wrong within ourselves and caused some of these problems? We need a time of healing.

Anything has side effects. The education that we had from Britain is good. We were quick to understand what they wanted. We complained very much, but later on they became our friends. I think the growth that we had is through them. Now the end of war has gone—ah, you forget it. They have helped us. They were the killer, they were the healer.

PART V

WAZEEHOOD

"FORGET THE PAST"

After Uhuru, people became proud to say that they were the Mau Mau, because they believed that it was them who brought independence. We were anxious to see what Kenyatta would do for [the] freedom fighters.

We thought that Mau Mau will benefit, especially from the European *shamba*s or money. We were hoping that we were going to get cattle. Europeans were fearing [this possibility]. They did not know what would happen when Kenyatta took over, because KANU was against the Europeans. But Kenyatta changed his mind very rapidly. He organized a big meeting for the settlers, at a place in the Rift Valley called Subukia. Even today there is a ceremonial [monument there].

"You have been fearing that when KANU takes over, I will kill you, each and every European," Kenyatta told them. "We are not killing you, but we want friendship. We are happy that we are independent, but we don't hate anybody. The constitution that we made protects individual property. We Africans shall never discriminate [against] anybody of color. Whoever says and believes he is African, you will live with us together, friendly, as Africans."

They could hardly believe Kenyatta. "We will forget what has passed," Kenyatta told them. "We know the good work you have done in this country. The only man whom we do not want in Kenya is the *bwana mkubwa*. Whoever feels that he cannot work with black people, he can leave at his own time. Please, we will give him a green card to go. If you work to change from *bwana* to Kenyan people, and you live together brotherly with us— feel free. You remain with your properties, and you will help us as Kenyan people to continue with the government."

"The dark turned to light." That's the words they [European settlers] said. The dark turned to light. They were seeing the dark on the side of KANU, and the good was KADU. But KANU joined KADU to say there was no war between colors. They clapped.

But we were no longer "boys." These people never recognized whether you are grown-up, initiated people. They called us "boy." So we said, "Why don't they recognize us as men, and we recognize them as men?" When they say *memsahib*, know that it is *memsahib* for us all.

Kenyatta said, "So feel free. Do your work. Keep your animals. We are not taking your money, but we are going to buy things." That's like the language Mandela would say.

Europeans were not chased away. Of course that was right. They were the people who had money, and they were paying good taxes from their farms. Even today they are paying good taxes, and the money goes to the government of Kenya. We couldn't live without them, and Africans could not manage those big farms then.

I cannot take your things [simply] because you are European—never. If you want to buy it, you can make an agreement with the owner. There was no time when Kenyatta declared that all *shamba*s belong to the blacks— never. The constitution which rules even today protects personal property. Anybody can acquire land anywhere as far as you're a Kenyan citizen. But *kina* Kaggia and others were not happy to see that Kenyatta turned from African to European.

When he came to us, Kenyatta had a big meeting. "My friends, Africans—thank you very much for the fight you have fought," he said. "We have liberated ourselves from colonialism. But, dear friends, revenging will never take us anywhere. Let us forget the past." That's the word he said. "Let us forget the past. Forgive each and everybody, because it was a brother who was killing you—now let us forget each and every thing. Work together. Live together. And let's go back to our *shamba*."

That's what he told us. Kenyatta made friends with the Europeans. And of course that was right. But with those words "forget the past," it affected Mau Mau seriously. We people who fought did not like the statement that he gave. Those who were detained and struggling together— after being released, they returned to their life. But all the things they had, had been stolen. People suffered. There was no compensation for anybody.

Kenyatta said to go back to our *shamba*s and work. So that's what I did myself. I heard what Kenyatta said. Let me go to my *shamba* and forget the past. In Meru we were lucky. We didn't lose the land. But if your *shamba* was taken, what *shamba* should you return to?

In Gikuyu areas, all of their land was taken by Homeguards, and the government of Kenyatta did not help them. Those who had *shamba*s had nothing left. Their coffee was uprooted. Whoever took the Mau Mau oath could hardly come back to his land. Even today they are in camps. They remain in the big villages where the Mau Mau were put—the very camps they made during the Emergency times. Only the people who could group up and work for a loan could buy a place from Europeans who sold their farms. Otherwise, even today people are spread all over the country searching for a place to live because they lost their land. People returned to be the workers of the Europeans, as they were, but not "boy" now.

In 1963 I was still doing my business of timber, but it was not very promising because it was black market. I knew one day my daughter, Muthoni, would go for higher education because she was clever enough. I was fearing that if I followed this business of timber, I could most likely miss [having] money when she needed it. I decided that it was the end of my timber business, but I never regretted my movement with timber. The knowledge that I earned from that business helped me very much.

It was time for me to join teaching again. Everybody knew that I was no longer Mau Mau. County council, not missionaries, was running the schools. I knew one of the school administrators, and I asked [him] if the Mau Mau were allowed to teach. "The mission chased away all the Mau Mau, but I am in charge now," said Mr. Kinyua. "I think I can employ you in one of the district schools. I don't think anybody will bother you."

The following month I reported to the school, and everybody was surprised to see me. They said, "Are the Mau Mau allowed to teach?" But I met some teachers that I used to teach with, and they welcomed me. I was paid very lowly because I started as a new man, but I claimed later on that I should get credit for the six years of experience that I had before the Emergency. So my salary raised from two hundred and fifty to three hundred and forty shillings a month.

Some people still did not like me and reported false things. "King'ua is teaching during the daytime, and at night he goes for the Mau Mau movement," they said. The chairman of the school talked to me, and I said they were mad [crazy]. I said, "Tell them to get a hold of me when they find me at night attending to this business, and bring me to you."

The chairman was a good man. During the meeting when people accused me of these things, he said, "If this man is teaching our children and doing Mau Mau at night, then get hold of him. You can even beat him. Carry him with you, and we'll put him in prison." Of course they could not.

Two years later I was teaching with Njiru when we saw a man being taken to the chief's camp. He had no clothes and was wearing sacks from the tea factory. We couldn't see who he was, but somebody came and reported that it was Safari. Safari was one of our Mau Mau fellows. We left him in the forest and thought he was shot or killed. We never thought anyone was still living in the forest. We even asked Mwariama when he came out if he had ever met somebody called Safari. He said no.

The men who caught Safari told us the story. I think they were hunting animals in the forest. One man, Kayaba, had known Safari during the Emergency. Kayaba saw Safari clearly, and they walked nearer to him. Kayaba shouted, "Safari!" Safari tried to run, but Kayaba said, "Stand where you are. If you go, we will shoot you!" Safari stood. "Safari! Who are you with? Where are you living?"

"I live alone," he said.

"What for?"

"You know me. I'm fighting for *uhuru!*"

"Eh, Safari, you are not. We are going to take you out." They took him to the chief's camp.

Later that afternoon I went to see him. I asked him, "Don't you know the Mau Mau ended? Uhuru came, and everybody is okay. Even some of the *wazungu* left. Who were you fighting?" He tried to talk [say] something, but I could never understand him. He said he could not find anyone to fight with in the forest. He never knew Kenyatta was president.

I didn't like to see him wearing those sacks. "Safari, all the women hang their clothes outside to dry during the daytime," I said. "Why didn't you come and collect those since they are hanging freely? Nobody would think of Mau Mau. Even when it was serious in the forest, we would manage to get clothes." Safari would come from the forest, a long way passing families and homes, and then steal sacks from the tea factory at night—sacks!

There was an old lady who used to talk about him. She would say, "Safari comes to our home." But nobody believed her. We said this woman is mad.

I said to Safari, "And what were you eating?"

"The food came back in the reserves," he said. "I could come and get food. I took yams from the *shamba*s. I was eating animals and honey." And he was getting fire the natural way, rubbing two sticks together. He wasn't even using a match. He didn't hear any shots, there was no bombing, but still—he was fighting for *uhuru.*

He stayed at the chief's camp for two days, and somebody, his son or relative, got him clothes and took him home. He was not detained anywhere. Safari was harmless. People laughed at him. Safari got lost in the forest for thirteen years, alone, eating honey and talking with animals. I think he was the last to leave.

Safari is alive now, an old man. He moves with a stick because he cannot walk properly. He used to pass here not long ago to attend the meetings for people working to get money from the Europeans for compensation. Safari used to say he will be paid.

You have educated people telling these hardcores that there is an agreement that the British will pay for the people who died in Mau Mau, for wives and children, but they are cheating.

One of our ex-ministers was a lawyer, and he was trying to gather Mau Mau to [supposedly] get their compensation. Today the group is registered, and they have a big union trying to see whether they will be paid because their family was killed by Europeans. People have contributed a lot. Even those who never took oath are contributing—their father was detained, and so he is a son of Mau Mau. It is interesting—today you will be surprised to see my son claiming to be a general of Mau Mau.

I attended a meeting at Meru to find out what these people were saying. I stood up and said, "Do you know me?" They said yes. "You are telling lies," I said. They were saying that the Europeans have agreed that they were going to get millions and that our check is pending at some office. They wanted to take the names from every district who needed to be paid for the Mau Mau, but for your name to be included, you have to pay three hundred shillings or some [similar] amount.

Even my family here, the wife and sons of my brother who died during the Emergency, have contributed. They believe they will be compensated because their father died. I told them they won't be paid. They said, "Ah, Nkungi has money, he has already been given money by the Europeans, so he doesn't want to help with this."

"Continue then," I tell them. That's keeping on of things because they are bitter. People have contributed, and they have died not seeing anything from it. Educated fellows are still cheating them. Don't the people see that those fellows are driving nice cars, bought by their money?[1]

My question is: who will compensate the other one? We burned a lot of European wheat. Many of them have died. Now, if they compensate us for the Mau Mau [Emergency], are we going to compensate them for the damage that we caused? They never count all the things of the people who died [fighting on the other side]. War is war. Germans did a lot of damage to other countries, but I doubt whether they were compensated. No.

To those who disagree, I say, "You were fighting for Kenyatta to become the leader of Kenya, and he became [that]. He gave the direction that we should forget the past and go back to our *shamba*s. Who is beyond Kenyatta?"

I WILL STOP DANCING WHEN I SEE MY CHILD COMING TO DANCE

It was Kenyatta's approach that we planted tea. The [European] KPA, the Kenya Planters Association, would not allow small farmers to plant tea. They said that it will spoil their market. None of the Africans could make a tea farm with the required number of stems or kilos.

Kenyatta formed a body called KTDA [Kenya Tea Development Authority] for small farmers to plant tea. We consolidated the little *shambas* to make one farm. Many farmers take their tea to one factory, and that factory will be equal to one *mzungu* farm. KTDA was formed to compete with large-scale settler farmers to see whether we can do as the Europeans were doing.

Kenyatta assured the Europeans that if we can't get the standards of tea that is equal [to] or higher than theirs, then the KTDA won't let it be sold to their market. Of course, KTDA produced wonderful, good tea—better even than [that of] the Europeans—because it was under terribly strict supervision.

In Kericho, where settlers planted tea, there's a *shamba* which has seven factories in one farm, producing a lot of tea with thousands of workers. They have primary schools and secondary schools within that farm. The owner died, but his sons are running it. They produce tea of any kind—some with the green leaves for Japan—to sell to all the people that need tea in the world. He's allowed to pluck with machines. People tried to resist it, [saying] that it would chase away workers, but he gave one big part to be plucked with machines for the green tea. They planted trees there to use for drying the teas, instead of using electricity. They kept the wonderful environment. There in Kericho you never know whether it is Kenya—you'll think that is somewhere in America.

But the way we planted, once you could afford to plant a thousand stems in your *shamba,* you could have tea. Every factory has field staff to see that the grade is the same, that the plucked tea is two leaves and a bud—they are the soft ones. Good plucking has two leaves and a bud. We have tea of the same kind and same grade, so it's easy to market it. The tea looks like it's from one garden.

We people here who were in the high bracken zones did a good job. The volcanic ash from Mount Kenya created organic matter in the soil. It is wonderful, acidic, powdery soil and [allows farmers to] harvest good crops on the equator.

We were not allowed to plant tea before we demarcated the land. The first thing we were to do was measure the land and agree whom it belongs to. We had already demarcated a bit by planting trees to show the family property. Every thing was measured by these officers, to know the acreage that every person had. Now, if I had ten pieces of land, they were measured separately, and then I was asked, "Do you want the *shamba* to be one? Because this is the time we can move the land around." And I would say yes because for farming, the bigger areas are more productive. We called that "gathering."

In the community we were in agreement to have a lot of acreage for the common lands. For development, we must put schools, markets, roads— the things that will come. We said that everyone should contribute to the common lands. For every twenty acres, you give one. Every twentieth acre that you own will go toward the common lands.

Now, the acres that are cut from your *shamba* create a vacuum in between the *shamba*s. Those portions don't belong to anybody, so the demarcation officer had the knowledge to ask, "Where do you want a school? And the markets? What about roads?" And the people will tell him where they want the common lands. We wanted a big land at Kinoro for the primary and secondary schools and the market, so we consolidated the common lands there and pushed some people who had *shamba*s there to other areas. The acres can float. But you could never move from a good *shamba* to a dry or stony place. The chairmen had to sign and make sure that when somebody moves, the [quality of the] land will be equal to the place you have left.

[Just after Independence,] tea was planted to the other side of the river at Kiangua, but our location here, in Igoji, refused to demarcate [at that time] in 1962, so we could not plant tea. That is how [when] Mr. Mate helped us. I spoke with him, and we approached the officer in charge of demarcating, who was a good African. "These people are behind," Mr. Mate told the officer. "They refused to do the demarcation at the right time, when others were doing it, and now—could you please help them to plant tea, even before they demarcate the land?"

I was told, "Japhlet, now you have different plots of land in different areas. Where do you want to live?"

"I want to live in my *shamba* that has thirty acres," I said.

"Good. Choose the place where you want your *shamba* to be, and the rest of the pieces will come there." If we are planting tea, we do not want complaints that somebody has taken their tea because of the move. So, what we said was, "Choose your *shamba* and then plant tea in the middle. If there will be a move, we'll make sure that it doesn't touch you where the tea is."

So that is how we planted tea before demarcation. That was me and Mr. Mate who convinced the *mzungu* from the ministry that there will be no argument, and the tea will never be uprooted. We tried to convince the people now, "If you plant tea in the wrong place, and you have to move—leave it. Never complain. Because we have clearly stated that there will be no complaints." Of course, some people didn't hear, but we managed. The gathering started in 1965, and the demarcation started in 1966 and '67.

Long ago we had a very nice tradition that if I needed a goat, I could give you a *shamba* of some acres, and you could give me a goat. Very many people bought land through goats and cows. Now, this agreement was very temporary. As soon as I could return your goat, I take back my land. But during development time, we knew that this is a very bad movement. Because during the time when you had the goat, it was very valuable. You could not get a goat unless you cut a portion of your land and sell it to someone else. But nowadays a goat is nothing. It's very cheap. If you want to give me a goat now for the goat that you took by that time—no, I will fight.

In 1956, Njuri Ncheke passed a declaration saying that no matter how little you paid for a *shamba*—whether a skin, for wearing—you cannot return it now. Today we never wear skins, and they are very many, but [at] the time you sold it to me, you could never get it. So you cannot bring that time now. The time remains very important, so the skin will remain very important, as it was. That *shamba* remains your *shamba*.

Njuri Ncheke declared that no matter whether you bought the land with a needle—one hundred acres or ten acres—you can never repay it. You cannot bring a dozen needles, no. The land remains of that man. I think that helped a lot, because otherwise very many people could have revolted and been chased from the land.

This *shamba*, the area where we are now, was bought by somebody. Seven acres—with one goat! My grandfather sold it because he was in an emergency. Very luckily, before the declaration, the man who bought it told me, secretly, "Do you know that your grandfather wants to repay me the goat, and then he will repossess it, but sell it to somebody else?"

He was an old man and a friend of me. "Now, please, never take the goat from my grandfather," I said. "Let me pay you back. This is our family *shamba.*" We made an agreement. He agreed to take forty-five shillings, plus I paid the goat to his son. We did that in the presence of somebody else, so we had a witness. It was serious—luckily, we did that before the declaration, otherwise, my *shamba* would remain of that man because I could not repay the goat. That was wonderful.

So Mr. Mate and I led the team to plant tea before we agreed to demarcation. Some people within the area were not allowed to plant tea because it was said that unless you plant three thousand stems, it is not economical. Some could not afford to buy all those stems, so I offered myself that anyone who could plant a thousand or fifteen hundred stems could purchase [them] under my name. Once you buy the minimum, you could buy any amount. So people within our area planted tea under my name. I wrote out the form and signed that I transferred my tea to So-and-So. Then that person remains with whatever he has planted under his own name. The tea officer agreed to this system.

I planted tea in 1966. I began with five thousand stems. The following year, I planted another thousand for my mother and three thousand for my father. Within two years, I had nine thousand tea stems. The whole seven acres were covered with them. They grew; I pruned them to make the whole farm look like a table, flat so the sun hits them evenly; and in three years, I harvested.

One afternoon, I met Dr. Irvine while I was teaching. He was coming from Nairobi to see how all the people, the missionaries, were. He happened to come to Kiangua, and he said, "Japhlet! Mr. Japhlet, did you come again to teaching?"

"Yes."

"How is it?"

"It is very well."

"I see that you have done good work. You have planted a lot of tea."

"Yes."

"And how is your madame?" I told Dr. Irvine that she was okay. That was all.

Once we planted tea in this area, I was the representative in the board of KTDA. I was the tea district committee chairman. We do everything in committees here. In '67, I became the head chairman for demarcation. That's the time I bought land and added to my *shamba*. From '65, '66, '67, '68—I acquired a lot of acres. The *shamba*s that didn't belong to anybody became within the Ministry of Land. So you could buy land during this time.

I used all the money that I had to buy land. [Eventually] I heard of somebody wanting cattle. I said, "If anybody wants to give me three acres, I will let him choose whatever he wants to take from my six head of cattle." I was hoping for that person to hear me. By that time, the price for an acre was three hundred shillings, and you could get a good cow for nine hundred. I meant to entice that gentleman.

That somebody said, "Repeat it again."

I said, "Do you know my cattle?"

"Yes."

"Go there and choose the best that you want and give me three acres." The following day, he came with his boy. He chose a good heifer with a good first calf. He said, "You give me that one, and I'll give you the land."

"Why not?" I said. "Let's go to the demarcation officer." He went there and signed [over] three acres for me. "Get your boy and come in the morning to take your cattle. If you want milk, you can milk it yourself."

But his acres were not near my land, so we arranged through the demarcation officer that whenever he sees a move [the common lands getting shuffled around], that he will call me. I said, "The lower that you go, the better, because coffee is not good in the altitude."

When there was a vacant place near the church, he squeezed in those acres of mine there. Nobody wanted to take that place, so it became mine, and I planted coffee. I got that portion of land for cattle. I had finished [used up] all the money that I had.

Around this time, I heard that my old chief, Nathan, had bought a lot of tea but had nowhere to plant it. He was from the area below where tea does well. He planted a few [stems], but the rest was rotting. I was thinking that everything was forgotten after Independence, and we were to say hello to one another. So I approached him and said, "Mr. Nathan, I have heard that you do have tea, and it is not planted. Would you like me to pay you back your money, and I can take those and plant them?" At first, he agreed. I told him, "Can you go and count and tell me how many [stems] they are?" He didn't give me the answer.

When I came with money, he didn't agree. So the whole lot of Nathan's tea got dried up. He didn't plant them and didn't let me plant them. His tea was rotting, dried, but he couldn't take my money. So I knew, "Uh-huh, the enmity is still in."

In 1969 I started plucking and was earning from my *shamba*. I meant to farm. By 1970, I had what I wanted.

In 1974, I opened a *duka* for selling beers. At night Jesca and I could sell beer. I had four children in secondary school. We had become poor, and we had to start again from the very roots. It was a hard time, and we were very busy. We knew the way we had to take until we reached where we were before. It was not our will that we lost it.

There was a time when I came to see that my eldest children—Kinyua, Kirimi, and Muthoni—were employed, and they could come and buy beer in the place where we were selling it. They were drinking in our bar. I said, "I don't want us to serve beer for Muthoni. I don't want to have beer with Kirimi, no. This is the place where we can misbehave and quarrel. This is the time for me, now, to leave this. My drinks should be limited."

In Kimeru we say that I will stop dancing when I see my child coming to dance. We have that saying in our culture—when you see the age group of our children is maturing, yet still you are behaving like a young man, then you must stop some of the jokes. Your age group's daughters, are going to dance. I was in a group of our fellow men, and we decided to leave it right then. "Today is the time for conversion," I said. "We have taken all [of] what we wanted. This is our child's time, not our time."

Now also in 1978 my *shamba* of coffee which had been producing over ten thousand kilograms per year gave me seven hundred and twenty-one kilograms. I had a loan, and my coffee—three thousand five hundred trees—gave me only seven hundred and twenty-one kilograms.

When I heard that, I was with Jesca there in the bar. I took a bottle of beer and then another one. I showed Jesca the slip, that our coffee was [worth] nothing. Our coffee *shamba* was bushy with dried branches. We weren't working for it. I asked Jesca, "Have we now come to our end? Does that show that we have settled? Have we forgotten all the times, the way that we came? Is it beer that has made us to forget?" I told her, "This will be my last beer."

I took four bottles, and she took two. We left the place and closed the bar. She was surprised to even see me throwing away the packet of cigarettes.

I said, "I'm going back again to my *shamba*, back to my coffee." That was [at] the end of 1978. In '79, I went and bought five lorries of *mbolea* [manure], a wonderful heap. I bought fertilizers. I bought a lot—more than twenty bags of fifty kilograms [each,] I think. Then back to my *shamba*. I pulled up each and every bit that was bad and put a mug of fertilizer with it.

I remember someone—Kabira—came to visit me. He was campaigning for the seat in parliament and met me in the *shamba*. He thought that I was mad [because I was working so hard]. He said, "General, can I see you?"

I said, "Ah, not now, Bwana Kabira, I will see you later. I cannot leave this place." I employed two people from the other side of Tigania who helped me. The rain followed in April and October. By April 1980, I harvested ten thousand and one kilograms. I cleared all the loan with the first payment. The second payment was my money, but by that time, the whole industry of coffee was collapsing, so I got very little pay. I counted the loss.

We went to the church. With all my life, I've been a wonderful Christian, although I was not complicated by some things in the Bible. When I was a teacher before the Emergency, I wanted freedom, where I could drink and do what I liked. So I was Christian in a way, but I did not want to be tightly linked with conversion things. Even the church people knew. They were pointing at me, saying "*This man*—ah." I had to joke with them. I said, "I have no time to carry the Bible. You read the Gospel, leave me to be a teacher. I cannot do both."

If you mix things, you will mess up. You can find people being very [much] hypocrites. The Pope and Catholic Fathers cannot not have children, but some do have them. Where do they get children from? Heaven? I say that if you decide to be a [Catholic] Father, make sure you become a Father. But if you become [a] Father of religious things and then become a father of children, then you're mixed up.

In 1982, I said, "I have come with the Bible." I learned the story of what Jeremiah the Potter said when he was told by the Lord, "I am the maker." God said, "All my creatures are made from this very clay. And they can be molded into different shapes. If I find one isn't doing as he should, I can smash him to the ground. But then when it grows and takes a different shape, it will be stronger." I liked that people can change shapes and mold to fit different circumstances and times in their life.

With the beer I said 'bye. I was confirmed as a church elder. "Now I have to reveal, to confess all the sins that I had through the beer," I said. "I'm no longer in there. I live for the company of the people." I started now the cooperative movement and joined [committed to] each and every bit of the movement. I corrected all the mistakes that I had done for five years. We became people again.

TOO MUCH OF ANYTHING IS POISONOUS

A family can be like the avocado tree. From the same tree, the fruit of one branch is different from the avocado of another branch. If you taste them, one avocado is somehow watery and without taste, and the other is good and sweet—from the same tree but different branches.

We have six daughters, and none are the same. Even my sons are not the same. Those whom I helped more may be the ones who don't even come to us. Those whom we think are not so attached are our friends who look after ourselves. We never know why, but it's true. Do you know what people want? People want their children to inherit their deeds. In Kimeru, we say, if you are a thief, and your child becomes a thief, then you will be very proud of him.

We have good children as far as I can see. They love us, and we love them. When we call our girls here, *kina* Kaari and others, we enjoy how they talk to people in the public about the way that they have been brought up.

Very, very unfortunately our first two [children] have gone. They were girls, and they have died. During Mau Mau, when we left them, I think they suffered. Muiti, our first lady, our first daughter, after having very many children, she died of this disease, HIV/AIDS. Our second daughter, Muthoni, was very clever. She performed very well and went to Alliance, the best school, where I had wanted to go but could not. But she had mental problems, and we had a hard time to live with her. When she was in the mental hospital in Nairobi, she left the hospital and disappeared. For two days, we never knew where she was, but later on she was found in Nairobi. She was killed by thugs.

We buried them. When our daughters were mature and married, they left their children. During Mau Mau—ah, they suffered.

And you know [my sons] Kinyua and Kirimi are very close [in age]—it was a difference of only six months. In Meru if you get a child with somebody who is not your wife, the child belongs to the father, and you have to take care of that child. That's Kinyua—Kinyua is of that kind. He has a different mother, from the same area where Jesca is from. Kirimi was born in December 1952, and Kinyua followed him in 1953. I was in the forest by then.

When I came back, I went to see the father and brother of the lady. I wanted to know whether the lady wanted to keep the child and make sure the child goes to school, or do they want me to take the boy? It was upon her to decide. I knew we had to educate that boy, because if he goes off, he will be the problem of my family, and I won't be able to help him.

For the first time [at first], she said she wanted to stay with that boy. I said, "I will pay for the school fees, and you buy the uniform." She agreed. Kinyua went to school.

I think when he reached class four, Kinyua became a big boy [thought he was grown-up]. He left school and started roaming with other boys who were not in school. The brothers of his mother called on her and said, "What did you talk about with Japhlet? He does not want the boy growing up not educated. If you want to solve the problem, take the boy to Japhlet."

She agreed. She did not even send anybody. She just told the boy, "Do you know your father's home?" Kinyua said yes. "And so now—go," she said. His school was at Kiangua, and he was with Kirimi. Kinyua came back here with Kirimi.

I said, "Kinyua, what happened?"

"My mom sent me to come here. She asked me to come up. She cannot keep me any longer," he said.

"Okay, then. Stay." Then I went to see the lady. We talked, and she told me the complications. I said, "Okay, now—let me remain with him." We agreed.

With Jesca—women—they don't like it. But Kinyua is her son. She fed him. She raised him within the family—he was never treated different. I was very careful, seeing whether there was a difference that might hurt him. Once you have that sort of family, you must manage it properly. You never like to have any difference between them, but when they grow [up]—that's okay.

Kinyua and Kirimi are brothers. *Kabisa.* You never know whether they're from different mothers, no. In my family, my father adopted two children—where from, I don't know. My elder sister—and she is my sister—was adopted by my father. I was not taught to know anything beyond that. They told me, "That's your sister." That was all. In my family, my mother had only three children, but she fed six. We grew [up] being six, but ours [of my mother and father] were only three. One of my relatives died, and the boy was taken into our family. My father's brother died, and we took his daughter.

In Kimeru, if my elder brother died, I could take the wife whether she has children or not. You keep them at your home. But if I died, my elder brother could not take my wife, because he helped me to marry, and she was like his daughter. My father had one more [child] with the wife of his brother.

Even my grandfather adopted a Maasai child of my father's age, so my father grew [up] together with him, being one family. You could never know who was the Maasai and who was our family. We never have any generation that has not adopted somebody. That's the inheritance [tradition] from Ncurungu's and Muthanya's time.[2] I've taken the same character.

One day, a mad woman passed here with a young girl. She left the girl in our premises and disappeared, so we took the girl, and people wondered. We said, "Let's feed the child. We have enough. We can educate her even. If this woman was mad, and the child is not mad—why should we leave her? Let's keep the child." We adopted her.

She was being called Waithera, but when she came to us, we changed the name. My wife said, "Let's call her Kangai, somebody who has been brought by the God—a gift from God." *Ngai* is Lord, our God who lives in Kirinyaga. So we called her Kangai—a fellow of God, God-brought.

She is our daughter now, making our daughters six. I don't know who is the mother or who is the father, but she is my daughter, and I like her. We educated her, she grew, and now she's employed at our SACCO, married, with two daughters. She is well looked-after, maybe even more than my real daughters, because I fear that people are looking to see how I will raise her. You can never know she's not of us.

When we took her, people said, "Ah, Nkungi doesn't care whether it's a woman or a man. This man is wonderful. He takes even this girl."

I didn't mind what they said. Later on, these people were saying that if there was another mad woman, they were going to direct that child to Nkungi and leave it with me. I asked them, "You have seen the same child. You have seen the woman—why don't you help the child yourself?"

They tell me, "Because not all the people, Nkungi, can do it."

In Meru tradition, you are to respect your father-in-law, and he is to respect you. I could play [joke around] with my father, but not with my father-in-law. My father could tell me to work for him, but if I had to do something for my father-in-law, I had to report to my father and tell him, "I promised my father-in-law that I will help him to do something. Please, could you excuse me, and I will complete your job when I come back from that?" I will be allowed.

But now[adays], I give my son-in-laws cattle. I've given cattle to every one of my girls. Instead of getting dowry, I give [it to] them. I said to their husbands, "I don't want cattle for them. I like you to stay well, rather than getting dowry. My girls were the milkers of my cattle. I want continuity of my girls milking cows. If you don't have a cow, I will give you one." I've never received any from them. I said, "Who is marrying—is it me who you were marrying?"

My age-mates fought for the Independence knowing that if these Europeans leave this country of ours, and we have children with education, they will take over all the work that was being done by white men, and our standard will come up very, very quickly. We fought thinking we will become like those people who colonized us. We never knew that not all the education people get is valuable. We have learned that practically from our children.

We came to understand that when these people go for higher education, they do copy, of course, what is being done by Europeans, by the white people. And when turning back to our people, they try to make their own higher classes. The other day I went to a conference in Nairobi. It was at a wonderful good hotel called the Safari Park Hotel, where all the presidents stay when they meet in Kenya. You can never enter it unless you belong.

I went to that hotel with Mwiti and another friend, and we ordered three bottles of soda. A soda, a small bottle, should be twenty shillings. I was left to pay the bill, and I gave a hundred shillings. The waiter was there, looking at me and wondering what I was doing. "How much?" I said. He told me it was four hundred and fifty shillings. They were a hundred fifty shillings per bottle, for these small bottles of soda—the very ones that you buy outside for twenty shillings. I gave the man an amount of five hundred shillings. So I thought, *What is being sold there is not soda but the class of the people who are supposed to go there.*

The people who want to eat inside do not want to be disturbed by common people. I think it's supposed to be like the Norfolk [in] going there. They put the cost so high that they don't have to mix with you. They want to see their class, how many there are, and then they become friends. That's for people who have lots of money and want to display it.

You find families being very sad because they live on comparison, comparing their lives with other big people. If you eat enough and then if you keep on eating and eating, it will disturb you, like a disease. Instead of being happy, you'll get trouble in the stomach.

If somebody says, "Nkirote is too rich," that "too" is not good. That "too" can mislead you and tempt you to do beyond what you think you can.

Too much of anything is poisonous. One of my friends was telling me when people say somebody is "too good," that means that person is foolish. Why not just "good"? That "too" means she is good to everybody, even to those who wrong her.

Kenyatta was a poor man who was hungry, and he ate too much. He ate beyond what he could carry in the stomach, and I think he died because of that. Once someone has suffered from poverty, no matter how clever, he can change into anything. Leading up to Uhuru, in Mau Mau and after, we were all for Kenyatta. Everybody believed that he had wonderful knowledge, and he would do the best for us. He had lived with Europeans for a long time and had a lot of experience. I didn't know anybody beyond Kenyatta. He was an old man, highly respected. But instead of respecting him, people came to fear him. When he said to forget the past, I forgot, myself. And those people who didn't forget, who went against him, they got lost. He had no sympathy.

Kenyatta spent his life fighting for independence, and he wanted to benefit. He wanted to change the laws that made him fight and acquire very big portions of land. That destroyed his integrity. He keeps the legacy, but we didn't take him in the way he emerged. He forgot the long story that he had and all that he fought for.

The corruption began during his time, and it was very serious. Kenyatta posted all the big Gikuyu people in government positions which paid a lot of money. When it came to sharing the government facilities, we wondered why some of the Gikuyu with very low education were honored to take very big ministries, while there were learned people with more knowledge who were to be assistants to the ministers.[3] All of the parastatal [state-run] businesses like the Kenyan airport authority were led by Gikuyu. Because of the government posts, the Gikuyu had money, and they organized their people to buy the land of any Europeans who wanted to leave.

The Gikuyu were the ones who were educated during the colonial time. Even some of them managed to go overseas and acquire degrees. They came back after the Emergency and bought the big farms in the Rift Valley which were European farms. But the land occupied in the Rift Valley used to belong to the Kalenjin. That's why the Kalenjin became annoyed—it used to be their land, but Gikuyu people acquired the land during the Kenyatta era.

The question is: If a European acquires land in Rift Valley, and he leaves his *shamba* and sells it to me—now, what did I buy from him? The areas of the Rift Valley were called the White Highlands. Europeans stole that land because they had cattle and wheat to cultivate. The *mzungu* never bought it. The land used to have people on it, but the European chased them from the land to other areas. Now what about myself—what did I buy from that European? Did I buy the land or the property? Because this land was not of that *mzungu*. If I bought cattle from Europeans, okay. If I bought wheat from Europeans, okay. But the land does not belong to the European. The *mzungu* didn't buy it from us. So, what did I buy from the European? The property or the land?

The original people who occupied the land are thinking: *You chased me from this land, and you paid nothing to me. You put your cattle on the land, occupied it, whatever you did. I ran away because you chased me away. I was fearing you because of power. Now you want to leave the* shamba, *but you sold it to somebody else, not me. Instead of the land going back to the original people, "black Europeans" came in and took all the lands. When the mzungu left, another black man became* mzungu.

When you go to [the] Rift Valley to these *shamba*s that belong to Kenyatta or Moi, you walk kilometers to the end of that *shamba*, and nobody is there. Most are kept by sons, or others are idle, but you cannot touch them. If the owner wants to sell, he divides it into so many acres and sells to groups who have already organized, and most of them are Gikuyu. In Meru we are least concerned because we don't have land in [the] Rift Valley.

The most important issue in Kenya is land—that's why people are fighting. Kenya is an agricultural country which produces a lot of crops—wheat, maize, pyrethrum, coffee, tea—but all these *shamba*s belong to big people. Even now some people have nowhere to live. They are poor. They can work, but they don't know where to work, because they don't have land. So the time comes to question what to do, and this is where we need judiciary [judgment]. We need proper regulation of the land. In our Kenya we are trying, but it will be a long struggle.

Now the danger is coming with these title deeds. In Meru before, no one could sell land, because it's not yours. It is family land. If you die, you left the land to whoever lives. In my family, my uncles had no sons. My father was the only man, so the whole land became his. This new adoption of title deeds—demarcating, consolidating the land, and having ownership—that's a danger to our community. Because if I want to sell this land, I have got a title for it. If I become poor or something happens to me, I will never mind about the family. I will sell the land, because at my age now the deed allows me to get money. What can we do with these boys who are selling the land after claiming it from their father? We are tied up.

People quarrel because of the *shamba*. I divided mine [my land] according to the number of boys that I had. The chairman of KTDA, Mr. Mutai, told me, "Why are you giving your sons land? Why don't you choose an acre or two, you put your buildings there, and you farm the acres without any interference?"

I said, "My children want to farm, so I'm going to give them portions."

"Now, it seems okay for you to give them portions, but are they going to have sons? They are going to give these small portions to their sons—after all, you'll find that there is nowhere to farm."

The areas we are occupying are good for tea and those big farms. Within a very short time, you'll find no *shamba*. Everything will be houses. These problems can be solved by getting people into towns. All the areas where we live need electricity and water. Choose a good site and let people move there. They have their schools, they have their hospitals, they have electricity. Leave all these *shamba*s for any good farmers who will farm the coffee, keep the animals, farm the tea. And leave the other side to be forest.

NOTHING CULTURE

In our age time, there was no money, and there was no need for money—what for? In some ways money is good because people can change bananas for money. I had no bananas, but with money I can choose the best because the one selling the banana needs money. The banana, no matter how sweet, is only there for eating.

When our fathers had little to feed with, people were very social, very friendly. If my father meant to kill a cow or a bull, that was shared. It was not of one man. We grew together—boys, manhood, *wazee*-hood. Governing was terribly serious. People were naturally disciplined through fear of whatever punishment. The teaching was even harder than Christianity. Once you [commit a] wrong in a way, you could be severely punished. Everybody would know [that] you wronged, and that story will carry on.

I grew [up] in skins, and I would have remained with it. We had no hospitals. We used herbals. We were very few before the Europeans came—very, very few. When Kenyatta took over from the British, we had only five million people. Now we are thirty-five [million].* We were dying in 1919 of hunger when plenty of food was at Embu—just sixty kilometers [away]—but we never knew. And it was difficult to go to Embu and get food and come back again on foot. We are as we are because of the Europeans who came to our country. They did a lot.

But the missionaries told us [that] each and every thing we did was sinful. They said it's not civilized, it's not a good thing—it's evil, as it doesn't relate to Western civilization. Our people who were Athome, the Christians, they left the whole custom of our people and cleared [away] all the traditions we were carrying. They think whatever was done was primitive. They have been bent in the Christianity way, where they had very little learning concerning our country's [Meru] culture. They read from the book but not from our tradition. They refused to pray to our God on Kirinyaga. They have known another God whom we do not see, neither do we know where He lives. They said He lives in heaven.

In our area people ran away from our nice culture with no system and no good leader. We took this white culture in a very wrong way. We did not even know their culture. We mixed our own culture and the other one, and something new came out. Nobody can tell which it is. It's not European culture, not Kimeru culture—I don't know. We call it "nothing culture."

But we're trying to change it *polepole*. We are trying to see whether we can refer our educated people back to the Kimeru traditions. It doesn't interfere with civilization, it doesn't interfere with religion—still, it modifies our life. It brings us back to our good culture. We have come to know that there's no harm with the education of Njuri Ncheke. It is training our people to be ourselves, as our former fathers were. It gives relationship. It gives the friendship. It gives the connectivity of the clans and also the fellowship of the whole Wameru. And I think they are coming now, with understanding, not as they were before.

People ask me, "General, South Imenti has tea, Kirinyaga has tea, Nyeri has tea—but how do you organize these people of South Imenti? They do their SACCO, they take loans, and yet you have some money to invest for other business—put up a building, make a school." I tell them you have to come to South Imenti, to see our SACCO.

---

*In 2013, the Kenyan population was approximately 44 million.

We had very many organizations, especially Meru Coffee, MACU, that is Meru African Coffee Union, and all this has fallen [away]. It was very difficult to reorganize, because [the] people who started it were with very good vision, but the rest who took over were only working for themselves, so the beautiful union of our coffee fell away without a mark.

As chairman, I have wonderful relationships with the members because I never cheat them. When things are bad, I tell them what it is and what we are doing. And we never do any project without their recommendation. I explain to them, tell them what we are thinking and why we are thinking so, and if they allow us to do what we are telling them, it will be beneficial for us and for the society.

With Mwiti and the staff, I say, "Make sure that you put your staff close to the board and close to the people." We go one way together. He's a good teacher, Mwiti. They fear him, and he works.

I was telling these people of the SACCO that if you don't save today, you will cry tomorrow. Because the things that we have are not ours. All the cattle that you have is not yours. All the *shamba* that you think is yours is not yours. There will be a time when even the food that you keep in the store will not be yours. Why? Because you won't be able to cook it. I have cattle, but I cannot milk—neither my wife cannot. So those animals are not ours, because you have to get somebody, and he or she has got a right to take any amount of milk because it is she who milks this cattle. You cannot fetch water even from the pipe. You cannot wash the plate that you are going to eat with; neither can you cook in the kitchen. With the meat I buy from the butchery, Jesca gets somebody to cook it, and she can eat any part of the meat that she wants. My things that belong to me are not mine—they are of other people.

In a meeting, I called together three people of my age, and I called Kimathi [in his thirties], the driver of our tea SACCO. I asked the SACCO members [hypothetically], "We are seeking employment. The three of us want one thousand shillings each, and we are going to pluck your coffee. Now, there's also this gentleman Kimathi, but he wants three thousand shillings. Whom will you hire?"

They said, "Kimathi."

"You are very right," I said. "Kimathi will pluck the tea or pick the beans of coffee and then carry them to the factory where they are needed. We ourselves who are old want to sit. These three people are out of date and don't have anything. Nobody wants our service. We voluntarily will work, but nobody will employ ourselves. We have to find our own means of feeding."

We've changed greatly through the cooperative movement. Our SACCO is doing very well. In 1998, I went on a ten-day trip to India for a SACCO conference. The trip was organized by the Ministry of Cooperatives. They said, "The old man from South Imenti, the Meru one—let him go." India has good planters of tea and harvests a lot. I went to see their tea plantations and how they managed their tea in South India, called Tamil Nadu, just next to the highlands.

They have people who do research to see which clone [tea strain] can give more tea. If one doesn't do well, they pull it off and plant a new one—to see which can give the best tea. They use tractors and machines to uproot [old plants] and plant the new. To us, that's very difficult to uproot and plant because we are doing things manually. With them, they are very advanced, even more than Kericho. I have never seen any [plant] being uprooted in Kericho for a new clone. Only I've seen them do it at Del Monte,[4] on the way coming from Nairobi. When the pineapples become old and give little fruit, they plow it, manure it, and plant new crops.

In India, they use machines to pluck. Also, they are plucking four to five leaves, so the grades that they have—they have all the grades, the first, second, third, and poorest grade. But they use it all, even the lowest grade, because Indians are very many. They consume more than three-quarters of the tea they produce. They sell a little tea to China, and they use the rest.

They differ from ourselves because we grow tea and then don't drink tea because we have finger millet porridge and other things to drink. We only grow tea for selling, and the same applies to coffee. Our market is controlled by the buyers, not the sellers. If you know that I don't use tea, then you can buy it at any price because you know that whatever price you give, I will sell it. Otherwise, I won't get money. So in India, they are getting money because they sell tea to themselves. In their market, the price is more stable according to the need of the tea.

If you have money, you can put up your factory even if you don't have tea. You are allowed to buy tea and process it if you wish to, and the farmers will sell their tea to you if you have [a] good price. In Kenya, once you are qualified and registered as a farmer and you comply with all the market rules of the KTDA, then you can have your own factory. But everything is regulated by the government. We farmers could never sell direct to a buyer—no, it must go through the KTDA.

India plants tea in the very highland areas with funny roads. It took us almost an hour to climb up, and it was very steep. We went with [by] *matatu* [minibus], and I was not comfortable, because it was so steep. In the area on top they had nice old gardens and a nice hotel which Europeans built.

Also in that place I noticed—ah, they have slaves. Up to this day, they are people with the very low caste. You know Indians have castes—the lower caste, the middle one, and the top, big people. The lower caste, men and women, they are the pluckers of tea and also the people who work in the factories processing tea. They go with bicycles. There's another group that manufactures the motorcars and machine spare parts. They are good people who move with the *boda-boda* [motorcycle]. There are very many bicycles for the lower castes, *boda-boda* for the other group, and the motorcars for the best, the *bwana mkubwa*, who owns the lands and the factories.

We were told that they have been that way, and they will die that way. It's difficult to move from one caste to another. It's graded [such] that you cannot move. Even schools—I don't know whether the locals go to school. It's terrible. The people are the same color but different castes. But [in] the worst class, they have black people, even some blacker than myself. Only you can notice they are Indian because of their soft hair. You will never believe whether they are Indian. You believe they are exported there from somewhere. They are completely slaves. You wonder. They were [under] British rule too, but the British didn't bother with them. They left the very traditional castes as they were. But when you go to the market, you see good, clean, white Indians. They are the owner of the *shambas*—some are as white as yourself [with blond hair].

I believe that Jesca and I have been living better than most of the people that I see. We live happily. We have lived in cooperation. I'm not telling you that Jesca and I didn't fight. When there was a mistake, and we can't come to a compromise, we could shout to one another, even use our hands, but we compromised. We had to sit and say why. We quarrel ourselves, and we reconcile ourselves. Nobody has ever had to listen to [mediate between] us.

Murithi was asking me, "When you and mother were taking drink, you quarreled and even fought, but we never knew in the morning why you quarreled. How did you live this way? How were you reconciling?"

I had to explain to him. I said, "Murithi, Jesca and I—we do not joke. We laugh, but we do not joke, because with joking, I may mean one thing, and she understands me another way. If you heard us fighting, whatever night, whether drunk or not, and in the morning, you never hear of it again, it is because we came to reason: Why did we fight? It is because we had a little to drink, or did you mean something? Instead of joking, why don't we speak as grown-ups as we arranged from the very beginning?

"If we wronged, then we apologized to one another. We asked who made the mistake. I could say sorry to Jesca if I have wronged [her]. And also, I preferred her to do the same. We came to an agreement, and we forgave one another."

I told Jesca, "The way that I am born, you won't ever change me. Leave me alone, and I will leave you as you are born. But as we do the common good, let us agree to our living. People say that you change over time. If you see that the character which has developed is such that we cannot fit to one another, then you have to decide." The thing which is dangerous is this: If men and women are new to one another, one can hide his character when he meets the other one. They pretend. People cannot keep together when they convert to different things every day.

Before marrying, say what you can do. Say, "I can only scratch where I can reach. Do not make me scratch on my back where I told you I could not reach." You find money interfering with relationships: "Now you want me to get some type of car, but when we met I told you I had a bicycle. You can ride on the back, there is a seat for you if you want. And when I'm tired, you should pedal. But this car business—ah."

There is nothing harder than two people trying to understand one another. If you understand one another, then you know each other's problems, and that makes you sensitive. Life becomes easy if you understand the problems.

Now Jesca complains that she has a lot to do, and I tell her now, "Instead of doing all these things, why don't you get people to help you? Get people—we have money!" I told her what an old man named Manyango told me: a story about an animal here called the *nkari* [anteater]. The *nkari*, when it is young, has long nails to dig [with]. He can make many big holes to look for ants to eat. But when [he] grows old the nails become weak, and he cannot dig into the ground as he used to dig. So he will be looking for ants in the holes he already dug. He gets what comes to those holes— ants or whatever—because he cannot dig new ones. From Manyango, we learned how to make holes during our youth time because we knew there would be a time when we could not.

Youth is the time to run. There will come a time when you see another group of people running ahead, and they are not your age group. You'll be left behind. That time will come automatically—never call it. If it doesn't come, work. That's what we read in the Bible. Work during the daytime, and the night will come.

But Jesca has never agreed that there are people that can work better than what she can do. She followed what her mother was doing. Every day, my mother-in-law was selling bananas in the road. Every day. One day, I asked her, "Supposing I bought all of your bananas today, right now, would you go home?" She told me she would go home to get more bananas to sell.

If you find Jesca in the house sleeping, then I must take her to the hospital. She is sick. She can complain at night that she is sick, but when it comes to the daytime—*polepole, polepole*—she disappears to go to the *shamba*. If she takes off her head scarf, you see a big mark [scar and indentation] across the forehead—that is from plucking, carrying the basket. Sometimes Jesca would be leaving the house, and I say, "Where are you going?"

"I'm not going anywhere," she says. When you go [to the fields], she is there. When it's raining, I say, "Jesca, why are you going?"

"No, I just want to see something," she says. Then she goes plucking. She comes back and tells me she plucked twenty kilos. Eh.

Finally I said, "Now, Jesca, you cannot continue plucking the tea as you are doing. You used to pluck thirty kilos in a day, and now you see that you only pluck ten or five. Leave it. I am older than you, and I will be joining you. Anything that you find you cannot do, tell me, and we have money to employ people. Don't think that I'm not farming because I am not with energy—I am! But we cannot manage this *shamba* ourselves, whether we like it or not. But we can use the money that we have, save a little from our work, and we will live."

She didn't believe me that we had enough money for other people to work. I told her that if she didn't believe me, she could open her own account. I said, "Why not open your own account, and when you want money, you will be seeing yours?" So she has her own account, and she never likes me knowing anything about it. She has lived that way. We got someone to work in the kitchen to do all the house chores. Jesca said, "I will go to my section and pluck tea, sell my eggs, sell the vegetables, work in the *shamba*—get somebody to work in the kitchen, and I will pay her salary and go with some too." That's a little arithmetic.

EPILOGUE

Now Is the Time I Prayed to See

When I had my first grade cattle, I told my father that we no longer needed a bull to serve [them]. I said, "They are not ordinary cattle, as we used to keep. My cattle will be served by a man who will come with the semen in a syringe and put it inside the cow. My cow will calve like that."

"I will come and see," said my father. So I called him when the veterinarian came, and my father saw how the man did it. "I will believe it when I come and see the calf that will be delivered," he told me. Then he left. After nine months, I called him during the daytime. "My cattle is calving," I said. "Now you come and see."

My father came straight away. The calf was with brown spots. My father looked at it and said, "Now, is this the heifer that was put [in] by the man's hand?" I said yes. "I don't want to jinx it, but if this is the method that we are following, where we can get calves from the cattle with no bull, I doubt whether your daughters will be getting married." Then he went home.

My mother was fearing to take the milk of that animal, because the cow was served by the man. But my father said, "No, no. Bring the milk. I saw the calf. It is exactly like the others. You can never tell whether it is a man's cattle put there by hand." And my mother had to follow and drink the milk as my father did.

My father knew that I was keeping different cattle, and he changed. When I meant to do it again, I called him to see, but he didn't bother. "I know what will happen. I have seen the first one, now you continue." He was satisfied, and he didn't follow me anymore. What I mean by this story is that we have to change. We have to change as things are changing. Can I live as my father and mother used to live? Never. I cannot live as my father lived; neither can Murithi live as myself. We have things in common. The handling of life is the same, but the life is different. You live in the situation that you meet.

You never believe how changes come. You're wondering about it, and things have already changed. But the young people never believe. They never recall any experiences from before. The youth are only seeing what is in front of them. That is natural. You never know what is behind you. You can tell somebody, "Unless you tell me what is behind me, I will never know." Old people know how things were.

The old people and the young people—they are parallel all the time. They never come close, and they're not supposed to, because of the age, or the mind—whatever it is, they are wired differently. It is useless for an old man to argue with the youth that he is not foolish. You yourself never agreed that old people were not foolish. Why do you want somebody to do what you did not do? You have to leave the child to grow and wait and see, because the time will come, and he will be referring to the story himself without anybody telling him, "Ah-ha! My mother was quarrelling with me, telling me this and that, and I never knew the way she was seeing it." He will have the very same story.

I talk to my sons and daughters who are grown up and married. "Your children are calling you '*mzee*,'" I say to them. "Be careful. If you knew that I was foolish because I was *mzee*, now you have taken the name. You are with me. Are old people as foolish as you thought they were?" If God keeps you, and you have time to see your grown-up people, you can become friends. *Kina* Kaari and Kaimuri—we are friends because they have seen their boys grow, and they can understand now.

When you are young it is the time that you can work, like the green leaves of the banana tree. The banana leaf, when it is young, is green and shoots up. Then it gets old and falls over, becoming very dry. We call it *kiragara*. You can use it to light the fire. There will be a time that you fall the other way and won't stand up straight again. I couldn't understand that until 1965. There was a high jump at the school where I was teaching. From the very beginning, I was doing high jump. I told my students, "Watch me. I'm going to do the high jump with this young fellow here, and I will show you how expert I was in that." I jumped, I don't know how many feet—I didn't even go four feet six inches—it took me a month to recover, with all the muscles aching. I could not move the following day. I regretted it, and I did not dare tell them what I did. I said [to myself], "Is this the time now that I'm becoming old?" I never knew whether the leaf had gone the other way—I thought it was still standing up. So youth changes, without your knowledge. All the strength that I had has gone. The places which once moved are stiff—the oil, or whatever it is, has gone.

Just recently I went to a meeting in Nakuru for the SACCO conference. On the last day, the committee organized a dinner. It was in a big hall, and they said, "We are going to dance." They put on a record of an old man called Kibaka, which was a dancing record of the Twist. Kibaka was during the 1940s. They said, "This is an old dance. Now we have the General here—he's the one who is going to show us how it was done." They wanted me to dance with a woman from Kiambu, the manager of the SACCO there. She was a young lady but not very young.

We had to open the dance together, me dancing the Twist with that lady. I knew how I was dancing in the old days, but when I tried to move— ah, I laughed, even myself. I could never move the way this lady was moving. From the young, green leaf, I have curled the other way to *kiragara*. Even today, some people are telling me, "Ah, General, you look like a young fellow." But it is me who knows who I am.

One of Jesca's friends told me, "Mwalimu, this is not a good time for us. If the time comes for somebody to be taken outside because he cannot move, then he waits outside until he is taken back in again—what is that for? It is like clothes put on the line outside, and whether they are dried or not, they cannot say that they are ready to come back [in]."

I called my children together not long ago, and I was telling them I don't fear death. "Baba, don't say those words," they said. I said, "I'm saying them because, for my own, I have done what I meant to do."

At eighty-seven [years old], why should I be driving? It is because I have work to do, and people want me to perform it, so I'm helped by God. Even I am happy because if I were idle, I would have gone very early. Once you are busy, you never become old, because you have a job. I have learned a lot from the countries where I have walked. Anybody can die anywhere, is it [right]? Death has no home. It is within one's body.

I'm very thankful to God. He brought me through the fearful stages, in the forest during Mau Mau, and I don't fear the remaining time. Now is the time I prayed to see. We try to tell these young people how we went to the forest, and they think that we were mad [crazy]. I'm telling you, they don't understand. "What made you to go there? What was in the forest? Who were the people whom we were fighting in the forest? What were you eating?" My grandsons could never survive one day in the forest. They can hardly understand the situation, how we could fight in our country. They never know whether the Europeans were all over here. They think the country was just as it is now, where people are getting weapons from

Somalia or Congo, whatever—you know, smuggling. There was none of that. Back then all the territories were European. There was no aid from anybody for Kenya. Mau Mau had no supplies—no help—from anywhere.

When I went to America [in 2006], I visited Mugambi in Georgia. He took me to a wonderful place, a mountain where the Americans were fighting during the [Civil] War. It was called Kennesaw. I was very happy to see where the American people fought, and I was trying to see whom these people fought with. When I saw that forest and the people there, I understood even the Americans had Mau Mau. I was shaking my head. In that big hill, I thought, *This is the real Mau Mau.* You see? When misunderstanding comes, people fight. So I think in Kenya, it will take time, but we are settling our things.

ACKNOWLEDGMENTS

This book took many villages. In Kenya, only the gracious cooperation of the General and the Thambu family made this work possible. Most especially, thanks go to Murithi, who provided me with every kind of logistical and personal support and convinced me that his father's life could and must be written. For keeping me in touch with the General despite the miles between us, thanks to Patrick Mwenda, IT director of Yetu SACCO, the South Imenti Tea Cooperative. For Kenyan hospitality and nourishment in many forms, I give thanks to John Mwiti Rukaria, Njiru, Chief Moses, Mwalimu Murithi Nyaga, Reverend Nyaga, Reverend James Kireru, Mama Bernice, Murithi Itunga, Julius Mwenda the *boda-boda* driver, Winnie, Mutwiri, Robert Kimathi Trappes-Lomax, and Wilson Mugambi Arimi.

In his acknowledgments in *Facing Mount Kenya,* Jomo Kenyatta wrote, "I owe thanks also to my enemies, for the stimulating discouragement which has kept up my spirits to persist in this task. Long life and health to them to go on with the good work!" I am thankful that in producing this book, I have encountered far more friends than enemies, though I agree with Mzee Kenyatta that criticism comes with many benefits.

Several careful readers of this manuscript provided feedback that helped me improve the story in ways I had not known were possible. I thank Peter Wood and Lil Fenn, who showed me how to organize the manuscript using the "sausage method" while sitting together at their kitchen table in Hillsborough, North Carolina, snacking on vegetables picked fresh from their garden.

To Hugh and Jocelyn Trappes-Lomax, who always paired criticism with a compliment, except when correcting my Kimeru misspellings and informing me that pineapples do not grow on trees—thank you.

I am indebted to Jeff Fadiman for writing the best book on Meru history and for always answering my calls when I was trying to write this one. Thank you, Susan Williams, for giving me the sage advice to get out of the way and let the General tell his story, and for saying it so kindly.

Mel Konner steered me toward the late Marjorie Shostak's brilliant books on the !Kung San people of the Kalahari Desert and believed in my ability to follow in her footsteps, in another part of Africa. Dr. K, your confidence meant everything to me.

Professor John Mason introduced me to African history in his undergraduate course at the University of Virginia. I am grateful that for our final exam, "Dr. J" asked us to write an essay as if we were Nelson Mandela crafting a letter from his cell at Robben Island to a comrade in the ANC. For your guidance at every step along the way, I thank you. Furthermore, it was you who showed this manuscript to Joe Miller and the editorial team at Ohio University. There could not be a more congenial home for this work. For the care that you have given to every last letter and punctuation in these pages, thank you to Nancy Basmajian, Sally Bennett Boyington, and Beth Pratt. Thanks to you, Joe Miller, and to you, Dave Robinson, and to my ultimate editor, Gill Berchowitz, for your hard work and your unstinting faith in this book. Thanks, too, for introducing me to Brian Balsley, cartographer extraordinaire, who created three outstanding maps from the rough ideas of a writer born without a sense of direction.

To Theodore "Dr. Ted" Rosengarten, thank you for writing "All God's Dangers" and for introducing the world to Ned Cobb. For sifting through my first messy pages and (somehow) responding, "This raw transcript is the source of all literature," I am indebted. In early drafts, you read for the message, then in later drafts, you were the most demanding stickler on form. That is how you inspire young people: Sort out the form after the idea gains confidence. To Dale Rosengarten, thank you for your positive energy and for your most thorough copyedits and for your investment in young people. I am grateful to be just one beneficiary of your belief and of your freezer full of ice cream.

I am grateful to Brussels Airlines for providing two tickets to Kenya so that I could return with photographer Mary Beth Koeth last December. If you are looking for someone to tell a story through pictures, you will find no better collaborator than Mary Beth.

To my brothers Pat and Eric, and my sister, Marisa, whose postgrad successes should have intimidated me right into graduate school, thank you for encouraging me to take the dirt road less traveled. I thank my mother, Muriel Patterson Huttenbach, for always "getting" this project and for giving me an infinite reserve of emotional support. You provide me a model to live by, one that I can only admire, because emulation would leave no time to write. To Granddad, Maurice Lee Patterson, thank you for writing letters and for telling me bedtime stories that made me appreciate the art of storytelling. By now, I hope you and the General have met. I thank my father, Dirk Huttenbach, for never failing to point out how valuable the work was—and how little money I stood to make from it. Thank you also for turning down the marriage proposal of the Zambian tour guide who offered you a brewery in return for me.

To the Satterlee family—Randy, Tom, Lauren, and Megan—for providing a space for me to write this book in Daytona Beach and to the Strachan family—Marijke, Russell, and Anneke—for your love and financial support, thank you all. To my fellow traveler Texys Morris, who suggested the crazy African backpacking adventure that led me to the General, I am grateful for everything except that Ethiopian meal.

Many people contributed in diverse and significant ways. Among them, I want to acknowledge Lindsay Tabas, Jessica Musick, Todd Kreidler, Thom Hartmann, Lynn and Larry James, Lisa Stockard, Clarissa Caldwell Foster, Jonathan and Abby Rosenthal, Kaitlyn Gentile, Daisy Ames, Cliff Hopkinson, Patty and Jim Fulcher, Ali Peyre, Ginette Prosper, Doris Dobrani, Christine Tunnell, the Vavasour family, Jessie Vossekuil, Karishma and Samir Naran, Rich Wilbur, Gregg Worley, Michelle McGreevy, Chas, Rachel, and Chuck Crawford, Emmakate Young, Katherine Fraser, Oto Ukpong, Yve Huttenbach, Barbara Huttenbach, Anna Westbury, Megan Wilson Stover, Katie Denny, Kerry Conant, Suzie Perry, Hadi Irvani, Ashley Morrow, Maxwell Bonnie, Judy Blase, Bill and Barbara Bear, Denege Blood, Alastair Newton, Jacqueline Sandberg, Lindsay Eriksson McGookey, Harry Clarke, Bieke Claes, Ashley Barnes, Carlin and Rafe Rosengarten, Courtney Cherry Ellis, the Arnetts, Robert Koehler, Ben Tan, Tanya Bhatt, Jim and Nancy Katzoff, the Elliots, Congressman John Lewis, Larry G. Deitch, Pat and Bob Brown, Ted Conover, Anne McNamara, Jocelyn Lebow, Brittany Fayard, Shannon Melton, Janet Silvera, Elizabeth Blase, Glenda Teabo-Sandoe, Markus Weisner, Anna Whitlow, Kitty Ganier, Alice Shin Thomas, Maria and Jennifer Thompson, Kenny Leon, Jason Setchen, Bailey Barash, Michael Diebert, and Mitchell Kaplan.

I end my thanks where I started, in Kenya, with the General, who never scolded me for what I did not know but commended my desire to be taught. Thank you, General, for teaching me that "people are people" and if we all share a common purpose, it is that "we live to learn." *Ibwega*, General.

JESCA AND THE GENERAL'S CHILDREN AND GRANDCHILDREN

Name	Year of Birth
1 Beatrice Muiti	1948 (deceased)

Children:

George Mbae
Bernard Mutegi (deceased)
Gaceri Kiria (deceased)
Gitonga Mboroki
Mwiti Mboroki
Karimi Mboroki
Murimi Mboroki

2 Susan Muthoni	1950 (deceased)

Children:

Denis Njeru
Robert Munene (deceased)
Alfred Murithi (deceased)
Muthomi (deceased)
Jeremy Mutwiri

3   Simon Kirimi
(Wife: Catherine Kainyu)   1952

Children:

Dominic Mutembei
James Kirema
Erick Kimathi
Purity Mukami
Kellen Kajuju

Simon Kirimi (children, cont.)

 Morris Mawira
 Martin Murithi
 Joel Bundi
 Doreen Kathambi
 Benson Mucui
 Tyson Muthugumi

4 **Frederick Kinyua**
  (Birth mother: Gladys;
  Wife: Catherine Murugi)   1953

  Children:

   Winnie Karimi
   Betty Gatwiri
   Brian Muthomi

5 **Rosemary Mugure**
  (Husband: Dunstan Miriti Mbae)   1956

  Children:

   Timothy Mbae
   Edith Gatune
   Ann Jesca Karimi

6 **Betsy Kaari**
  (Husband: Francis Mburugu)   1959

  Children:

   Kenneth Muriungi
   Paul Mwenda
   Rehema Joy Gatwiri

7 Florence Kaimuri
   (Husband, Rev. Martin Mworia)   1961

   Children:
      Nancy Gakii
      Ann Mwendwa
      Kellen Gatwiri

8 Jeremiah Nyaga
   (Wife: Medrine Gaceri)   1965

   Children:
      Elosy Nkatha
      Timothy Mwandiki
      Micheal Mwenda
      Bramuel Mwirigi
      Peterson Mwaki
      Lorna Monah Ngugi
      Judith Kainyu
      Ibrahim Allan Nkungi

9 Palmer Murithi
   (Wife: Zipporah Njambi)   1967

   Children:
      Jessica Kawira
      Timothy Mutai
      Phoebe Nyokabi
      Billy Mwiti

10 Dorothy Kangai
   (Husband: Paul Mwenda Ikiara)   Adopted 1976

   Children:
      Nelly Gakii
      Sharon Mwende
      Philip Mutembei

ABBREVIATIONS

CID	Criminal Investigation Department (also referred to as "Special Branch")
DC	district commissioner
DO	divisional officer
KADU	Kenya African Democratic Union
KANU	Kenya African National Union
KAR	King's African Rifles
KAU (pronounced "cow")	Kenya Africa Union
KCA	Kikuyu Central Association
KTDA	Kenya Tea Development Authority
MP	member of parliament
PCEA	Presbyterian Church of East Africa
SACCO	Savings and Credit Cooperative Organization

NOTES

Introduction

1. "Kenya: The Oath Takers," *Time*, June 13, 1960.

2. Robert Ruark, *Something of Value* (New York: Pocket Books, 1957), xi.

3. The Gikuyu, or "Kikuyu" as the British wrote the name, are the largest ethnic group in Kenya today, at 22 percent of the population. The General's ethnic group, the Meru, share some traditions with the Gikuyu. Both are Bantu-speaking, and both descend from ancestors who entered the Kenya area from the west around 1000 BC. The Luhya (13 percent) and the Akamba (11 percent) are other Bantu-speaking groups in Kenya. The second-largest ethnic group in Kenya is the Luo, who descend from ancestors coming from the north in southern Sudan and live mainly in the rolling hills around Lake Victoria. Other Nilotic-speaking groups include the Kalenjin (11 percent) and the Maasai (2 percent) pastoralists in the low dry plains of the Rift Valley. In Kenya's desert northeast live the Cushitic-speaking Somali, Borona, and Turkana peoples, related to others in Ethiopia. These three ethno-linguistic groups—Bantu, Nilotic, and Cushitic—are as distinct from one another as Latin-, Slavic-, and Germanic-speaking peoples of European origin.

4. "Contrary to public perception, only thirty-two European settlers died in the rebellion, and there were fewer than two hundred casualties among the British regiments and police who served Kenya over these years. Yet more than 1800 African civilians are known to have been murdered by Mau Mau, and many hundreds more to have disappeared, their bodies never found. Rebel losses were far greater than those suffered by the British security forces. The official figures set the total number of Mau Mau rebels killed in combat at 12,000, but the real figure is likely to have been more than 20,000." David Anderson, *Histories of the Hanged* (New York: Norton, 2005), 4.

5. Jomo Kenyatta quoted in Caroline Elkins, *Imperial Reckoning* (New York: Holt), 360–61.

6. Mwai Kibaki quoted in Wanjohi Kabukuru, "The Truth behind Britain's Mau Mau Payout," *New African*, July 2013, 23.

7. Our initial interviews took place shortly after the 2007/2008 contested presidential elections, when violence broke out in areas of mixed settlement like the Rift Valley, where Europeans had occupied land. In the election's aftermath, 1,200 people died and 500,000 people were displaced.

8. In Meru naming tradition, the first-born male and female are named after the paternal grandparents. The next-born will be named for the maternal grandparents,

followed by great-aunts and great-uncles. Naming is according to the character or actions of the person. For instance, a child can be named "Muthomi," a boy who likes to study, or "Kawira," a hardworking girl, if their relatives demonstrated such qualities. If a child dies, the next child born will be given a nonhuman name like "Kiura" or "Kirugu," meaning frog or banana, respectively, in an attempt to confuse God so that He does not take away another baby. One man at the General's church was called Mzungu because white people, it seemed, always live long, healthy lives.

9. Though the Kenyan shilling is the national currency, the General often spoke in terms of dollars.

10. James Olney, *Tell Me Africa* (Princeton: Princeton University Press, 1973), 5.

11. The Yetu Sacco Society was formerly called the South Imenti Tea Growers SACCO.

Part I: How I Grew

1. "There was a poor tradition that if you get twins of the same sex, you only take the first one," said the General. "The other one was not taken as a child. Twins were only known as boy and girl. This was a dirty thing that we were doing. It is good that we stopped it." In this case, though, both twins died of natural causes.

2. The Carrier Corps was an organization of African porters created by the British to assist them in fighting the Germans in East Africa (modern-day Tanzania). The name came from the work of the corps, which was to carry supplies. "Thousands died from exhaustion, hunger, and disease. The diseases they brought home spread through Meru, killing thousands more." Jeffrey A. Fadiman, *When We Began, There Were Witchmen: An Oral History from Mount Kenya* (Berkeley: University of California Press, 1993), 390.

3. The Magadi Soda Company, located eighty miles southwest of Nairobi, is the largest soda ash—sodium carbonate—manufacturer in Africa. Soda ash is used in the manufacture of glass, detergents, and industrial chemicals.

4. Salty tears stung the open wounds, teaching girls not to cry.

5. Indians, from the subcontinent, were brought to Kenya as indentured servants in the late 1880s to build the railroad from the coastal city of Mombasa to Lake Victoria in Uganda. Later, many Indians became shop owners and employed Africans.

6. "Born into a communal tradition, they felt that justice came not through punishment but reconciliation. To merely whip or jail the guilty failed to reimburse the victim. Both might then harbor resentments so intense that their conflict emerged once more." Fadiman, *When We Began*, 192.

7. In "Colonizer's Logic," Nigerian poet Chinweizu wrote, "These natives are unintelligent— / We can't understand their language" (*Invocations and Admonitions* [Lagos: Pero, 1986]).

8. "Each stoning was preceded by a 'prayer song,' sanctified by generations of use, imploring everyone who sympathized with the offender to come forward and 'buy him.' Should someone stand forth, he could shield the offender from execution by placing cows between the judged and his judges." After the prayer song,

"the stoning could begin only when offense had been given so often that no one in the whole community stepped forward." Fadiman, *When We Began*, 267.

9. The African tradition of taking oath was abhorrent to missionaries. For a civilized alternative, Christians presented people in Meru with the Bible. In one interview, a Meru elder, Reverend Kireru of the Reformed Baptist Church in Chuka, said: "The problem has been that Christians say that traditional oaths are sinful. They say to put your hand on the Bible and repeat words. That's why we have people in court [today] who speak lies. They never believe in what they are holding, so the oath on the Bible doesn't bind them."

10. Ernest Carr was a successful British contractor living in Nairobi. He offered to bankroll construction and chose Chogoria as the site for the new mission, which had a nearby waterfall that could provide hydroelectric power and irrigation. Carr offered the missionary post to his daughter and new son-in-law, Dr. Clive Irvine. Fadiman, *When We Began*, 237.

11. Class five, also called standard five, is equivalent to American fifth grade.

12. Kithinji likely suffered from what was called yaws. Dr. Irvine used an arsenic-based medicine called Galyl to treat the disease. Fadiman, *When We Began*, 240.

13. Colonial officials, however, did not take note of the name change. Issuing his *kipande,* they used "Kithinji." Nowadays, he explained, "we don't have Mto names any longer. The boys now don't follow this tradition. They keep the names of their mothers along with the baptized name and the father's name."

14. Embu did not suffer famine in 1940. "It rained in Embu, I don't know why," said Mr. Thambu. "Even today sometimes it rains in Embu and does not rain here."

15. In one interview, a Meru elder, Reverend Kireru, pulled out his Bible and read from Leviticus 11. God told his people, "These are the beasts which ye shall eat among all the beasts that are on earth." Only cloven-hooved animals that chewed their cud were to be consumed. Pigs were "unclean." People must not mix dairy and meat. Reverend Kireru elaborated on many Meru beliefs that coincided with Jewish practices.

16. Also known by its acronym, KAR, the King's African Rifles was a British colonial regiment composed of East African soldiers. During World War II, KAR fought against the Italians in East Africa, the Vichy French in Madagascar, and the Japanese in Burma.

17. The General traveled to Israel in 2001.

Part II: Black Market

1. Alliance High School was founded in 1926 by the Alliance of Protestant Churches. Located twelve miles west of Nairobi, the school was the first secondary school in Kenya to accept Africans.

2. The Kamba people are a Bantu ethnic group living in eastern Kenya, known for their dancing, agility, and athletic ability.

3. The vernacular method uses one's mother tongue instead of the official national languages, Swahili or English.

4. Bernard Mate (pronounced "MA-tay"), an age-mate and friend of the General's, would be elected as one of the first African members of parliament in Kenya in 1957.

5. Chiggers are tiny mites that burrow into toes and itch until removed.

6. Known as the year when men ate thorns, *mpara ya kiaramu*, the 1919 famine was a result of a two-year drought beginning in 1917. The Meru population, already weak with famine, drought, and dysentery, were defenseless when the worldwide influenza struck in November 1918. Colonial records estimate that more than 10 percent of the Meru population died as a result. Fadiman, *When We Began*, 258.

7. Pyrethrums are chrysanthemum plants that are dried and used to make insecticide.

8. Some 75,000 Kenyan soldiers were shipped across the Indian Ocean to fight for Britain in the Far East. Kenyan soldiers of the Eleventh (East African) Infantry Division joined Indian, British, Australian, and West African soldiers to comprise the Fourteenth Army (also known as the "Forgotten Army") in Burma.

9. On March 14, 1922, the British arrested Harry Thuku for being "dangerous to peace and good order" and held him for deportation. Africans took to the streets in Nairobi to protest. Crowds swelled to over seven thousand, and police opened fire. Looking on from the terrace of the Norfolk Hotel, white settlers reportedly joined in the shooting. When people dispersed, at least twenty-one Africans, including four women, lay dead. Anderson, *Histories of the Hanged*, 16.

10. Johnstone "Jomo" Kenyatta, KCA secretary and founding editor of the monthly newsletter *Muigwithania* (*The Reconciler*), would be elected prime minister in 1963.

11. Thuku had encouraged Kenyans to burn their *kipande*s. He led protests for the restoration of Gikuyu land and against the hated hut and poll taxes. Thuku was exiled to Somalia without trial.

12. Regarding the land issue, Chief Koinange headed an official delegation to London in 1931, and the British created a land commission. "Kikuyus wanted the land that had been taken from them for European settlement to be returned, amounting by their own estimation to some 60,000 acres. . . . [T]o prove his case, Koinange took the commissioners onto the European farm in question, identified the site of his grandfather's grave, and had the bones exhumed in front of the disbelieving commissioners." Nevertheless, in 1934, the commission "decided to confirm existing European title." Anderson, *Histories of the Hanged*, 22.

13. From the Hindi word *sahib* (master) plus *ma'am*, *memsahib* was used to address white women during colonial times.

14. The Nanyuki bar was the Sportman's Arms. These businesses are still in operation.

15. Eliud Mathu was Kenya's first African Oxford graduate and the first African member of the Legislative Council in 1944. Anderson, *Histories of the Hanged*, 29.

16. Known as Meru oak, the species *Vitex keniensis* is not of the oak genus.

17. There are other explanations for the origins of the name. One of the General's friends said that "Mau Mau" was an acronym for Mzungu Arudi Uingereza,

Mwafrica Apate Uhuru—Let the European Return to England and the African Obtain His Freedom. Another plausible explanation comes from forest fighter Karari Njama, who wrote in his autobiography, "The first African who disclosed the secrets of the society at Naivasha police station told a European officer, 'I have been given MUMA,' an oath. The European being neither able to pronounce or spell MUMA correctly, created his own pronunciation . . . Mau Mau." The Naivasha trial that Njama mentions took place in May 1950. Nineteen Africans—seventeen Kikuyu, one Maasai, and one Kisii—were accused of administering an illegal oath that bound its followers to a certain secret "Mau Mau" Association. The name stuck. Later that year the government banned the "Mau Mau Society" as an unregistered, and therefore illegal, organization. Barnett and Njama, *Mau Mau from Within*, 53.

18. A World War II veteran and militant trade union organizer, Bildad Kaggia served as KAU secretary. He would be arrested with Kenyatta in October 1952 and put on trial at Kapenguria.

19. Mau Mau assassinated Chief Waruhiu on October 7, 1952. The government's top-ranking African civil servant, a devout Christian, and an outspoken critic of Mau Mau, Chief Waruhiu represented Britain's model African, even being dubbed "Africa's Churchill" by London newspapers. Mau Mau supporters rejoiced at the news of his death. Elkins, *Imperial Reckoning*, 35.

20. Tom Mboya was a popular Luo leader and trade union organizer.

21. In northern Kenya, Kapenguria was a closed district where "visitors from Nairobi or elsewhere would require a government permit in order to attend the hearing," thus allowing "the government to hamper the KAU in organizing Kenyatta's defence by refusing permits to certain lawyers and delaying the issuing of documents to witnesses for the defence." Kapenguria also "gave the government a far greater degree of control over how it would be reported and represented in the media." Despite thin evidence, Kenyatta was found guilty of leading oathing campaigns and "having preached the gospel of Mau Mau violence to his followers." Kenyatta was sentenced to seven years "in the dusty, dry heat of the prison camp at Lodwar." Anderson, *Histories of the Hanged*, 62–63.

22. Two people on the government's black list managed to escape before Operation Jock Scott—Dedan Kimathi and Stanley Mathenge fled to the Aberdare forests and directed armed resistance there.

23. Tom Mbotela was murdered on November 26, 1952. He was found lying facedown in a puddle near the Burma Market in Nairobi. Following the discovery, the police burned down the market. Elkins, *Imperial Reckoning*, 38.

Part III: The Forest

1. General Martin's real name was Isaac M'Ithinji. General Simba's was Moogi.

2. Also known as the Aberdare Mountain Range, the forests of Nyandarua were 150 kilometers west of Mount Kenya. Thousands of Mau Mau fought in Nyandarua.

3. The General is still haunted by his memories of women taking higher-level oaths. He would begin talking but stop short, shaking his head and clicking his tongue against the roof of his mouth, because his reflections seemed too troubling to say aloud.

4. *Kugera ngero* means "to cause grievous harm."

5. Jesca recalled a similar story: "[My husband] left just before dawn and within minutes the colonial solders were at my doorstep. I was really scared because I thought for sure they had met the others, and they were coming to arrest me. It was at this time I realized God really must have loved the Mau Mau because if they didn't meet each other that day—it was a miracle."

6. According to the General, the ranks of the forest fighters followed British military designations. "When you first enter, you are a constable, an *askari*. Then you have corporal, which was the lowest rank, then a sergeant. From sergeant, you go to RSM—regimental sergeant major—then captain, captain major, lieutenant, followed by general and full major general." Each promotion had an additional oath ceremony, and nobody could attend the officer meetings without being ranked. The frequency of meetings depended on events: "Whenever there was an event, there was a meeting. If a big man surrendered within the camp, the leaders have to meet to know the changes that you can make. If a big man is killed—a chief of a *mzungu*—then we have to meet to know where the [colonial] army is going to search. There was a protocol line, and we always had people in the reserve, loyal to Mau Mau, who could give us good information. If there was a meeting of big people around Mount Kenya, the secretary was there to take the minutes."

7. Waruhiu Itote, fighting under the nom de guerre General China, was captured on January 15, 1954, as he was moving between Mount Kenya and the Aberdares. Having already been in the forest for nearly two years, China was said to be the leader of over four thousand men in the Mount Kenya region. He, too, had gained military experience while fighting against the Japanese in World War II. "China's capture caused great euphoria amongst the British, who were starved of positive news," wrote historian David Anderson. The British intelligence team arranged for a white settler, Ian Henderson, who spoke fluent Gikuyu, to interrogate China. Though originally sentenced to hang, China received an alternative proposal from Henderson: "Would China help to offer a surrender deal to the Mount Kenya armies? The Governor [Baring] would pardon China if he agreed." China was convinced "to write letters to instigate a process of negotiation," and on March 4, 1954, "Baring announced to a startled Kenyan public that General China had been pardoned." From intelligence gained through China's cooperation, the British waged war more effectively on the Mau Mau forest armies. Anderson, *Histories of the Hanged*, 232–34.

8. "The stock itself was fashioned from the wood of the Muthiti or Thirikwa tree, which never cracks under any weather conditions. The barrel, generally made from water pipes, was fastened to this, and a smaller pipe or piece of iron, one which would fit smoothly within a barrel, was used as a hammer. The

hammer was released by a mechanism built out of a barbed wire spring and a piece of car or bicycle tube." Waruhiu Itote, quoted in Clough, *Mau Mau Memoirs*, 149.

9. The British conscripted soldiers from within Kenya and other parts of Africa—especially the Somali and Turkana and people from Uganda, Tanzania, and Mauritius—to fight in the King's African Rifles brigade.

10. Jesca recalled, "The government had their spies, so it was extremely hard for us." Late one night, a group of men came to her door claiming they were Mau Mau and needed food. Jesca had a feeling she was being set up, so she refused to let them in. The men broke down the door, demanded dinner, and said they would return in a few days to collect further provisions. When they came back, they used the coded Mau Mau knock, but Jesca said, "I'm sorry, but we do not open the door for anyone. Please leave us alone. You remember even the last time, you broke the door. We don't entertain anybody, I'm sorry. We cannot open." Through a small hole in the wall, she watched as the men reported to an officer carrying a gun in the distance. Coming back, the men said, "Okay, sorry—if you don't want to open the door, okay." The following day, she was arrested.

11. On the day of her arrest, Jesca sent the two elder daughters, ages five and three, to her mother-in-law's home. She kept their baby son, Kirimi, who was still breastfeeding, in her arms. At Kisumu Prison, the jailer ordered her to get rid of Kirimi because "prison was no place for a baby."

"But he is one year old," she pleaded. "How can he possibly survive without his mother?"

She was allowed to keep him in her cell until an intestinal infection sent her to the hospital. "It was probably the *ugali* from the jail that was not good," she said. When she returned, Kirimi wasn't there. She prayed that he had been sent back to her mother-in-law. "I had no way of knowing where he was. I would always pray and tell God, 'God, I know—I don't pray that I find those kids to be in good health, but let me find them alive.' When I came back and found them, I cried because of how they looked, but I remembered my prayer to God. It was true—the only thing they had was life."

12. Jesca recalled, "[The colonial army] pulled down our house and used the timber and the materials to build the chief's camp at Igoji, where we were finally detained." After losing her home but before being arrested, Jesca said, she "moved to the mud hut that we used for our kitchen. After some little time, they burnt the hut, too, so I moved in with a friend with my three children. I just prayed a lot."

13. Most sources cite March 26, 1953, as the date of the Lari Massacre.

14. "Herodian swore that he would kill my children," recalled Jesca. "My son Kirimi would be killed because his dad went to the forest. He [Herodian] said that when he became chief, he would be throwing maize on the ground for us, and we would have to peck at it like chickens. He was very cruel. Of course we told the Mau Mau in the forest about this."

15. General Kassam passed away at ninety years old in August 2011.

16. King George died on February 6, 1952, when his daughter, Princess Elizabeth, was vacationing at the Treetops Lodge in Aberdare National Park. She returned to England as Queen Elizabeth II.

17. In a letter to his wife, General Erskine wrote, "They [the white Kenyan settlers] are all middle class sluts. I hate the guts of them all." He blamed a "rotten administration" for Kenya's troubles. The country needed not just martial law but real political reform, "a new set of civil servants, and some decent police." Erskine quoted in Anderson, *Histories of the Hanged*, 260.

18. A good friend of the General and current treasurer for the South Imenti Tea SACCO, Njiru had two brothers who fought in Mau Mau.

19. "There was a big campaign to try and urge him [General Nkungi] to come out," said Jesca. "Homeguards and the British came and got his father, Baba King'ua. They would go in the Land Rover with a loudspeaker and drive into the forest. His dad would be shouting to implore his son, 'Please do come out of the forest. If you don't come out, these people have decided now they will come and kill you.'" When nothing happened, the *askari* took Jesca and her sister-in-law to Nkubu to do the same. "They put us in a Land Rover, and we would comb the forest, calling loudly on the loudspeakers, 'Please, come out of the forest. It's very important because if you don't they will kill you.' We did that for two days. On one of the days, they told me, 'Now you—your husband is not coming out, so we are going to leave you in the forest with this loudspeaker. You keep shouting—at least he's going to have mercy on you, and most likely he'll come.'" Jesca looked at the soldiers. "Over my dead body," she said. "I'm not getting left here." They took Jesca back to Nkubu.

Part IV: Uhuru

1. Jesca said that her children "were in bad shape. Kirimi of course was the worst because without milk and no good substitute diet, he was with a bloated stomach and anemia. Muiti was okay but was heavily infested with lice. Muthoni was the better of the three. She had a bit of scurvies, an infection, but it was not so bad."

2. *Ferangera* was likely pellagra, a deficiency disease caused by a lack of Vitamin B or protein and characterized by dermatitis, diarrhea, and mental disturbance. It is often linked to overdependence on corn as a staple food. At detention camps in Kenya, "high incidences were reported for dysentery, diarrhoea, [and] pneumonia, and for deficiency diseases including scurvy, kwashiorkor, and pellagra. These conditions indicate serious shortages of vitamins in the diet. Pellagra was the most common, especially in the larger camps. . . . The prison authorities noted Vitamin A deficiencies among many inmates, but also observed that the improper preparation of the maize consumed by prisoners might have been a principal cause of pellagra." Anderson, *Histories of the Hanged*, 320.

3. The screening teams designated a suspect's allegiance to Mau Mau through a color scheme. "'Whites' were clean and repatriated to Kikuyu reserves," while

"'greys' were considered more compliant oath takers and sent down the Pipeline to ordinary work camps in their home districts, and 'blacks' were the so-called hard core who went up the Pipeline for softening up in the special detention camps." Elkins, *Imperial Reckoning*, 135–36.

4. Kimathi was hanged from the gallows of Nairobi prison on the morning of February 18, 1957. "In the final tally, the British hanged 1090 Kikuyu men for Mau Mau offences." Anderson, *Histories of the Hanged*, 291.

5. In 1959, Mboya organized the Airlift Africa Project, together with the African-American Students Foundation in the United States, through which eighty-one Kenyan students were flown to the United States to study at American universities. A notable recipient of their scholarships was Barack Obama Sr., father of future American president Barack Obama.

6. Mugure was a result of his visit with Jesca right after General Nkungi left the forest. The Catholic Father had given them a private room.

7. The Agricultural Ministry gave them scholarships.

8. The General still has the pair of trousers that DC Cumber gave him. Holding them up to his waist, the General said, "Look at it! I am funny in these ways. I have been moving with them throughout all the houses. I like remembering the way I came. I took them to be washed the other day. I tried to make them fit me, but they couldn't." They were at least three sizes too small.

9. Bernard Mate was one of three MPs elected from the Central Province. J. G. Kiano and Jeremiah Nyagah were the other two.

10. Born in the coastal town of Kilifi, Ronald Ngala graduated from Alliance High School and Makerere University and became a teacher. In 1957, he was elected to the Legislative Council and accepted the position as secretary of KAU. Daniel Arap Moi had served as a member of the Legislative Council for the Rift Valley in 1955. In 1967, he served under Kenyatta as vice president; in 1978, he succeeded Kenyatta and became the second president of Kenya, ruling the country until 2002.

11. James Gichuru was a founding member of KAU in 1944 and acted as president until Kenyatta came back from Great Britain.

12. Formerly the Gold Coast, the West African country of Ghana achieved independence from Britain in 1957 under the leadership of Prime Minister Kwame Nkrumah.

13. "No one would buy my milk," recalled Jesca. The General's alliance with KADU made it difficult for her to sell or buy anything in her community.

14. Raila Odinga became prime minister, elected in 2008.

15. Kisoi Munyao, famed Kenyan mountaineer.

Part V: Wazeehood

1. On June 6, 2013, after decades of denial, "Her Majesty's Government in Britain took an unprecedented move by settling out of court a case that was filed in 2009 by five Mau Mau veterans" for reparations from the Mau Mau Emergency. Though more than five thousand people have filed claims for compensation, the

General did not intend to. Quotation from Wanjohi Kabukuru, "The Truth behind Britain's Mau Mau Payout," *New African*, July 2013, 23.

2. Ncurungu is the General's great-grandfather, and Muthanya, his great-great-grandfather.

3. "While the Gikuyu could easily be described as the most exploited group of Africans in Kenya, at the same time a tiny minority of them would become among the greatest beneficiaries of colonial rule." Elkins, *Imperial Reckoning*, 19.

4. Del Monte Kenya Ltd. produces and processes 250,000 metric tons of pineapples and 20 million liters of juice per year. It employs six thousand people and is located on the outskirts of Nairobi. The pineapple plantation spans five thousand acres. The General often bought a supply of pineapples there on his way from Nairobi back to Meru.

GLOSSARY

Aindi	Indians (Kimeru plural).
amerikani	Swahili word for unbleached calico. See also *shuka*.
askari	Soldier, guard, or policeman.
baba	Father.
barabara	Road, street, or path.
bas	Stop, enough.
bendera	Flag.
boda–boda	Motorcycle taxi.
bushy	Uncultivated land with weeds and scrub.
Bwana	A respectful title, usually designating authority, like "Master." Africans were expected to address white settlers as "Bwana." *Bwana* can also refer to a priest.
Bwana Mdogo	Little master. Africans were expected to address white children in this manner.
Bwana Mkubwa	Big Man.
chai	Tea.
chapati	Flat Indian bread.
dawa	Medicine.
duka	Store, shop, or stand.
fulani	So-and-so
gicee	The hut where the circumcised young man goes to recover in the month or two following the procedure.
gikama	An oath whereby the accused has to carry a hot piece of iron to prove his innocence. Also a tool for branding livestock.
gikunia (or *nkunia*)	The hooded informants used by the British to identify suspects.

gitambaa	Synonymous with *shuka*, a white sheet or loincloth, a headscarf or handkerchief.
*hoho*s	Peppers.
jambo	"Hello," or "Greetings!"
juju	Grandmother, grandfather, granddaughter, grandson, great-aunt, or great-uncle (used in addressing an elder), niece, or nephew.
kabisa	Completely, entirely, wholly.
kaborio	Homeguards, the loyalist colonial army.
kali	Root meaning is "sharp," as in *kisu kikali*, "sharp knife." It usually means hot, happening, strong, or fierce.
kibanda	Little hut.
kidogo	A little bit.
kina	Common Swahili word that precedes a person's name; it literally means "people such as."
kipande	An ID card or passbook that the colonial government required Africans to wear around their necks in a metal tin in order to get employment or move from one district to another.
mabati	Corrugated iron sheet.
machege	Chains, handcuffs, or leg cuffs.
majimbo	A federal system of government.
matatu	Public minibus.
mbaya	Bad.
mbolea	Manure.
Memsahib	From the Hindi word *sahib*, "master," plus *ma'am*, *memsahib* was used to address white women during colonial times.
miraa	The leaves from this plant, *Catha edulis* (grown mainly in Meru North in the regions of Igembe and Tigania), are a stimulant; it is also called *khat*.
Mto (or M')	Mister (or Mr.), used to address a man after he has been circumcised.
muga (or *mugo*)	Traditional healer.

mugwati	The person appointed by the family who cares for a young man just after he has been circumcised.
Muindi	Indian (Kimeru singular).
munanda	Cattle dip.
murani	Warrior or young man who has been circumcised.
murithi	Herd boy.
murogi	Poisoner or witchman.
mwalimu	Teacher. This is also used as a title attached to the name to address a teacher respectfully.
mwiriga	Clan.
mwonyo	"Sweet water," mineral water. There is a well-known spring not far from the General's home, the water from which (like other *mwonyo*) can be used to calm stomach problems and soften hard vegetables when cooking.
mzee	Old man. This is also a respectful form of address for a male elder.
mzungu	White person, European, or foreigner.
Njuri Ncheke	The highest council in Meru, the Council of Elders, on which the General served as chairman.
nkunia	Hooded informants used to identify Mau Mau suspects in the detention camps.
nthuki	Age group, peer group, or age-mates.
nyama choma	Roast meat or barbeque, usually goat.
panga	Machete, used for digging, planting, and clearing the bush. A common tool in rural Kenya. During Mau Mau, this was the most common weapon.
piki-piki	Another word for *boda-boda*, a motorcycle.
pluckers	Tea pickers or harvesters.
pole (pronounced "pole-ee")	Sorry.
polepole (pronounced "pole-ee, pole-ee")	Slowly or gradually.

riika	Age group.
rupiah	Currency from India; nowadays the term is used to mean two shillings.
salama	Peace.
sana	Very much.
sema	To say.
shamba	Farm or garden.
sharia	Law or laws.
shuka	White sheet or loincloth, which resembled a toga. *Amerikani shuka* includes the Swahili word for "unbleached calico."
siasa	Politics.
stima	Electricity.
thigu	A game in which a child fits a pronged stick over a tire or rim of a tire and runs behind the tire, pushing it to keep it upright. For girls, it can also be "hula hoop."
ugali	A Kenyan staple, ground maize-meal porridge, cooked into a thick paste like grits.
Uhuru	Freedom, Independence.
Wathome	Christian (negative connotation).
wazee	Old men, old people (plural of *mzee*).
wazungu	White people, Europeans, foreigners (plural of *mzungu*).
Whey!	"Wow!" or "Goodness!" or "You wouldn't believe!" or "Oh no!"

FURTHER READING

For readers wanting to learn more about the time and place in which the General lived, I am including this selection of books from which I have learned a lot, with brief comments on how these various works "converse" with the General's life story.

Dreams in a Time of War: A Childhood Memoir, by Ngugi Wa Thiong'o (Pantheon, 2010), Kenya's most celebrated author, is a beautiful chronicle of the author's childhood near Limuru, northwest of Nairobi, Kenya, in the late 1930s and early 1940s. Thiong'o, born sixteen years after the General, grew up in a compound with his mother and his father's three other wives. His recollections of Mau Mau are gleaned from what others have told him or what he has read in history books. Though he clearly recalls conversations with family members, teachers, and older acquaintances, his reporting on Mau Mau for the most part is shrouded by a "mist" (a word he uses several times) in his memory. "The events," he admits, "were largely abstract, happening in a misty land far away, like a story in a distant landscape, alternating between dream and nightmare."

Histories of the Hanged: The Dirty War in Kenya and the End of Empire, by David Anderson (Norton, 2005), is a well-researched, tightly written account of a teetering colonial government that employs all the military and propaganda assets at its disposal to preserve a social order that is slipping irretrievably into the past. Using court records sealed to previous researchers, Anderson turns the tables on the oppressors and puts the colonial authorities on trial, depicting the British as ruthless aggressors in a "dirty war" directed from the highest levels of state. The author comes close to achieving his goal of writing the definitive history of Mau Mau, but at a cost: the nonexpert, non-African reader may get lost in a maze of acronyms that punctuate the lengthy narrative. And for all its success in profiling the colonial government and the white settler community, the book leaves the Africans themselves rather faceless. Still, Anderson's insights into Mau Mau as a rebellion not just against the colonizer but against traditional African leadership, and into British propaganda tactics—largely successful to this day—of deflecting attention from British imperial aims and exploitative white settler culture to the brutality of Africans toward their own, make this the book to go to for a picture of the complex setting and reputation of the Mau Mau.

"If Africans were left in peace on their own lands," Jomo Kenyatta speculates, in *Facing Mount Kenya* (Random House, 1962), quite possibly the finest ethnography ever written by an African president, "Europeans would have to offer them the benefits of white civilization in real earnest before they could obtain the African labour which they want so much." Kenyatta wears many hats in this literary anthropology of his people, the Gikuyu, who likely suffered the greatest displacement under colonial rule. They lost their best lands as they were pushed off into the towns and cities where, ironically, they went to schools that were meant to train them to serve their British masters but exposed them to global currents and taught them to think strategically, thus creating an opposition. Kenyatta was educated to serve, but rose to rule. In this book, he skillfully combines his personal story with a formal study of Gikuyu life and death, work and play, sex and family. In his own inimitable way, the General does the same for his people, the Meru. Though the General respected Kenyatta during and after Mau Mau, he joined the opposition party before independence in 1962—the year Kenyatta's book was published. After a few years with Kenyatta at the helm, the General sensed a change. "As we used to love Kenyatta, we came to fear him," he said. "You could hardly oppose Kenyatta. He had no sympathy." Now, more than three decades after his death, Kenyans are debating the legacy of their first president. The General's story is certain to fan the fires of the discussion.

When We Began There Were Witchmen: An Oral History from Mount Kenya, by Jeffrey A. Fadiman (University of California Press, 1993), is a unique and hence immensely important collection of the oral traditions, religious beliefs, and folklore of the Meru people. Oral history in East Africa is "swiftly dying," Fadiman observed twenty years ago. He got there just in time. This rigorous, beautiful book ends where the General's story of his adulthood begins, when thousands of Kenyans were enlisted to fight with the British in the Second World War. Deeply versed in Meru rules of witchcraft, rituals of reconciliation, and social controls, Fadiman provides a kind of out-of-body memory, an archive, for remembering where the Meru have come from. He understands the riches as well as the baggage with which the Meru confront the modernizing forces that have descended on

Kenya. Kenya as a nation is an alien idea to the Meru of old, and it is a distinction of the General's that he has a foot in both camps, both identities, or rather, both feet in the ethics of the old ways and simultaneously both feet in the material progress of the new.

Imperial Reckoning: The Untold Story of Britain's Gulag in Kenya, by Caroline Elkins (Henry Holt, 2005), won a Pulitzer Prize, touching off a firestorm of criticism and defense. The work was praised for setting straight a history made difficult to tell by the willful destruction of records by the British, both on the ground in Kenya and in the Colonial Office in London. Elkins set out to document the system of prisons, detention centers, and work camps that the colonial government built in the name of "rehabilitating" Mau Mau collaborators. After an exhaustive search for official reports led her to a dead end of confidential files, burned documents, and empty shelves, Elkins turned to survivors for their testimonies. The evidence she collected supported her thesis that Britain deliberately ignored its own domestic and international laws in order to crush the Mau Mau movement through torture, assassination, and indefinite detention. Though the argument has not been refuted, Elkins has been attacked for being "one-sided" in her determination to rectify propaganda stereotypes of Mau Mau. Her critics fault her for inflating casualty figures and overlooking atrocities committed by Africans against Africans. The dispute over numbers has not been settled, and the latter critique strikes me as an assault on her sympathy for the oppressed.

In 1962, Donald L. Barnett, an American graduate student of anthropology, met a forest fighter named Karari Njama. From an extensive series of interviews, the two produced *Mau Mau from Within: An Analysis of Kenya's Peasant Revolt* (Monthly Review Press, 1966). Njama was raised on squatter land in the Rift Valley and, like the General, was one of the few literate fighters, having been educated at Alliance High School. Njama was stationed in the Aberdare Mountains and was the right-hand man to Dedan Kimathi, the ultimate leader whom the General knew only by name and picture. Editor Barnett interjects helpful figures in his introductions to Njama's words. Barnett informs us, for example, "By 1934 some 6,543,360 acres of land had been alienated for occupation by 2,027 settlers; an average of 2,534 acres per occupant, of which only 274 acres were under cultivation."

Njama describes the hypocrisy and corruption of British rule. He hints at a conspiracy theory that perhaps the British were behind the Lari Massacre, where the Mau Mau slaughtered troops from the loyalist Home

Guard and their families. Even if they weren't, he concedes, Lari "made me think that the British believe that killing by a gun or bomb is right, while killing with a *panga* is evil. To me, it made no difference whatsoever. But who has killed more innocent women, British or Mau Mau? I wondered whether the bombs dropped on towns and cities by the British during the First and Second World Wars—and in many other wars—spared the lives of innocent women and children for which they are blaming us."

For a knowledgeable tour through the autobiographies and life stories of Mau Mau veterans, visit Marshall Clough's *Mau Mau Memoirs: History, Memory, and Politics* (Lynne Rienner, 1998). Clough focuses on thirteen "memoirs," beginning with the publication of J. M. Kariuki's *Mau Mau Detainee* in 1963, the first full-length narrative of the uprising from the African perspective. "The pages seemed to echo British memoirs of Japanese prison camps along the Burma Railway, but in this case the British themselves were the brutal camp officers and their African detainees were those who suffered, died, or endured to gain their freedom." Clough weaves together excerpts from and commentary on Barnett and Njama's *Mau Mau from Within* (1966), General China's *"Mau Mau" General* (1967), Charity Waciuma's *Daughter of Mumbai* (1969), Kiboi Muriithi's *War in the Forest* (1971), Joram Wamweya's *Freedom Fighter* (1971), Karigo Muchai's *The Hardcore* (1973), Ngugi Kabiro's *Man in the Middle* (1973), Mohamed Mathu's *The Urban Guerilla* (1974), Bildad Kaggia's *Roots of Freedom* (1975), H. Kahinga Wachanga's *The Swords of Kirinyaga* (1975), Gucu G. Gikoyo's *We Fought for Freedom* (1979), and Gakaara wa Wanjau's *Mau Mau Author in Detention* (1988). For a reader seeking an introduction to the rich literature inspired by the need to tell about the Mau Mau, Clough's volume is the place to start.

One of the books that Clough examines is the biography of Waruhiu Itote, aka General China, *"Mau Mau" Detainee* (East African Publishing House, 1967). Itote was born the same year as the General in Nyeri, a Gikuyu town that the General called a "hot place" for politics, where most people wound up taking the oath of Mau Mau. The first six pages of the memoir, in which Itote recalls his experiences as a KAR soldier fighting on the Burma Front in the Second World War, give insight into the development of awareness on the part of the persecuted. From three conversations—with a British soldier in Burma, a black American soldier in Calcuttta, and an Indian man—Itote realized that he was on the lowest rung of racial hierarchy in his own country and that he was fighting a war from which he would not benefit. In the jungles of Burma, he also learned guerrilla fighting techniques and how to use contemporary weapons. Returning to Kenya with his newfound nationalism and understanding of race, Itote drifted toward politics and Mau Mau. He went to the forest a year and a half before the General and was caught less than a year after the General entered. China then cooperated with British intelligence and even orchestrated a meeting of Mau Mau leaders to discuss terms of surrender. While Itote was regarded as the most important general of Mount Kenya, the General said, "I don't have much to say about China" because their time in the forest did not overlap for long and because the General was "disappointed" by China's dismissive attitude toward Meru General Mwariama. Furthermore, after Independence, the General was miffed that China, a mostly illiterate man who happened to be Kenyatta's friend, was appointed to an executive position in the National Youth Service, while more educated Kenyans from other ethnic groups were denied similar opportunities.

Alexandra Fuller's witty *Cocktail Hour under the Tree of Forgetfulness* (Penguin, 2011) takes the reader on a bumpy ride through southern and East Africa with Fuller's mother, Nicola, as host and guide. Nicola's outlook on relations between the races is familiar to readers of Isak Dinesen's (Karen Blixen's) Eurocentric classic, *Out of Africa*. Expect the African landscape to be breathtaking and the Africans to be in need of civilization. Born in Scotland in 1944, Nicola Fuller bounced from London to Africa and landed in western Kenya in time for the Mau Mau Rebellion. Her father once accidentally shot a Gikuyu man and was taken to court, but the "accident" lay not in the gunshot but in the timing. "A few days later and it would have been fine for my father to shoot a Gikuyu," said Nicola Fuller, "because the British had declared a state of emergency." A powerful storyteller, Alexandra Fuller is less accomplished as a historian of Kenya. She devotes the better part of thirteen pages of Mau Mau coverage to the murder of a white family by their machete-wielding servants. Mau Mau, as she tells it, routinely engaged in bestiality and cannibalism. "The one good thing that came out of Mau Mau," mused her mother, a white African without a trace of angst, was getting a good deal on a prized mare named Violet because "jittery settlers made plans to leave Kenya" and "everyone was trying to get rid of their animals." No character like the General makes an appearance in Fuller's pages. He tells another side of the story—about a subjugated people's ambitions for acquiring human rights and sovereignty in a new nation.

With his plainspoken narrative, *The Worlds of a Maasai Warrior: An Autobiography* (Random House, 1986), Tepilit Ole Saitoti invites readers into the realms of an East African man born in 1949. Reviewers uniformly praise the book and recommend it to Western travelers before their African safaris. Saitoti is a Maasai, a traditionally nomadic people at home on the vast savannah divided between Kenya and Tanzania, where they raise cattle and resist the two governments' efforts to have them abandon their wandering ways and adopt a sedentary life. As a boy, Saitoti was rewarded with early circumcision for killing his first lion. As a young man he traveled to Germany and the United States, where he ate McDonald's hamburgers, watched go-go dancers in Hollywood, and enjoyed the Jungle Ride at Disneyland. As an elder, with a sense of fatalism but an openness to surprise, he weighs the temptations of modern life against the satisfactions of tradition. Unlike the General, Saitoti shows no interest in condemning or even evoking the colonial past.

Nisa: The Life and Words of a !Kung Woman, by Marjorie Shostak (Harvard University Press, 1983), is the absorbing life story of a hunter-gatherer from the southern African desert, in modern-day Botswana, as told to an adventurous, newly minted anthropologist from Harvard. The book, now appreciated as a work of art as well as a classic field study, appealed at first to readers who, in the aftermath of the civil rights movement in the United States and independence movements in Africa, wanted to "know" Africa. Shostak took the search a step deeper and elicited an African woman, dignified, competent, thoughtful, and humane. Yet Nisa is surely a member of one of the most remote and least visible people on earth. Shunning a conventional social or ecological study, Shostak focuses on the personal connection, weaving her own journey as a woman and a researcher in unknown terrain into Nisa's story. Thus the text that emerges is a dual memoir that, to one reviewer, reveals "the universality of women's experiences and feelings despite vast differences in culture and society" (*Choice*).

INDEX